SOUTHERN BUSINESSMEN AND DESEGREGATION

EDITED BY
ELIZABETH JACOWAY & DAVID R. COLBURN

LOUISIANA STATE UNIVERSITY PRESS
BATON ROUGE AND LONDON

DESIGNER: ROD PARKER
TYPEFACE: VIP CLARENDON LIGHT
TYPESETTER: GRAPHIC COMPOSITION, INC.
PRINTER: THOMSON SHORE, INC.
BINDER: THOMSON SHORE, INC.

THE EDITORS WISH TO THANK OXFORD UNIVERSITY PRESS FOR
PERMISSION TO REPUBLISH PORTIONS OF WILLIAM H. CHAFE,
*CIVILITIES AND CIVIL RIGHTS: GREENSBORO, NORTH CAROLINA AND
THE BLACK STRUGGLE FOR FREEDOM* (1980)

Library of Congress Cataloging in Publication Data

Main entry under title:

Southern businessmen and desegregation.

Bibliography: p.
Includes index.
1. Afro-Americans—Civil rights—Southern States—
Addresses, essays, lectures. 2. Industry—Social aspects—
Southern States—Addresses, essays, lectures. 3. Southern
States—Race relations—Addresses, essays, lectures. I.
Jacoway, Elizabeth, 1944–   II. Colburn, David R.
E185.92.S683   323.4'08996073075   81–19362
                                       AACR2
ISBN 0–8071–0893–6

TO OUR CHILDREN
TIMOTHY AND TODD WATSON
AND
KATHERINE, DAVID, AND MARGARET COLBURN
WITH HOPE FOR THE FUTURE

CONTENTS

ACKNOWLEDGMENTS

The editors are grateful to a number of people for their generous contributions to this project. We owe a great debt to Morton Sosna, who suggested the idea and gave valuable assistance in the early stages of its development. We also appreciate the efforts of the friends and colleagues who helped us locate our contributors, especially Dewey Grantham, Bell Wiley, Blaine Brownell, Stephen Channing, Neil McMillen, Daniel Hollis, Ernest Lander, and David Goldfield. Our thirteen contributors have been unfailingly prompt and cheerful in responding to continuing requests for stylistic changes and additional information, and we appreciate the spirit of cooperation which has made the development of this project both instructive and enjoyable. Professors Carl V. Harris and Numan V. Bartley read the manuscript in various stages of completion, and their thoughtful criticisms and suggestions have improved it immeasurably. John Easterly has been a delightful co-worker and editor who has saved us from errors too numerous to mention. Our typists, Dolores Mingo and Adrienne Turner, have performed faithfully and without complaint through many drafts. Finally, but certainly not least, we are grateful to our spouses, Tim Watson and

Marion Colburn, who endured through many dull weekends and missed vacations, and whose patience and understanding sustained us in this effort, as in all others.

In addition Carl Abbott wishes to thank the Research Committee of the Old Dominion University School of Arts and Letters for a grant which assisted him in his research for his Tampa essay.

David R. Colburn acknowledges gratefully the support of the Division of Sponsored Research, University of Florida, Gainesville, and the American Philosophical Society in preparing his study of Saint Augustine.

Robert G. Corley wishes to thank the Birmingham Metropolitan Study Project for grant funding used in the preparation of his article on Birmingham.

Elizabeth Jacoway gratefully acknowledges the financial assistance of the National Endowment for the Humanities and the American Philosophical Society for research for her Little Rock essay. She also wishes to thank William Leuchtenburg, James Lester, Charles Bolton, T. Harri Baker, and Robert M. Collins, whose criticisms and suggestions clarified and redirected her thinking in important ways.

SOUTHERN
BUSINESSMEN AND
DESEGREGATION

ELIZABETH JACOWAY

AN INTRODUCTION

CIVIL RIGHTS AND THE CHANGING SOUTH

Several years ago Dewey Grantham suggested that recent southern history has reflected a continuing tension between opposing forces of continuity and change; torn between twin desires, southerners have wanted to hold on to the certainties of the past and also to reach out for the opportunities of the future.[1] Nowhere is this tension revealed more clearly than in the efforts of southern white businessmen to come to grips with the demands of the civil rights movement. In the 1950s and 1960s, white businessmen across the South found themselves pushed— by the federal government and civil rights forces as well as by their own economic interests and values—into becoming reluctant advocates of a new departure in southern race relations.[2]

Although they often perceived themselves to be progressive builders of a "new" South, in 1954 most southern white businessmen shared the racial values and prejudices of their region.

---

1   I owe a great debt to my coeditor David Colburn. He was an active participant in the writing of this introduction—counselling, criticizing, and cajoling at every stage of the process. I am also grateful to August Meier, Blaine Brownell, and Willard Gatewood for their helpful criticisms and encouragement.
2   Dewey Grantham (ed.), *The South and the Sectional Image* (New York: Harper and Row, 1967), 1–7.

Prior to the 1950s, few had any reason to question this apparent contradiction. Henry Grady, early prophet of southern industrialization, had elaborated an ethic that tolerated and even exploited segregation; and then throughout the first half of the twentieth century southern progressives, for the most part, had busied themselves with economic remedies for the region's ills, leaving disturbing questions of race beyond the ken of their concern, if not of their consciousness. With the momentous decision of *Brown* v. *the Board of Education of Topeka, Kansas* in May of 1954, however, law-abiding southerners found some of their most cherished institutions and deeply held values stripped of the sanction of law; and many of them faced, for the first time, the necessity of reconciling their progressive pretensions with their region's racial realities. Southern leaders, and particularly southern business leaders, thus embarked on a painful quest for order, for stability, and for reassurances that their progressive "image" could somehow remain untarnished. The story of the ensuing process of change that these leaders and their communities experienced is filled with ambiguity, irony, and frustration; but however limited the gains—especially when compared with the equalitarian goals of the civil rights movement—when measured against the record of the southern past, the change was significant.

Of course a handful of black children in previously all-white schools did not constitute meaningful desegregation, but it did represent meaningful *change* in a society that for three hundred years had insisted on almost total social separation of the races. In terms of numbers it was a minimal change, at first, and it was accepted only under extreme pressure; against the backdrop of the southern past, however, even this minimal softening on the fundamental issue of race—and this new willingness on the part of the businessmen to yield to the pressures for change—constitutes a historical phenomenon worthy of careful examination and analysis.

This volume traces the response of the business community in fourteen southern cities to the challenge of desegregation. The contributors to this volume do not suggest that the South's business leadership became partisans of the civil rights cause; in fact, they often demonstrate that southern businessmen responded to the civil rights challenge in a fashion that was cal-

culated to preserve the "image" of progressiveness while yielding a minimum of desegregation. Nonetheless, although these
articles contain a variety of interpretations of the nature and
meaning of the business elite's response to desegregation, taken
together these articles do suggest that the South's white businessmen yielded to the demands for change because of a fundamental reordering of their priorities: although the maintenance
of white supremacy remained a cherished objective, somewhere
along the way it slipped from its traditionally dominant position
and the primary objective for the South's business leaders became economic growth. Although not all of the contributors included here would agree, the editors feel that this conflict between competing values—with the ultimate resolution in favor
of "progress"—represents a significant new departure in southern life and thought.

From the beginning southern culture had been different from
that of the North. Agrarian rather than commercial, hierarchical rather than equalitarian, slave-holding rather than free,
southern society became militantly different—and the apolo-
gists for southern "superiority" increasingly vocal—in the
years before the Civil War. In the wake of military defeat and the
traumatic experience of Reconstruction, white southern culture
became even more different from that of the North as the will to
resist northern assaults on southern values and the southern
"way of life" intensified. Into this milieu stepped a group of new
men with a set of new ideas that promised to build a new South
out of the ashes of defeat. Battling a majority sentiment that
clung to the past, these prophets of the New South called for
economic diversification, sectional reconciliation, and a more
enlightened approach to race relations; in short, as Paul Gaston
has suggested, this New South Creed carried with it the promise
of American life for the southern people. In the 1870s and 1880s
many leading southern businessmen, editors, and politicians
thus prodded the South toward plunging into the nation's economic mainstream; but despite much-heralded advances toward
this goal, the revolts of Independents and Populists in the late
1880s and 1890s demonstrated unmistakably that the logic of
the New South ideology had not swept all before it. Indeed, these
minority movements notwithstanding, the values and culture of

the Old South continued to flourish well into the twentieth century.[3]

Emerging in the 1920s the second generation of New South prophets bore the stamp of their time and place, but they were, nonetheless, clearly heirs to the New South tradition. George Tindall has called them "business progressives," because not only did they seek governmental support for business imperatives, they also worked to achieve governmental efficiency and to expand the public service concept of the state. The quest for northern capital and "harmonious" race relations continued, although the impulse toward sectional reconciliation increasingly found expression in a desire to attract federal dollars. The business-progressive impulse remained the norm in southern state politics in the following decades, but the demands of the Depression diverted southern leaders from the economic development that had so long eluded them. Similarly, the excesses of fundamentalism and Ku Kluxery indicated the extent to which the South continued to resist submersion in the nation's mainstream, economic or otherwise.[4]

With the conclusion of World War II and the return to a peacetime economy, the South began to awaken on a large scale to the possibilities of participation in the national economy. Young southerners who had been away to war had gained a vision of the advantages of a more prosperous economy; southerners who lived near military installations had gained an altered point of view from the presence of outsiders in the neighborhood; almost all had experienced the heady sensation of higher wages and loose change as a result of wartime inflation and defense spending in the South. The result was that by the early 1950s chambers of commerce and state governments across the South had, with widespread popular approval, renewed and expanded their efforts to attract industry to the region, and the South's industrialization process at last went into high gear.

For a brief moment one could almost have believed that Henry Grady and his tribe of New South prophets might be smiling down from their ethereal reaches on the movement they had inspired, when once again there loomed on the horizon the

3   Paul M. Gaston, *The New South Creed: A Study in Southern Mythmaking* (New York: Knopf, 1970).
4   George Brown Tindall, *The Emergence of the New South: 1913–1945* (Baton Rouge: Louisiana State University Press, 1968).

specter of racism, the South's ancestral weakness. In this extremity southern businessmen reacted as southerners first and businessmen second. While preoccupied with their own fears, resentments, and deep-seated prejudices, they allowed racial extremists to capture control of their communities. Gradually, however, they came to perceive, dimly at first, that their racism and abdication of leadership were taking a heavy toll: they were losing to other cities the industry they might have had; they were losing their carefully guarded images as progressive communities; they were losing their schools; they were losing their self-respect. Galvanized into action at last by pressures from the federal government and civil rights activists as well as by the unmistakable evidence of their own losses, these men finally yielded to the desegregation effort. Of even greater significance, they also used their influence to lead their communities into a reluctant acceptance of the dreaded changes in southern life.

Although the southern business leaders were not advocates of meaningful desegregation, they did become active agents of change (and not simply passive recipients of the results of that change), for they used their influence in their communities to press for the alterations in southern racial patterns that they had come to believe were necessary. If they had remained recalcitrant, if they had used their influence to stand against the tide, the desegregation process would have been much more difficult, the maintenance of national unity much less tenable. As it has developed—and on some levels the southern business leadership must have realized this—the changes they accepted were the entering wedge for the much greater changes that have since taken place in southern life and race relations. Although the analogy must not be pressed too far, in some ways it is fair to say that with the coming of the civil rights movement the New South ethic at last achieved dominance in southern thought.

The changes in southern race relations did not come without causing considerable tension among the businessmen who contributed to the process. As Atlanta *Constitution* editor Ralph McGill described the effects of the postwar southern industrial boom, southern leaders seeking new enterprises "never saw themselves as carriers of the virus which was to destroy the *status quo* in their towns . . . and also, therefore, the old 'way of life in the South'. . . . They sought with a kind of desperation to maintain the *status quo*—all the while laboring to bring new industries and payrolls which could only accelerate the changes." For a brief space, southern business leaders allowed themselves to believe that they could maintain the traditional pattern of the South's race relations at the same time that they pursued industrialization and progress; the civil rights movement made them realize that they had to choose. In choosing, they accepted a new ordering of their values and priorities, placing economic imperatives above racial ones. In other words, the "common resolve indomitably maintained" that the South should preserve white supremacy yielded primacy in the hierarchy of values of the South's business leadership to a new resolve to share in the nation's prosperity. This is not to suggest that these leaders lost their racial prejudices in this process; it is to suggest, however, that their racial fears and anxieties subsided sufficiently to allow other concerns to achieve dominance in their thought. In southern life, this was change of the first magnitude.[5]

One could perhaps argue that these men simply acted as urban businessmen anywhere would have done—when they placed the quest for profits and "progress" above all other considerations. Do not businessmen always, one might ask, place business objectives above other values and goals? This is precisely the point. These men *were* acting as urban businessmen anywhere would have done; somewhere along the way, they had become nationalized to the extent that they now behaved in the very *un*southern manner of consciously and explicitly placing other considerations above racial ones.

More to the point, one might ask whether these businessmen really had a choice in their response to desegregation. Was continuing, unremitting resistance a rational, viable course of action for these men and their communities? Again, with economic considerations paramount, the answer was clearly no; but if traditional southern values had prevailed, the answer would have been a resounding yes. The South yielded to change, finally, not only because of federal and civil rights pressures, but also in response to the reordered priorities of significant elements of its own leadership.

5   As quoted in Wilma Dykeman and James Stokeley, *Neither Black nor White* (New York: Rinehart and Company, 1957), 332–33; Ulrich Bonnell Phillips, "The Central Theme of Southern History," *American Historical Review*, XXXIV (1928), 30–43.

Finally, one might ask whether the southern business leadership actually experienced a change of mind with regard to race relations. Did they not simply, one wonders, reach the point where they had to yield on the race issue, given the increased cost of maintaining the status quo? And did they not then work to yield as little as possible, even developing, thereby, in James Ely's words, "a more subtle form of resistance"? Scholars have suggested this repeatedly—so often, in fact, as to have made this argument an article of faith in the literature of the civil rights movement. But the behavior of businessmen in cities across the South has brought this conclusion under serious scrutiny. In city after city, as the articles in this volume reveal, the southern business leadership consciously chose to abandon traditional racial patterns, even in the full knowledge that they were abandoning the old "southern way of life." To be sure they yielded as little as possible and they held to their traditional racial attitudes. But the important point is that they confronted the alternatives available to them, examined their values and priorities, and chose, ultimately, to place economic growth before white supremacy. This choice represents significant change, and it would seem to be as much of a change of "mind" as a pragmatic adjustment to reality.[6]

Of course, cities are not the whole story in the South. But as Blaine Brownell and David Goldfield have recently argued, southern cities have always served as "links between the traditional South and the contrary influences of northern capitalism and the American 'mainstream,'" and thus have functioned as agents of change. Although the cities were clearly in the vanguard, the acceptance of a new ordering of priorities, especially with regard to the fundamental issue of race, heralds the dawn of a new era in southern history.[7]

Following a line of interpretation that has gained acceptance in many quarters, Neil McMillen recently characterized the civil

6   James W. Ely, *The Crisis of Conservative Virginia* (Knoxville: University of Tennessee Press, 1976), 132. See especially Numan V. Bartley, *The Rise of Massive Resistance: Race and Politics in the South During the 1950's* (Baton Rouge: Louisiana State University Press, 1969).
7   Blaine Brownell and David Goldfield, *The City in Southern History: The Growth of Urban Civilization in the South* (Port Washington, N.Y.: Kennikat Press, 1977), 8.

rights movement as "a time of social revolution accomplished by federal power and civil rights activism." The articles in this volume suggest that this characterization is incomplete. Indeed, these studies of individual southern cities suggest that the gains of the civil rights movement, although demanded by federal authority and sustained by civil rights activism, also stemmed from a growing awareness of the need for change on the part of significant elements within the white South itself—not only liberal racial groups, clergymen, newspaper editors, and college professors, but also such traditionally conservative elements as state and local political leaders, and particularly, businessmen. Specifically these articles demonstrate that southern business leaders emerged from their confrontations with racial anxieties, federal force, and economic loss with a new understanding of the necessity—and even the inevitability—of change, and that they then became a significant if ofttimes reluctant element in the desegregation process.[8]

In city after city, essentially the same scenario unfolded in the 1950s and 1960s. After an initial reaction of shock, surprise, and resentment in response to federal and/or "outside" intervention, the city's business leadership lapsed into silence, thus creating a power vacuum and permitting the ascension to power of extremist elements. As the months passed and the realities of economic loss began to become apparent, as the federal courts and civil rights activists held firm, and especially as the inevitability of change became clear, the business leadership began to awaken to the consequences of their silence and their city's continuing resistance to the federally mandated changes in southern race relations. Resuming their traditional positions of community leadership and organizing themselves into biracial committees and pressure groups, the businessmen then began to cast about for issues with which to oppose extremist elements and/or state officials; they generally seized on issues that sidestepped the central question of integration versus segregation, arguing instead for such things as open schools, community stability, and social order. With the return of the traditional leadership and their emergence as advocates of change, the de-

---

8   Neil McMillen, "Black Enfranchisement in Mississippi," *Journal of Southern History*, XLIII (August, 1977), 351–72.

fenses of segregation began to crumble and the South took its first halting steps toward becoming a desegregated society.

Everywhere the gains were limited, and in some places the attempts at "tokenism" were more blatant than in others, but in all the cities studied here—in every state of the old Confederacy and then some—important elements of the southern leadership made the intellectual leap from one set of values to another, from a rock-ribbed defense of white supremacy to a determination to restore and preserve their city's progressive "image." As one Little Rock leader expressed it: "We sort of felt, even those of us that were archconservatives, that Faubus had tried, and failed, and now let's get on with the game and comply with the court order, but still not with any great rushing out, just keep it in low profile and do what we had to, to get off the front pages." The process was halting and often ambiguous, as such workings of the historical process usually are, and it was neither conducted with fanfare nor accompanied by much mention in the press; but when set against the backdrop of the southern past, the performance was impressive.

Of course not every city studied here found itself embroiled in a racial crisis. Many cities learned from the experiences of their southern neighbors, and their leaders set about early to avoid becoming "another Little Rock." In some cities, such as Norfolk, New Orleans, Birmingham, and Jackson, the businessmen acted, in Carl Abbott's words, as "a rearguard rather than as pioneers"; but in others, such as Tampa, Columbia, and Dallas, the businessmen took the lead in preparing their communities for the inevitable changes. In the vast majority of cities, however, whether early or late, the influence of the community's own leadership, in concert with federal and civil rights persistence, turned the tide and ushered in a new era in southern race relations.

In his analysis of the businessmen's response to desegregation in Dallas, William Brophy concluded that that city avoided the "hatred, violence, and mental anguish" that characterized the desegregation effort in other cities because its leaders "wanted to prevent violence and preserve the community's image" and because its biracial committee "was able to convince whites that the old order had to be changed and blacks that it had to be changed gradually." In describing developments in

Birmingham, Robert Corley has written: "By 1963, the blacks' demands for desegregation had reached the point where they threatened not only the economic vitality of Birmingham, but its social order as well. . . . The end of segregation in Birmingham was dramatically hastened because King and his demonstrators threatened chaos in a city whose leaders were now desperate for order." John Quincy Adams and Charles Sallis found that "when Jackson's businessmen became convinced that sustained racial upheaval would imperil economic development, they provided a climate for change in southern customs by taking a stand on upholding 'law and order.'" In Norfolk, according to Carl Abbott, "If the participants in the Committee of 100 did not serve as the major force for change . . . they did assure a peaceful process of desegregation. By openly ratifying the inevitable, the city's business leaders helped to make desegregation respectable." Simply stated, as Steven Lawson has concluded about Tampa, southern merchants and businessmen "calculated that ugly racial incidents did not make good dollars and cents."

In most cases, the southern business leadership felt more concern about the image their cities projected than about the substance of real or meaningful change in their region's racial patterns. In Augusta, for example, James Cobb found that civic leaders "used tokenism and ballyhoo to create an illusion of cooperation and harmony—and crusaded for expanded prosperity without further compromising their racial philosophies or their economic or political advantages." Similarly, in the historic community of Saint Augustine, David Colburn noted that "only when business leaders realized there was no turning back, and their economic viability and the celebration of the town's four hundredth anniversary were tied to the amelioration of the crisis did they oppose the reemergence of racial violence." Or as William Chafe concluded about Greensboro: "From one perspective, Greensboro had achieved a new maturity of race relations. . . . From another perspective, however, the older forms of control had simply taken on a new appearance." Nonetheless, although image was the businessmen's major concern, they understood that change was the product of their actions.

The articles in this volume trace the process of change the civil rights movement initiated in southern life. From these fourteen studies some generalizations about that process can be drawn. For instance, those cities that experienced comparatively mild racial disturbances during this period—in particular, Atlanta, Tampa, Dallas, and Columbia—tended to have historically good race relations prior to 1954 and experienced dramatic demographic and economic changes after World War II. These communities eagerly embraced the economic growth of the postwar period, actively soliciting new industry and northern migrants. The dramatic nature of these socioeconomic and demographic changes seems to have focused attention in these communities on matters other than race: jobs, housing, schools, transportation, police and fire protection. Most of these communities also developed a dialogue between the races that helped to alleviate past tensions. Additionally, southern traditions in these communities suffered a further blow with the immigration of people who did not share southern racial attitudes and perceptions.

Little Rock appears to be a notable exception to the pattern outlined above; for while it experienced substantial economic and demographic changes and while it had a history of relatively harmonious race relations prior to 1954, violence erupted during the school crisis in 1957. An important variable that may help explain developments in Little Rock and elsewhere is the role of the governor. Urban racial crises appear to have been alternately heightened or lessened by the nature of the governor's involvement. Thus, governors such as Orval Faubus, George Wallace, and Ross Barnett severely complicated and exacerbated the racial crises in Little Rock, Birmingham, and Jackson while governors in South Carolina, Kentucky, and Georgia helped moderate racial tensions.

Those cities that underwent little or no population or economic growth in the postwar period—in particular Saint Augustine, Augusta, Louisville, and Memphis—typically experienced considerable racial turmoil during the civil rights era. The populations of these cities remained relatively homogeneous and tradition played an important role in the lives of the people. Most of these communities sought new industry and a civic renaissance but were unsuccessful in their efforts. Because these communities remained relatively stable, they appear to have held firmly to the racial heritage of the past.

Those cities in which active civil rights organizations had been established prior to 1954 generally avoided violence. Such black organizations had established lines of communication with the white community, thereby gaining visibility and credibility for their activities and establishing some momentum for racial change. Communities in which blacks established vocal organizations after 1954 usually experienced considerable racial tension as whites felt themselves and their society threatened by demands for change.

No correlation seems to exist between the size of the black community and the extent of racial violence. Saint Augustine's black population was 21 percent compared to 17 percent for Tampa. Birmingham had a population that was 40 percent black, but so did Atlanta. Furthermore, while cities of the Deep South were more likely to encounter racial turmoil than those of the border states, there were certain notable exceptions, such as Atlanta and Columbia; similarly, Little Rock and Saint Augustine were in border states and yet had severe problems.

These studies suggest that where there were no efforts by the business leadership to prepare the community for change, as in Memphis and New Orleans, violence ensued; on the other hand, where biracial committees kept open the lines of communication between the races, as in Dallas, Tampa, and Greensboro, violence was minimized or avoided. Later cities learned from the experiences of Little Rock and New Orleans and thus were able to plan more rationally; apparently their leaders' realization that change was inevitable was a major factor in their decisions to yield rather than attract unfavorable publicity. In sum, the process of change in the South seems to have involved a variety of factors, not least among which were the leadership and involvement of the white business community.

Several years ago C. Vann Woodward wrote an article attacking the notion that the South's industrialization process had contributed to a change in—or a moderation of—southern racial attitudes and behavior. Arguing that the maintenance of white supremacy had long been important to the exploitation of black and white labor in the New South, Woodward contended that claims of a hopeful new role for southern leaders growing out of their desire for new industry constituted a "New South fraud." While the desire for new industry did not cause southern business leaders to become supporters of black protest or champions of civil rights, the articles in this volume suggest that it did lead to a willingness to modify southern race relations. The desire to attract new industry and to maintain a progressive image was one very potent force leading to the southern willingness to abandon segregation.[9]

More recently, Numan V. Bartley traced *The Rise of Massive Resistance* and concluded that the South's ultimate acceptance of token desegregation was "a conservative reaction in defense of southern continuity and represented no real break with the past." As Bartley described it:

School closures in Arkansas and Virginia brought to a head the fundamental dilemma facing a region seeking both the maintenance of past customs and the advancement of economic and technological progress. The Supreme Court refused to surrender to southern opposition, and the Eisenhower administration's intervention in Little Rock demonstrated that southern state governments would not be permitted to ignore court orders. State officials could only close the schools and stand defiantly in the face of federal authority. Such a policy of calculated anarchy assaulted public education and threatened the whole structure of southern society, the region's economic future, and the vested interest of southern institutions. Thus the dialectic was once again rephrased, and the future of public education and the stability of the governmental process, rather than segregation and desegregation, became the central issues. This situation led to a general shift away from massive resistance, a shift that was conservative rather than reformist, that sought social stability rather than social change.[10]

This examination of the southern business leaders' response to desegregation suggests that Bartley's dichotomies—"conservative rather than reformist," "social stability rather than social change"—were too sharply drawn. The response of the South's business leaders *was* conservative—in the sense that these men were not motivated by a desire for reform—but it nonetheless involved the conscious acceptance of a fundamental reform of southern society. Similarly, these men did seek social stability, but in the process they accepted social change. Else-

9   C. Vann Woodward, "New South Fraud is Papered by Old South Myth," Washington *Post*, July 9, 1961, p. E3.
10   Bartley, *The Rise of Massive Resistance*, 342–43.

where Bartley argued that the southern shift to moderation was "based on the ethics of cost-accounting rather than human justice." Clearly Bartley was right, but his conclusions, and those of many others, have drawn attention away from the fact that a fundamental reordering had occurred in the priorities and value systems of the South's businessmen.[11]

One cannot deny that in the face of federal and civil rights pressures southern leaders attempted to hold the line and do the minimum necessary to restore order, assure stability, and preserve at least a facade of "progressivism." One also cannot deny that in the context of southern history, the changes these leaders were willing to accept represented a significant break with the past—a softening on the fundamental issue of race. Substantively the change was negligible at first, and from the black perspective practically meaningless. Qualitatively, in terms of the southern white mind, it represented a significant new departure in southern history. Southerners did not abandon racism, but they did choose, for the first time, to place other considerations above the maintenance of white supremacy.

Some students of the phenomenon (including some of the contributors to this volume) have argued that the response of the South's businessmen to desegregation was simply a strategy to maintain social control or to minimize the effects of change. The articles in this volume, however, when read as a unit, suggest an alternative hypothesis. These articles suggest that the response of the southern leadership to the desegregation challenge was an accommodation to what was perceived as inevitable change—an accommodation based on a conscious choice between the past and the future. Under the unremitting pressure of the civil rights movement, these southern leaders carefully examined and ultimately rearranged their most cherished values and priorities; although they did not moderate their racial attitudes, they did allow racial considerations to slip from the dominant position in their hierarchy of values. In response to the altered stance of its own leadership as well as to the unrelenting pressures for change, the South, at last, for good or ill, cast its lot with the future.

11   *Ibid.*, 320, 27.

ELIZABETH JACOWAY

TAKEN BY SURPRISE

LITTLE ROCK BUSINESS LEADERS AND DESEGREGATION

When Harry Ashmore's *Epitaph for Dixie* first came off the presses in 1958, many readers believed that the Arkansas editor had penned his lament prematurely. Events in Ashmore's own city had stunned the world the previous autumn, and the Little Rock crisis seemed to many convincing proof that Dixie was indeed alive and well. Ashmore liked to think of himself as a prophet, and in this instance, the description fit; for Ashmore was in fact documenting a phenomenon that was about to happen.[1]

In essence, Ashmore argued that economic self-interest—the balance sheet—would lead the South away from racism and violence. Realistic businessmen, Ashmore argued, "are willing to put up with a good deal of nonsense, [but] they aren't willing to pay for it." In Ashmore's words:

The fact is that the dominant economic interests in the New South—granting a few local exceptions—not only are not engaged in any calculated effort to keep the Negro in his place, but are providing a sig-

1 Harry S. Ashmore, *Epitaph for Dixie* (New York: Norton, 1958); interview with Harry S. Ashmore by the author, November, 1976. Ashmore denies that the book was premature.

nificant counterbalance for the incendiary activities of the Citizens Councils and the reborn Klans. It is not that the bustling gentlemen at the local Chambers of Commerce or the state Industrial Development Commissions are particularly concerned with race as a moral problem; on the contrary, they, like most of their fellow Southerners, wish the matter of integration would quietly go away, and many of them privately share the views of the Councilmen and the Klux. But they also recognize that sustained racial disorder would be fatal to their effort to lure new industries and new capital from the non-South, and that the existing level of tension isn't doing their handsomely mounted promotional campaigns any good.

Ashmore was describing here with prophetic insight the impending transformation of southern life—the final stages of metamorphosis from an agrarian into an industrial civilization. Involving a redefinition of values as well as of economic arrangements, this process of transformation had been under way for decades before the 1950s, but in response to the challenge of the civil rights movement it came to fruition in the southern mind. The dynamics of this change—this redefinition of values—can be observed in the two-year experience remembered as the Little Rock crisis.[2]

Although the chronology of the Little Rock crisis is well known—from Orval Faubus' calling out the National Guard to President Eisenhower's sending in the army, from empty school houses to teacher purges—not so well known is the reaction to these events of key elements of the community. Especially in the response of dominant elements of the business community are there lessons to be learned about the profound changes that the second half of the twentieth century has wrought in southern life.

The literature of the 1957 crisis in Little Rock suggests a curious absence of leadership within this beleaguered city; the governor is there, and the president, and nine courageous black children, but until May of 1959 one finds few references to the traditional leadership of the city itself. The silence of Little Rock's leading citizens in the face of turmoil in their city is one of the most intriguing phenomena of this two-year experience,

2   Ashmore, *Epitaph for Dixie*, 131, 118. William Hord Nicholls, *Southern Tradition and Regional Progress* (Chapel Hill: University of North Carolina Press, 1960), analyzes this process.

for this silence, this impotence, is an integral part of the process of change that communities all across the South experienced in the 1950s and 1960s. As Harry Ashmore wrote in *Harper's* in 1958, describing the "substantial and silent mass of plain citizens" of Little Rock: "When emotion triumphed over reason they did not actively join the crusade of the governor and the Citizens Councils; rather they simply subsided into troubled silence and by so doing withdrew their support from those few who attempted to stand against the tide. And because they were silent, their attitude went largely unreported. The press took due note of the fact that in fairly short order Governor Faubus was in command of the field; but . . . it did not explain why—which is the heart of the story."[3]

   During this period of "troubled silence," much was happening in the minds of Little Rock's social and business leaders, and the leaders ultimately would be the ones to shape their community's response to the challenge of desegregation. Who were the traditional leadership in Little Rock? Fortunately for this analysis, that question can be answered fairly easily, for the community's leadership had identified and mobilized itself in a campaign to clean up city government just one year before the outbreak of violence at Central High School. The Good Government Committee was composed of 150 men who were invited to participate by a coalition of leading citizens. The committee's original four were K. August Engle, publisher of the Arkansas *Democrat*; J. Ned Heiskell, president and editor of the Arkansas *Gazette*; J. V. Satterfield, president of the First National Bank and former mayor of Little Rock; and S. J. Beauchamp, citizen extraordinaire. These four men immediately drafted Clyde Lowry—another citizen with a lifetime of public service in Little Rock—to spearhead the Good Government campaign. Other groups that could be added to this nucleus of social and business leaders would include the members of the prestigious Committee of 100 (organized to promote Little Rock's economic development), the past presidents of the Chamber of Commerce, the Rotary Club, and the Community Chest, the members of the Little Rock Country Club and the downtown Little Rock Club,

---

3   Harry S. Ashmore, "The Untold Story Behind Little Rock," *Harper's*, CCXVI (June, 1958), 10ff.

the husbands of Junior League, Garden Club, and Aesthetic Club ladies, and the fifteen men who composed the exclusive all-male fraternity called XV. Of course there was much overlap among the various groups; but the combination of all these elements of the community yields a list of a thousand men and women who can fairly be identified as Little Rock's elite. The vast majority of these men were either the owners or managers of commercial or industrial operations or the accountants, lawyers, and other professionals who served the business community. If points are awarded for participation in each of the above groups, an inner core of thirty-two men can be obtained, and observation of their behavior and the subtle shifts and clarifications of their attitudes in response to the crisis in their city yields important insight into the changing nature of southern society at mid-century.[4]

Emphasizing gentility, graciousness, and a leisurely pace within a hierarchical, ordered world, Little Rock's civic elite had long pursued "the good life" in an unhurried, self-satisfied fashion. They were disturbed, of course, by the many reminders of their state's poor standing in the national economic picture, but in the years before World War II they had launched no great schemes to improve the Arkansas economy. World War II changed all of that. According to one of the leaders of Little Rock's social and business communities:"We were pretty well satisfied with ourselves previous to [the war], and then there came a great influx of people out at Camp Robinson [the army base across the river] . . . and you bring a whole group of people from other sections of the country where things *were* done, and that gave an added stimulus to us to get on the ball. . . . So we realized that Arkansas had to balance itself ['balance agriculture with industry'] if we were going to pull ourselves up from forty-eighth or forty-ninth where we'd always been."[5]

By 1952 the Little Rock Chamber of Commerce had taken

4   The author conducted interviews with nine of the inner circle of thirty-two (thirteen others are deceased) as well as with five school board members and six other community leaders who, for one reason or another, did not appear in the tally of the civic elite (three of them are Jewish and thus were excluded from many clubs) but who are known to the author to have played key roles in resolving the crisis.
5   Interview with A. Howard Stebbins III by the author, December, 1977.

upon itself the task of creating an industrial district on the out-skirts of town that would attract northern capital with pre-ferred sites, tax advantages, and occasionally outright subsi-dies. Civic leaders also lured an air base to the area, formed a blue-ribbon Committee of 100 to promote economic develop-ment, and began to clean up the corruption in city politics by lobbying for the more "efficient" and "professional" city man-ager form of government. What was taking place in Little Rock was, as one of the leaders has described it, an "awakening" to the possibilities of life in the modern world and the creation of a broader vision of what life could be for Arkansas and her people.[6]

By the mid-1950s Little Rock's leadership had reason to be proud of the transformation they were working in the economy of the city and the state. Industry was moving to Arkansas at an unprecedented rate; jobs were being created and the standard of living was beginning to rise; new construction on every hand bore eloquent testimony to heightened aspirations and the ca-pability to meet them. No one would have believed that in a mat-ter of months all of this would be jeopardized, but then no one would have believed that Little Rock—a town long noted for its enlightened racial policies and practices—would soon be the scene of the first major confrontation between state and federal powers over civil rights.[7]

An integral part of the postwar awakening in Little Rock was the growing awareness among civic leaders of the inequi-ties of segregation and a consequent commitment to the im-provement of black life in the community. As one student of this phenomenon has written: "There seems to have been a genuine movement of conscience among the white civic leadership, aided by a general willingness among the average white citizenry to permit the exploration of avenues of racial cooperation. . . . The

6   *Ibid.*
7   Garry Fullerton, "New Factories Thing of the Past in Little Rock," Nashville *Tennessean*, May 31, 1959; Griffin Smith, Jr., "Localism and Segregation: Racial Patterns in Little Rock, Arkansas, 1945–1954" (M.A. thesis, Columbia Univer-sity, n.d.); see also William Peters, *The Southern Temper* (Garden City, N.Y.: Doubleday, 1959), 69–71. The thesis of Little Rock's racial harmony is also pur-sued in Irving Spitzberg, "Racial Politics in Little Rock: 1954–1964," unpub-lished manuscript in possession of Spitzberg. See also "Researcher Says LR Prospered, Grew from Race Crisis," Arkansas *Democrat*, June 23, 1977.

failures of the city in the postwar decade were not failures of goodwill, but rather failures on the part of both races fully to comprehend what was required to make the Negroes 'first class citizens.'" Important community institutions began to respond to pressures for change—from the school board to the parks commission to the public library. According to one study, "the Negro changed his status more from 1945 to 1954 than he had in the previous fifty years, and the efforts to modify segregation in his favor met much more often with success than with failure." In short, this study concludes, "Segregation was weakening from within, and federal pressure was only one of at least three direct forces which contributed to its weakness. More significant by far were the developing social and civic consciousness among Negroes and the corresponding 'movement of conscience' among whites." Although this study may attribute too much to conscience and too little to business pragmatism, the conclusion does seem warranted that the status and opportunities of Little Rock's black citizens improved considerably in the postwar decade.[8]

In 1953 the Little Rock School Board hired a dynamic, hard-driving school administrator named Virgil Blossom to be superintendent of schools. Abreast of Supreme Court decisions with regard to desegregation in education, Blossom understood fully the implications of the recent rulings, and within days of the *Brown* decision in May of 1954, he and his school board announced their intent to comply with the Court's decision. One of Blossom's close associates later described his thinking on this issue at the time: "The NAACP pressure had nothing to do with Little Rock coming forward with a plan. That was evolved out of Virgil Blossom's reading of the decisions . . . about Negroes' pay, and giving them equal opportunities in schools. . . . Then he was watching *Brown* v. *Board of Education*, and when he read the decision on that, he spontaneously, voluntarily started working on his plan. He wasn't scared. He wasn't running from anyone at the time. He was really trying to cooperate, and do the right thing." The "Blossom Plan," as the plan for compliance came to be called, provided for a gradual program of integration beginning at the high school level and resulting in integration at all levels within six years.

8   Smith, "Localism and Segregation," 19, 99.

Unveiled in the spring of 1955, the plan was not scheduled to go into effect until September of 1957, by which time a new high school would be completed in the fashionable, lily-white Heights section west of town. Blossom apparently sold his plan to many of the city's civic and social leaders by pointing out that their children would not have to attend integrated Central High School. This points up a persistent complicating factor in any attempt at analysis of the Little Rock crisis: the existence of deep-seated class divisions within the community. The civic leadership exacerbated these divisions by calling for changes that would affect the power relations and customs and mores of the lower economic classes of whites without making similar demands of themselves. Some of these changes were in city government. The old mayor-alderman form of government, tied as it was to wards, drew representatives from all sections of the city, whereas the new manager-commissioner form drew its representatives almost exclusively from the fifth ward (the Heights), where the city's elite resided. The changes in city government thus removed power from the rest of the city and concentrated it in the affluent fifth ward; the changes in education necessitated by the Blossom Plan did not materially affect the fifth ward. In short, the civic leadership abdicated responsibility for bearing any of the unpleasant burden of change.[9]

In the two years before his plan was to go into effect, Virgil Blossom made scores of speeches before social and civic groups across the city, and by the spring of 1957 he and his school board were convinced that they had prepared Little Rock's citizens to accept the inevitability of integration and the workability of their plan. They were given heartening evidence of their success in the school board elections of that spring; although

9   Interview with A. F. House, August, 1971, Columbia University Oral History Program, on file at the Dwight David Eisenhower Presidential Library, Abilene, Kansas; Blaine Brownell and David Goldfield, *The City in Southern History: The Growth of Urban Civilization in the South* (Port Washington, N.Y.: Kennikat Press, 1977). For the text of the school board statement promising compliance with the *Brown* decision, see Virgil T. Blossom, *It HAS Happened Here* (New York: Harper, 1959), 11–12. The charge of Blossom's duplicity was first reported to the author in an interview in October, 1976, with Mrs. Daisy Bates, who was president of the Arkansas NAACP during the 1957 crisis. Interview with Daisy Bates by the author, October, 1976, Southern Oral History Program, University of North Carolina, Chapel Hill, North Carolina. Several white leaders, who have asked not to be identified, have corroborated this charge.

the newly organized Capital Citizens Council launched a frontal
assault on the Blossom Plan and ran two die-hard segregationists for the vacant school board positions, the "moderate" candidates who had declared their support for the plan carried the
election by a better than two-to-one margin. (Opposition to the
plan was concentrated in the working-class wards of the city.)
In essence a referendum on the Blossom Plan, this election suggested to Virgil Blossom and his supporters that the dominant
sentiment in Little Rock was a willingness to accept, however
grudgingly, the *Brown* decision as the law of the land. As one of
the school board members later recalled: "We had convinced the
community that there was no way to avoid it and that the intelligent, rational way of voluntarily planning the sequences of
events would have been much better than to be forced to do
things we didn't plan on doing."[10]

Despite a vigorous Citizens Council campaign throughout
the summer, capped by an incendiary rally featuring speeches
by two staunch segregationists, Georgia's Governor Marvin
Griffin and Roy V. Harris, the school board felt fairly complacent
until the last week or so in August, when they began to fear that
Governor Faubus might be contemplating a move to obstruct the
Blossom Plan. After numerous frustrating meetings with the
governor had ended in stalemate, the school board members began to consider the possibility of delaying implementation of
their plan. In the following days one of the representatives of
the segregationist Mothers' League of Central High School obtained an injunction in chancery court against the school board;
the federal district court struck down the injunction, and the
board found itself under court order to proceed with its desegregation plan.[11]

10   Blossom, *It HAS Happened Here;* interview with Harold Engstrom, December, 1970, Columbia University Oral History Program, Eisenhower Library. As
one of the moderate leaders realized later, "The supporters of the Blossom plan
were probably not representative of the community." Interview with W. S. Mitchell by the author, December, 1977.
11   Interviews with R. A. Lile, Henry Rath, Harold Engstrom, Wayne Upton,
and Richard C. Butler, Sr., by the author, all in December, 1977; interview with
R. A. Lile, August, 1971, Columbia University Oral History Program, Eisenhower Library. One of the best guides to the chronology of the Little Rock crisis
is included in *Crisis in the South: The Little Rock Story* (Little Rock: Arkansas
Gazette, 1959), compiled by the staff of the Arkansas *Gazette.* Other excellent

In a surprise move the day before school opened, on September 2, 1957, Orval Faubus called out the Arkansas National Guard and stationed them around Central High School, to what end it was not immediately clear. Faubus' motives in this action have been much debated, but it was generally believed at the time that he acted out of a desire to win an unprecedented third term in the statehouse; Faubus maintained then, and he still claims, that he acted out of a desire to prevent violence and bloodshed. Whatever the explanation, the black students who attempted to enter the school were turned away, and the governor of Arkansas had undertaken a test of one of the central tenets of the "massive resistance" philosophy by "interposing" the power of the state between its citizens and the power of the federal government. At various points across the South Orval Faubus became an overnight hero in the struggle against a "centralizing" federal government, but among Little Rock's civic leadership there was little rejoicing. Astute businessmen saw all that they had attempted to create being jeopardized. They saw their city's image as a progressive, stable community being superseded by the hated and, they believed, distorted characterizations of themselves as backwoods rubes and racists, and they knew a great sadness and a smoldering anger.[12]

After three weeks of inconclusive maneuvering, including a conference at Newport, Rhode Island, between Faubus and President Eisenhower, Federal District Judge Ronald Davies enjoined the governor and the Guard from interfering further with integration. Faubus removed his troops from around the high school, the Little Rock police moved in, and the city settled down for a tense weekend of waiting and anticipation. Monday

---

sources of information include Numan V. Bartley, *The Rise of Massive Resistance: Race and Politics in the South During the 1950's* (Baton Rouge: Louisiana State University Press, 1969), and Corinne Silverman, *The Little Rock Story* (Rev. ed.; University, Ala.: University of Alabama Press, 1959). Except in specific instances, citations will not be made to indicate the source of information on the unfolding chronology of the Little Rock crisis.

12   Interview with B. Finley Vinson by the author, December, 1977. Brooks Hays claims that when Roy Harris of Georgia heard that Faubus had called out the troops he wondered if Faubus had "called 'em out *for* us or *agin'* us." Brooks Hays, *A Southern Moderate Speaks* (Chapel Hill: University of North Carolina Press, 1959), 134. For a full discussion of this phenomenon see Bartley, *The Rise of Massive Resistance.*

morning the worst fears of all were realized as a surly crowd gathered about Central High School, breaking forth into a seething mob as word spread that the nine black children had slipped into the school through a side entrance. Two days of random violence left the city's business leaders heartsick about affairs in their community, but many of them were dismayed nonetheless when President Eisenhower made the fateful decision to send federal troops into an American city. As the "screaming eagles" of the 101st Airborne Division rumbled across the Broadway bridge into Little Rock, the community's leaders responded to the eerie spectacle with a mixture of resentment and relief. As one of them recalls the initial reaction: "Once you laid down the gauntlet, which the government did, I think many of us felt like we should rally behind the only leader we've got right now and that's Faubus; and I think many of us were weak in not standing up against him but rather feeling like 'Well, he's sort of a martyr to this cause.' Now you can criticize that attitude, looking back on it, but at the time, why we hadn't had federal troops since '67! That was so shocking that we didn't know whether we should support the government or not."[13]

The initial resentment was compounded by the national press coverage of the crisis. As one of the city's business leaders described the widespread feeling: "It was difficult to believe it had happened in the first place . . . and the reaction of the news media in making it seem more dramatic than it was was the second shock. . . . There was *not* the militant situation here that was played up; there was *not* an armed camp; there was a flurry, not a war."[14]

In this situation of confusion and strong emotion, clear thinking was at a premium. "There was not an absence of thinking and discussion in the business community," one business leader has suggested, "but to marshall the proper leadership and community sentiment into a cohesive direction couldn't be done by turning on a light switch." Furthermore, he recalls, "We

13 Interview with S. J. Beauchamp by the author, December, 1977; interview with Cooper Jacoway by the author, October, 1977; Hays, *A Southern Moderate Speaks,* 166–73; Engstrom interview, Columbia; Stebbins interview.
14 Vinson interview.

were fragmented to an extent, and we were resentful of the whole incident. It was making something of our town which we were ashamed of. We were, we *knew* that we were more progressive in the beginnings of racial integration than most of the South, and most *all* of the North, so our feelings were: Why us?" Another close observer has suggested that there was more involved here than the race issue: "There was also resistance to compulsion, especially among some self-made businessmen who were not accustomed to having people tell them what they could and could not do. . . . Orval Faubus drew great support from people of that nature . . . and some of these would have been way out front in any community development program."[15]

Despite the confusion and the resentment and the growing suspicion that perhaps integration was not inevitable after all—that perhaps Orval Faubus was right—Little Rock's business leaders began in a very short time to rally. The response of the business community from this point forward went through four stages of development, beginning with the businessman's traditional approach of seeking to work "behind the scenes." Although they shared a growing understanding that eventual compliance with the desegregation mandate was inevitable, they nonetheless worked feverishly for a number of months in an effort to secure a delay—a breathing space, a cooling-off period—during which time the community and the schools could be more properly prepared (or ways could be found to deal more effectively with the governor). This strategy failing, and the economic impact of the crisis becoming daily more apparent, the business community then moved out from behind the scenes and made an attempt to take over the school board, but they were only partially successful. After several months of inconclusive maneuvering within the school board they finally seized the opportunity to take their case to the people, elected a third school board dedicated to the "moderate" position of reopening the schools, and stationed one of their own leaders as president of the board. The immediate crisis having passed, the business community now moved into the fourth stage of its development, whereupon the most prestigious and influential of the downtown leaders, working in concert with selected representatives

15   *Ibid*; anonymous interview no. 1 by the author, December, 1977.

of the black community, assumed responsibility for assuring desegregation of all the city's public facilities. With each of the four stages of this crisis, Little Rock's businessmen achieved a greater understanding of both the economic impact and the moral imperatives of the situation that had been thrust upon them; although the economic arguments were used with much greater frequency, it is nonetheless clear that the businessmen of Little Rock experienced a growing awareness of the moral dimensions of the crisis.

Shortly after the arrival of the 101st Airborne, Clyde Lowry, president of one of the city's largest insurance companies and a leader in every area of civic life from the Community Chest to the country club, called together the twenty-five past presidents of the Chamber of Commerce, who then began meeting daily in an effort to arrive at some resolution of the conflict. They met, and they talked, day after day, but feeling was running too high in the group—in too many different directions—to arrive at any meaningful course of action. As one participant in these discussions has recalled, "There was much argument between those who were fiercely independent and those who were more realistic. The former thought the crisis would not hurt Little Rock economically," and only the passage of time convinced them of their error.[16]

At length the businessmen did issue a rather bland plea for peaceful compliance with court orders, but for the most part they failed to use their enormous influence either to challenge the governor or to lead public opinion. Not wanting to force the governor into an adversary position, and understanding the strong segregationist sentiment out in the state, they settled instead upon a plan of working behind the scenes to persuade the chief executive not to call a special session of the legislature. (Brooks Hays has suggested that the businessmen feared that if called, a special session of the legislature would, "unless the political climate changed, result either in closing Central High School altogether or penalties such as withdrawal of state aid.") In this they were successful, although they failed completely in

16   Hays, *A Southern Moderate Speaks*, 177. Others who were instrumental in organizing the businessmen were W. H. Sadler, W. M. Shepherd, Raymond Rebsamen, Sam Strauss, Walter Guy, and Warren Bray. Hays, *A Southern Moderate Speaks*, 183–84; anonymous interview no. 1.

their efforts to persuade Faubus that a stand for segregation would, in the long run, prove a less effective political force than a strong stand for law and order.[17]

Convinced, finally, that no progress could be made in the atmosphere of tension and high emotion prevailing in their city, the twenty-five business leaders began to concentrate on persuading the school board to abandon its plan and seek a delay from the federal district court. Virgil Blossom resisted this idea with great vigor, however, whereupon he and his board fell increasingly into disfavor with the city's business leadership. Day by day the six school board members found themselves increasingly isolated—from the segregationists, from the governor, from the federal government, and now from their own community leaders—and only their conviction that they were right, and their devotion to Virgil Blossom, sustained them through the difficult and tedious days.[18]

As one of the school board members has suggested, the businessmen were scared. "The traditional leadership *hid*," he claims, "mainly because of greed—they were afraid they'd lose business if they openly supported the school board. It took a long time for them to realize that the crisis was hurting everybody." Another school board member has suggested, with greater feeling, that the business leaders were "chickens." "They were trying to figure out some way to run," he recalls,

and avoid the problem. You know they wanted to back up, they wanted to fire the school board, they wanted to go back to the Supreme Court and ask for mercy. They wanted to go on their knees to Faubus, or anything they could do to get this terrible thing off the back of the community. . . . [They were scared of this] terrible calamity which no one was removing, and they were just looking for a way out. . . . They'd take any kind of agreement with segregationists or integrationists or anyone if they could just get this thing to move to Jackson, Mississippi, or Fort Smith, or Memphis, or anywhere except Little Rock.

17   Hays, *A Southern Moderate Speaks*, 183; Henry Gemmill and Joseph Guilfoyle, "The Quiet Force in Arkansas," *Wall Street Journal*, October 8, 1957, clipping in the Brooks Hays Papers, John Fitzgerald Kennedy Presidential Library, Waltham, Massachusetts; interview with Sam Strauss by the author, December, 1977.
18   Hays, *A Southern Moderate Speaks*, 181; anonymous interview no. 2 by the author, December, 1977; anonymous interview no. 3 by the author, December, 1977; Upton interview; Rath interview.

They thought that it was going to be the end of the good life here in Little Rock. They thought we'd never recover.[19]

Many suggestions could be offered for the failure of the community's traditional leadership to exert a more positive influence on affairs in their city. Many businessmen feared the crippling or destruction of their businesses; many others felt an obligation to stockholders, clients, and employees to protect their jobs and investments; numerous leaders hesitated to jeopardize the November "Good Government" election—the campaign to elect the first slate of city commissioners—by allowing that campaign to become associated in the public mind with the desegregation conflict.[20] Despite all these considerations, however, probably the best explanation of elite behavior is to be found in the admission by one member of the group that "in their hearts" most civic leaders believed that Orval Faubus was right; they might not come right out and openly support the Citizens Council, but they tacitly agreed with the arguments these people were making. After all, racial prejudice had flourished for over a hundred years in Arkansas, and it could not be expected to subside overnight.[21]

19   Anonymous interview no. 3 by the author; anonymous interview no. 2 by the author.
20   Interview with Frank Lyon by the author, December, 1977; Butler interview; Beauchamp interview. The fear of economic loss was well founded; as one observer recalls: "When Faubus closed the schools here, and the Eastern Arkansas people [where Arkansas' plantation wealth is concentrated] threatened the banks in Little Rock with 'we will move our money to Memphis' . . . the businessmen of Little Rock were afraid to buck them, and therefore we didn't have any community support." Interview with Terrell E. Powell, November, 1972, Columbia University Oral History Program, Eisenhower Library. As one business leader recalls: "Either their institution or their industry or their business would be almost immediately boycotted, not by a few but the majority. And you say, 'Well, that's a poor excuse, that's putting money before principle,' but a lot of these businesses aren't owned by these people. . . . [A businessman] has got to look at the other people in there too. In a matter like that when you're getting ready to *destroy* something you can't just say, 'Well, here's the way I feel.' You must take into consideration not only the people who work there but the people who own it." Lyon interview. Although the Citizens Council ran a full slate of candidates on an openly segregationist platform, the Good Government Committee refused to inject the racial issue into the campaign, and the "moderate" candidates won six of the seven seats on the city commission.
21   Interview with Robert D. Lowry (Clyde Lowry's son) by the author, December, 1977. See also "A random report on EFV's [Emory Via] Little Rock trip,

By February of 1958 the Chamber of Commerce group, and the unyielding crisis in Little Rock, had worn down the resistance of the school board. The board's representatives had attempted repeatedly to arrange an audience with President Eisenhower or his aides, and they had carried on an extensive correspondence in pursuit of this goal. They had also prepared an impressive slide and chart presentation that demonstrated the negative impact of desegregation on the quality of education in Little Rock and had presented it to a number of the members of Congress—hoping thereby to achieve some executive or legislative support, or at least understanding, in their dilemma. The school board finally agreed to allow one of its attorneys, Richard C. Butler, Sr.—who was also, not incidentally, one of the past presidents of the Chamber of Commerce—to place a suit before the federal district court in Little Rock seeking a postponement of integration until: "(1) the concept of 'all deliberate speed' could be defined clearly, and (2) effective legal procedures for integrating the schools could be developed in a manner that would not impair the quality of the educational program." The businessmen's group knew that Governor Faubus also desired a delay—so that the state's segregation legislation could be tested in the courts—and since the Dallas School Board had recently been granted such a breathing space, there was some reason to hope for success. As Brooks Hays has written: "One should keep in mind that the Governor had steadfastly held to the idea that time was the key to the solution—that delays in integration orders were essential. He continued to maintain that, in Arkansas, no state functionary should be compelled to support federal orders until the constitutionality of the interposition and other statutes approved by the people was determined."[22]

February 14–16, 1958," February, 1958, Southern Regional Council Papers, Southern Regional Council, Atlanta, Georgia, which suggests that the executive director of the Arkansas Council on Human Relations "feels that the business community supports Faubus' general position."

22   Hays, *A Southern Moderate Speaks*, 187–89; Butler interview; R. A. Lile to Dwight David Eisenhower, January 18, 1958, and R. A. Lile to Senator Richard Russell, February 1, 1958, both in Richard Russell Papers, Richard Russell Memorial Library, Athens, Georgia; Sherman Adams to R. A. Lile, February 19, 1958, R. A. Lile to D. D. Eisenhower, February 21, 1958, and Memo from "Mary" to "Governor" (Sherman Adams), March 21, 1958, all in Official File, White House Central Files, Eisenhower Library; Lile interview.

On February 20 the Little Rock School Board formally filed its petition requesting a delay, and NAACP lawyers requested, unsuccessfully, that the court dismiss the petition without a hearing on its merits. Throughout the spring of 1958 Federal District Judge Harry J. Lemley of Hope, Arkansas, considered the board's request, occasionally asking for further information and clarification. Governor Faubus, in the meantime, mounted a dazzling campaign for a third term, which he won handily the following summer.[23]

On June 21, 1958, Judge Lemley granted a delay of integration in Little Rock until January of 1961. He conceded that the black students had the constitutional right to attend the white schools but held that, given the school board's testimony concerning the chaos and tension at Central High, the time had not yet come for them to enjoy that right. Immediately the NAACP appealed this decision to the Eighth Circuit Court of Appeals in St. Louis, and on August 18 that court set aside the Lemley delay order. Within a week Governor Faubus had called a special session of the Arkansas legislature to deal with the integration problem, and the Little Rock School Board had appealed the circuit court decision to the Supreme Court.[24]

Before an unusual called session of the United States Supreme Court in September of 1958, Richard Butler argued the case for the Little Rock School Board and Thurgood Marshall argued for the NAACP. On September 12 the Court handed down its finding in the epochal decision *Cooper* v. *Aaron*, which established the principle that community opposition was not a sufficient cause for delaying integration, and which ordered the Little Rock School Board to proceed with its integration plan; thereupon Orval Faubus signed into law a bill passed by the special session of the legislature that empowered him to close all the city's high schools. Plans were then set afoot, unsuccessfully, to lease the public school buildings to the newly formed Private School Corporation, and Little Rock's parents began a frantic search for some form of schooling for their children.

The school closings introduced a new element into the Little Rock crisis. Many people who had failed prior to this to see the

23   Arkansas Council on Human Relations, "Progress Report, Second Quarter, 1957–1958," Southern Regional Council Papers, Atlanta, Georgia.
24   *Crisis in the South*, 97.

implications of the Faubus position now found themselves directly involved, and in a most uncomfortable fashion. As one school board member recalls: "That was the first . . . deep hurt that they got. Of course their pride was hurt when the troops came and their pride was hurt when we became sort of a national spectacle, but not very deeply felt. But when you close a school and your number one son doesn't have a place to go to school, and all your hopes and dreams have rested on him, it's a very deep hurt."[25]

On all sides the cost of all-out resistance was painfully apparent, and at this point many "ordinary" citizens found their voice. Most hopeful of all the responses was the formation, under the leadership of one of Little Rock's great ladies, Adolphine Fletcher Terry, of the Women's Emergency Committee to Open Our Schools. Conceived originally as an organization to work for racial justice, the Women's Emergency Committee quickly scaled down its objectives when the leaders realized the timidity of the ladies and the possibility of using the schools issue to build a broad base of support for a more enlightened position on the integration question. Housed in the Heights and drawing its support primarily from the affluent fifth ward, the Women's Emergency Committee was a hopeful indicator of a change in attitude and awareness on the part of Little Rock's civic elite. As the businessman husband of one of the ladies has suggested, the women could speak out when often it would have been economically dangerous for the men to do so.[26]

---

25   Anonymous interview no. 1, December, 1970, Columbia University Oral History Program, Eisenhower Library.
26   Vivion Lenon Brewer, "The Embattled Ladies of Little Rock," unpublished manuscript in the Vivion Lenon Brewer Papers, Sophia Smith Collection, Smith College, Northampton, Massachusetts; interview with Vivion Lenon Brewer by the author, October, 1976, Southern Oral History Program, University of North Carolina, Chapel Hill, North Carolina; interview with Frank Lambright by the author, December, 1977. Mrs. Terry, a Vassar graduate, was the wife of a former Arkansas congressman and the sister of one of the "Nashville Agrarians," Arkansas' poet laureate John Gould Fletcher. As one businessman describes her, at any point during the crisis "the phone would ring and it would be Mrs. Terry, who must be ninety, saying 'Grainger, what are you businessmen going to do about this now? We must get busy!' Always you'd hear this voice—a rather remarkable woman, who wasn't afraid of the Devil himself, you know, and whom everybody respected even when they might disagree with her." Interview with E. Grainger Williams, December, 1970, Columbia University Oral History Program, Eisenhower Library.

Downtown businessmen also developed new insight into the Little Rock crisis in the fall of 1958. As Chamber of Commerce committees began to make industrial recruiting visits to cities in other states, only to learn that no one was interested in moving to Little Rock, the impact of the crisis on the community's economy became all too apparent.[27]

At this point one of the city's most successful business leaders, William F. Rector, stepped into the fray. Although he resented what he perceived as northern self-righteousness and federal force as much as any man in town, Rector was on the Chamber's industrial committee, and he had also had the sad experience of losing a ten-million-dollar shopping center because of the continuing difficulties in Little Rock. In November, 1958, the school board resigned in despair because the community had abdicated its responsibility for education and had allowed the integration dispute to become a fight between Faubus and the school board. As one of them recalls: "We resigned because we had tried every avenue open to us, and had failed, and we had no other options. . . . They kept referring to it as 'our problem,' and we thought it was the whole community's problem, and by this action, the community had no other choice. We made it their problem." With the resignation of the school board, Rector took it upon himself to organize a "businessmen's slate" to fill the vacant positions and to get the city off dead center in its confrontation with federal authority. The ensuing school board elections in December reflected fairly accurately the divisions within the community: three of the "moderate" businessmen were elected by a combination of votes from the affluent sections of the city and the black precincts; precinct majorities in the working-class sections of the city also added three arch-segregationists to the board. Unfortunately this three-three split on the school board precluded any positive action toward resolving the impasse, but as the months passed, the conviction spread that the schools must be reopened, even if that meant integration.[28]

27 Anonymous interview no. 1 by the author. In fact, Little Rock would not gain another new industry until 1961. Fullerton, "New Factories Thing of the Past in Little Rock."

28 Vinson interview; *Crisis in the South*, 96; "15 Candidates File for School Board; Karam Withdraws," Arkansas *Gazette*, November 16, 1958; interview

At the beginning of the new year the incoming president of the Chamber of Commerce, E. Grainger Williams, shocked the crowd assembled to hear his inaugural address by calling for an end to the crisis. Discussion of the events in Little Rock had long been taboo in refined circles, for one was never sure of the convictions and sentiments of one's peers and associates; and so when Grainger Williams called for an evaluation of the cost of education and "the cost of lack of it," a gasp went through the crowd, followed shortly by a wave of applause. At last someone in a position of authority had spoken out publicly, and soon public discussion of the crisis became acceptable and widespread.[29]

Under Grainger Williams' leadership the Chamber of Commerce board soon asked the general membership to vote on two questions: (1) Do you favor Little Rock's continuing with closed public high schools? (Yes—230; No—632; Not voting—285), and (2) Do you now favor reopening the Little Rock public high schools on a controlled minimum plan of integration acceptable to the federal courts? (Yes—819; No—245; Not voting—83). In March the Chamber's board issued an official policy statement which concluded with the observation that: "The decision of the Supreme Court of the United States, however much we dislike it, is the declared law and is binding on us. We think that the decision was erroneous and that it was a reversal of established law upon an unprecedented base of psychology and sociology. But we must in honesty recognize that, because the Supreme Court is the court of last resort in this country, what it has said must stand until there is a correcting constitutional amendment or until the Court corrects its own error. We must live and act now under the decision of that Court."[30]

By May of 1959 the respectability of opposing Governor

---

with Everett Tucker, Jr., by the author, December, 1977; anonymous interview no. 3 by the author; anonymous interview no. 1, Columbia; "Two Slates and One School Board," Arkansas *Gazette*, December 9, 1958; "The School Vote," Arkansas *Gazette*, December 9, 1958.

29   Williams was also an active worker in the Urban League and the Southern Regional Council affiliate, the Arkansas Council on Human Relations. Williams interview, Columbia; anonymous interview no. 1 by the author; *Crisis in the South*, 102.

30   "Position of the Little Rock Chamber of Commerce, March 23, 1959," in Wilson Record and Jane Cassels Record, *Little Rock USA: Materials for Analysis* (San Francisco: Chandler Publishing Company, 1960), 141–42.

Faubus had been established (although it was still far from "fashionable"), and many people were seeking an issue with which to challenge the governor's hold over the city. A rump session of the school board (the three moderates had walked out) handed such citizens the issue they needed when the three segregationists on the board summarily fired forty-four teachers and administrators, including some of the most beloved teachers in the system, for supporting compliance with the desegregation order. No immediate explanation was given for the firings but school board president Ed I. McKinley later admitted that a stand in favor of integration was "part of the criterion." Here was an issue around which all "right-thinking" people could rally, and within thirty-six hours the PTA of Forest Park School (in the Heights) was calling for a movement to Stop This Outrageous Purge (STOP) by recalling the offending members of the school board. The segregationists responded with a Committee to Retain Our Segregated Schools (CROSS), which called for the recall of the moderate school board members.[31]

Led by Will Mitchell and Ed Lester, two lawyers of undisputed influence and respectability, the STOP campaign was the point at which the civic elite found its voice. In this brief space the issues were crystal clear, and they involved nothing more threatening than fairness, educational opportunity, and economic growth for all. As one of the leaders of the effort recalls, "A lot of people that worked on the STOP campaign wouldn't go with us on opening the schools integrated; they didn't want to get in that black and white thing, but they wanted their voices to be heard because they felt like they ought to be doing *something* in this crisis, and this was something they could do. . . . They could get on that bandwagon and do it without feeling that they were being unfaithful to anything they'd been taught." After a fervent campaign in which many businessmen openly endorsed the program of the STOP forces and many others opened their pocketbooks to pay for a massive advertising and propaganda campaign, the STOP forces prevailed and the three segregationists were removed from the board, soon to be replaced by three men of a more "moderate" stamp. The determin-

31   "Attitude Not Sole Factor in Releases; But Board President Admits Integration Stand Considered," Arkansas *Democrat*, May 6, 1958.

ing factor in the STOP victory was the alignment of voters in the fifth ward with those in black precincts. This alignment also brought victory for moderate forces in the city commission elections of November, 1957, and the school board elections of March, 1957, both of which had strong racial overtones.[32]

The STOP campaign was the turning point in Little Rock. Although the issues were always argued in terms of fairness to the teachers, everyone understood that the real issue at hand was compliance or resistance, schools or no schools, integration or segregation. Although by a slim majority, the people of Little Rock in May of 1959 voted for integration, for schools, and for a return to sanity in their community. They had played out their fears, and their resentments, in the year and a half since Faubus first called out his troops, and they had come to understand the price of holding to the "southern way of life." It was a price they were not willing to pay.

Symbolic of this new disposition in Little Rock was the new president of the school board, Everett Tucker, Jr., grandson of a Confederate veteran who had moved to Arkansas and established a profitable cotton plantation, Tucker had attended Washington and Lee and Harvard Business School. Married to a Vassar graduate who was the granddaughter of a United States senator from Arkansas, Tucker returned to Arkansas after serving in World War II, but he had no desire to settle down to farming. Instead, sharing in the postwar awakening in his state, he became the industrial director for the Little Rock Chamber of Commerce, where he was instrumental in developing the Little Rock Industrial District and the air force base.[33]

---

32   Of course the deeper divisions involved issues of class as well as race. Injecting the ever-present class issue into the campaign, as he always did with great skill, Governor Faubus labeled the STOP forces "the Cadillac brigade," and addressed his remarks to the "honest hard-working" lower and middle classes. "The Intervention of Orval Faubus," Arkansas *Gazette*, May 26, 1959; interview with E. Grainger Williams by the author, December, 1977; William Starr Mitchell Scrapbook, in possession of W. S. Mitchell, Little Rock, Arkansas. See also Samuel Lubell, *White and Black: Test of a Nation* (New York: Harper and Row, 1964), 73–75.

33   Everett Tucker, Jr., was William F. Rector's best friend; interview with Everett Tucker, Jr., August, 1971, Columbia University Oral History Program, Eisenhower Library; interview with Everett Tucker, Jr., by the author, December, 1977.

Not only did Tucker's abandonment of rural values set him apart from an older southern tradition; his racial attitudes also reflected a changing South. Describing himself as having been "typical of the conservative enlightened southern viewpoint" in 1957, Tucker recalls that:

You rebelled against the doing away with what you had grown up knowing, and without any personal vindictiveness or any ill feeling toward the colored race, you'd just always gone to separate schools, and this was the way it was supposed to do. This is what you learned at your mother's knee, and you don't learn anything bad at your mother's knee. Once you got over the shock of the realization that this was coming to an end, this way of doing things, then I would say . . . that I regarded Virgil Blossom's plan as being a very practical, intelligent, token approach to easing into the thing. . . . [Now] I've gotten to where I think really it's for the good of both races to adopt sensible programs for letting white and Negro children go to school together.

In the year that Everett Tucker became president of the Little Rock School Board, his wife became president of the exclusive Aesthetic Club, oldest literary club for ladies west of the Mississippi; the Tuckers represented the quintessence of respectability in Little Rock, and when they called for the reopening of the schools, when they spoke of the need to attract industry to Arkansas, when they challenged the hold of Governor Faubus over their city, people listened.[34]

After the successful STOP campaign the community's business leadership lined up solidly behind Everett Tucker and his allies. The Citizens Council brand of thinking had been thoroughly discredited by this time; as one business leader recalls: "Citizens Council influence was practically nil. . . . Their leaders didn't have any influence or public leadership in the community, and successful people didn't want to be identified with them." At last leading citizens found themselves willing to step forward and proclaim publicly: "We may not agree with the decisions of the Supreme Court of the United States, but they are the law of the land and will so remain until changed by constitutional process." When the schools reopened in August, six black students enrolled, and the Little Rock crisis was over.[35]

34   Tucker interview, Columbia; "Aesthetic Club Yearbook, 1957–1958," Aesthetic Club Papers, Little Rock Public Library, Little Rock, Arkansas.
35   Vinson interview; "Committee for the Peaceful Operation of Free Public

Of much greater significance, in the long run, was the formation of a "secret committee" of the city's leading merchants, bankers, and Chamber of Commerce representatives—and also selected black leaders—which committed itself with considerable success to desegregating all the city's public facilities. As one member of this committee describes it: "This was a natural step after the STOP campaign. It resulted from the cohesiveness of the business community that began with the STOP campaign . . . and it reflected a firm forward movement that didn't ever stop."[36]

Indisputably, the work of Little Rock's secret committee had positive economic consequences for the city. Little Rock finally began to prosper economically in the 1960s, and there can be little doubt but that this boom was facilitated by the business leaders' ability to guarantee stability and racial "harmony" in their community. But these economic rewards and realities should not obscure the larger truth that many of Little Rock's businessmen had also transcended the South's traditional preoccupation with race and white supremacy and had arrived at last at a willingness, for whatever reasons, to allow black people to move beyond the confines of segregation and caste.[37]

This is not to suggest that racial attitudes in Little Rock, or even the attitudes of the elite, underwent a significant transformation in response to the civil rights challenge. In fact the elite in Little Rock sent their children to all-white Hall High School and thus were spared the anguish and adjustment of parents with children at integrated Central. Furthermore, William F. Rector, one of the leaders of the 1958 movement to reopen the schools, later spearheaded the development of all-white Pulaski Academy—an exclusive private academy in western Little Rock.

Schools, Statement by Chairman J. Gaston Williamson," July 29, 1959, Southern Regional Council Papers, Atlanta, Georgia.

36   Anonymous interview no. 4 by the author, December, 1977; Vinson interview.

37   Orval Faubus has argued consistently through the years that Little Rock's economic slowdown in the late 1950s was a response to a national economic recession, and that the Little Rock crisis had no adverse effect on Little Rock's economy; Orval Faubus to author, October 9, 1979. The Women's Emergency Committee to Open Our Schools compiled and circulated a *Little Rock Report* in 1959 that documented graphically the adverse impact that the crisis was having on Little Rock's economy.

Nonetheless, upon realizing the cost—in dollars and in self-respect—of allowing the crisis to continue unabated, Little Rock's businessmen used their enormous power and influence not only to put an end to what had become a racial spectacle, but also to move their city beyond traditional patterns of race relations. What emerged from the Little Rock crisis was one community's growing awareness that, if the priorities had to be faced squarely, economic growth was more important to her than absolute white supremacy.[38]

In the years since 1959, race relations in Little Rock have undergone significant changes. Initially tokenism was all that the school board was willing to concede, and Little Rock's public schools could not in reality be described as integrated; in the 1960s, however, with the development of effective black protest, the city adopted a system of busing that led to meaningful integration. By the end of the 1970s, Little Rock's public schools had become more than 50 percent black, and the private school movement and "white flight" were the primary threats to effective public education. On the other hand, Central High School had climbed to its precrisis levels of excellence under the leadership of a popular black principal, and the ratio of black to white had increased steadily at the University of Arkansas at Little Rock. During the 1960s and 1970s blacks assumed a far more active role in the life of the community—serving on the school board and the city commission and at every level of city government—and black faces became much more in evidence in clerical and managerial positions across the city. Old patterns of suspicion and mistrust persisted on both sides of the color line, but new areas of communication and understanding were developing. Little Rock was far from being a truly integrated society, but a meaningful start had been made in that direction.

In 1954 most Little Rock people responded to the *Brown* decision, if they thought about it at all, with the belief that "it can't happen here"; but the progressive leadership of the school board led them by 1957 to at least a grudging willingness to accept

38 See Earl Black, *Southern Governors and Civil Rights: Racial Segregation as a Campaign Issue in the Second Reconstruction* (Cambridge, Mass.: Harvard University Press, 1976), 338, and Richard Cramer, "School Desegregation and New Industry: The Southern Community Leaders' Viewpoint," *Social Forces*, XLI (May, 1963), 384–89.

the inevitable. By 1957 there was a range of sentiment within the business community, as elsewhere, from a moral conviction that integration was right, through a pragmatic understanding that it was inevitable, to a willingness to believe it could be averted, to an all-out will to resist. The dominant sentiment in 1957 seems to have been about midway between the suspicion that integration was inevitable and the hope that it would some-how just go away. With Orval Faubus' defiant bid to prove that integration was not inevitable, many members of the business community, as in the community at large, took heart that south-ern culture and traditions could be preserved, and only the im-pending destruction of their community—made clear by the closing of the schools and the massive loss of business and in-dustrial development—shocked Little Rock's traditional leader-ship into a willingness to accept the dreaded changes in their customs and mores.

Once again the range of feeling was very broad in the busi-ness community by 1959, but unmistakably the whole scale had shifted appreciably to the left. By 1959 many business leaders shared Everett Tucker's pragmatic assessment: "We sort of felt," Tucker recalls, "even those of us that were archconservatives, that Faubus had tried, and failed, and now let's get on with the game and comply with the court order, but still not with any great rushing out, just keep it in low profile and do what we had to, to get off the front pages." On the other hand, many other business leaders shared Chamber of Commerce President Grain-ger Williams' commitment to getting the schools open "on what ever basis we could in the framework of the law as it had been interpreted." Both points of view—that espoused by Tucker and that by Williams—represent a significant break with the past in response to the realities of the present.[39]

The role of Little Rock's businessmen in the crisis in their city reveals in microcosm the dilemma of responsible men and women across the South. Confronted with a situation for which they were totally unprepared, Little Rock's leaders recoiled from the reality of facing their deep-seated racial anxieties and fears; only months after the crisis had developed were they able to re-harness their emotions and identify the real issues confronting

39   Tucker interview by the author; Williams interview, Columbia.

their community. Other cities learned much from Little Rock, and their leaders were able to take a more active role in preparing their communities for the inevitable changes; the evidence of Little Rock's economic decline was a potent deterrent to other southern leaders' desires to resist federal and civil rights pressures for change.[40]

Based on the assumption that ideas are the handmaiden of economics, a Marxist analysis of the Little Rock crisis would undoubtedly conclude that Little Rock's business leaders abandoned their commitment to white supremacy when it was no longer useful to them economically. Viewed from one angle this study could, perhaps, support such a conclusion. Viewed from another, this examination of Little Rock's business leaders could support a quite different, non-Marxist hypothesis. The Little Rock experience could suggest that the southern determination to maintain a "progressive image" reflected more than simply a desire for economic gain, and that even the push for new industry stemmed from more than economic self-interest and greed. The Little Rock experience could suggest that the emphasis on "image" also reflected a desire to join, at last, the American mainstream—to be shed of the image of backwoods rubes and racists, to put an end to northern moral superiority, to lay down the burden of second-class citizenship. As Paul Gaston has suggested, the New South impulse from the start reflected a desire to share in "the promise of American life."[41]

These are powerful considerations that go deep in the southern psyche. From the beginning of this nation's history southerners have been different, outside the mainstream, and subject to criticism and attack. Throughout the first half of the twentieth century, as C. Vann Woodward argues in *The Strange Career of Jim Crow*, southerners congratulated themselves on their progressiveness and their growing kinship with other Americans, and thus they were doubly shocked and dismayed at the renewed northern assault on southern institutions in the "second Reconstruction."[42]

40   "Business in Dixie: Many Southerners Say Racial Tension Slows Area's Economic Gains," *Wall Street Journal*, May 26, 1961, p. 1.
41   Paul M. Gaston, *The New South Creed: A Study in Southern Mythmaking* (New York: Knopf, 1970).
42   C. Vann Woodward, *The Strange Career of Jim Crow* (3rd ed.; New York: Oxford University Press, 1975), 111–88.

Southerners had grown weary of being outsiders. They had feasted briefly at the table of national unity and prosperity in the era of segregation and had developed a taste for the bounty—material and spiritual—of that board. When the civil rights movement forced the southern people to come to grips with the realities of their departure from acceptable patterns of behavior, their desire to "belong," to be freed of the stigma of being different—coupled with a healthy regard for the balance sheet—led them into a willingness to forge a new pattern in southern race relations. The experience of the Little Rock crisis reflects this change. Although a determination to maintain white supremacy had been the cardinal tenet of southern thought throughout most of the region's history, the behavior of Little Rock's businessmen in the midst of crisis in their city reveals that these southerners' values had undergone a fundamental transformation. Although racism had by no means gone by the board in Little Rock, a desire for economic growth, and for sharing in all aspects of America's bounty, had taken precedence over the desire to maintain white supremacy. Little Rock would still have to wrestle with the legacies of slavery and segregation, as would the rest of the nation, but now that struggle would be couched in terms that placed this southern city, at last, squarely in the mainstream of American life.

WILLIAM CHAFE

GREENSBORO, NORTH CAROLINA

PERSPECTIVES ON PROGRESSIVISM

During the civil rights era many cities became bellwethers of the larger struggle, but perhaps none more consistently than Greensboro, North Carolina. The night after the Supreme Court handed down its historic ruling in *Brown* v. *Board of Education*, Greensboro's school board declared its intent to comply with the desegregation edict. Three years later the city became one of the first to engage in token desegregation—and then almost immediately adopted a posture of resisting any further integration efforts. Partly as a result of that resistance, Greensboro became the birthplace of the sit-in movement in 1960. In 1963 renewed massive demonstrations helped to propel a young man named Jesse Jackson into national prominence. By the late 1960s Greensboro had become the regional center of the Black Power movement. Finally, in 1971, the city became one of the last major urban areas in the South to accept full-scale desegregation—nearly two decades after *Brown*.

Irony abounds in this history. Although in accepting token desegregation in 1957 Greensboro appeared to be a pioneering symbol of the New South, the city was also helping to preserve segregation by blocking a class action suit against the entire

North Carolina school system. As school board chairman John Foster told segregationists at the time, "Dammit, we're holding an umbrella over your head," using the presence of Negroes in one white school to ensure their exclusion from hundreds of others. When the sit-ins began, Greensboro's white leaders succeeded in retaining their image of moderation by urging negotiations. Yet after token concessions on lunch counters in 1960, and then on cafeterias in 1963, white city leaders refused to promote further integration in jobs, government, or schools. Instead, one white executive said, it was up to the Negro "to take a responsible position . . . [and to show] that he is a responsible element." As a result one of the South's most "progressive" cities actually lagged behind more overtly bigoted areas in securing integration and racial justice.[1]

Business leadership played a central role in bringing about this paradox. Greensboro served as the corporate headquarters of numerous textile empires, including Burlington Industries, the largest textile firm in the world, and Cone Mills. It also was a major insurance center, serving as the headquarters of Jefferson Standard and Pilot Life insurance companies. During most of the 1950s and 1960s executives in these companies helped to shape Greensboro's civil rights history in two ways: they insisted that city *appear* moderate and enlightened in its approach to race relations, and simultaneously they refused to initiate or support substantive changes toward racial equality beyond the minimum necessary to sustain a progressive image. With primary emphasis on maintaining a public appearance, there was little chance that any action would be taken on the underlying problems of racism that pervaded the community. Thus during the 1960 sit-ins, business leaders convened a negotiating committee to stop the demonstrations, but refused to force Woolworth's and others to desegregate. Only when blacks took mat-

1   Research for this article is drawn from a combination of oral and written sources. See William H. Chafe, *Civilities and Civil Rights: Greensboro, North Carolina and the Black Struggle for Freedom* (New York: Oxford University Press, 1980) for a full listing of these sources as well as a report on the larger research project of which this article is one part. The quotation from John Foster is from the author's interview with Foster, February, 1973. The white executive's comment appears in W. O. Conrad to William Thomas, September 9, 1963, in the David Schenck Papers, a private collection made available to the author by David Schenck, Jr. Schenck was mayor of Greensboro during the mid-1960s.

ters in their own hands with an economic boycott and further demonstrations were the lunch counters integrated. Similarly, in 1963 black protesters had to push the city almost to the point of martial law before business executives could be mobilized to support concessions, and even then the primary goal was to do the minimum necessary to prevent further demonstrations.

Nowhere was this concern with image over substance more present than in the school board's attitude toward desegregation. Dominated throughout these years by business leaders, the school board repeatedly insisted that Greensboro's action in accepting token desegregation in 1957 proved her liberalism and let her off the hook as far as further desegregation was concerned. Two episodes illustrate this approach. When the parents of four black children sued the board in 1959 for denying their youngsters entry into a previously all-white school, the board first argued that it had already integrated its schools. Then, in an effort to defeat what the school board attorney called "as important a suit . . . as has arisen in North Carolina," the board said it would accept the black children. But subsequently it transferred every white student and teacher out of the school, replacing them with blacks. The board could thereby argue in court that the suit by Negro parents was "moot" since their children were now enrolled in the school to which they had applied. In a similar subterfuge a few years later the school board boasted of its freedom of choice plan, yet provided no transportation for children in black neighborhoods who wished to attend predominantly white schools.[2]

By the late 1960s such policies had produced a series of confrontations with angry blacks and the federal government.

2 *McCoy* v. *Greensboro School Board*, 283 F. 2nd 667 (September, 1959); Greensboro *Daily News*, February 25, April 21, July 22, September 24, 1959, November 16, December 17, 1960; Greensboro *Record*, August 29, 1958, July 22, September 1, 1959; American Friends Services Committee staff memorandum, June 25, 1959, in American Friends Service Committee Papers, Philadelphia, Pennsylvania. For a full discussion of Greensboro's position on freedom of choice, see Chafe, *Civilities and Civil Rights*, 232–38. See also Greensboro *Daily News*, April 20, May 23, October 13, November 20, 1968; Greensboro *Record*, April 17, 18, May 16, September 13, 1968; "Evaluation of a Team Visit of HEW to Greensboro Schools—April 17–18, 1968," an internal Greensboro school board document; interviews by the author with George Evans, February, 1978, George and Anna Simkins, July, 1972, Kay Troxler, June, 1973, Cecil Bishop, October, 1977, Otis Hairston, August, 1972, Hal Sieber, November, 1974, and Joan Bluethenthal, July, 1977.

When HEW urged Greensboro to use geographical zoning, curriculum reform, and grade clusters to promote integration, school leaders responded: "We will stand pat with freedom of choice." Although forty-two of Greensboro's forty-seven schools were immediately identifiable as black or white, sixteen were totally segregated, and 92 percent of blacks went to schools that were more than 95 percent Negro, the school superintendent claimed that "no child has been denied a desegregated education in Greensboro since 1957." As in the past it appeared that only massive action by blacks, or a crisis directly threatening the city's progressive image, could evoke a response by political and business leaders in support of change in race relations.[3]

Just such a situation developed in Greensboro during the spring of 1969. Over the preceding two years young black activists had mobilized increasing support for a Black Power alliance of students and adults, working-class and middle-class blacks. Using local colleges as a base, the activists recruited high school students, one of whom—Claude Barnes—ran for student body president at Dudley High. When school authorities barred Barnes's candidacy (giving no reason), students elected him anyway with write-in votes. After school officials declared the election illegal, students marched out in protest. Eventually the demonstrating erupted in violence, police attacked with tear gas and billy clubs, and the National Guard was mobilized. Within days a student had been killed by a shot through the head (students accused police and the police denied responsibility), armored personnel carriers rumbled through black neighborhoods, and troops mounted a massive military sweep of North Carolina A & T college dormitories to eliminate snipers. That same month the school board threw down a gauntlet of defiance to HEW, insisting that it would resist federal orders to desegregate all the way to the Supreme Court if necessary. The city's reputation for tolerance, urbanity, and progressivism lay in shambles.[4]

3   Greensboro *Record*, May 16, September 13, 1968, May 16, 1969; Greensboro *Daily News*, November 20, 1968, June 8, August 1 and 20, 1969, February 27, 1970, May 1, 1971; interviews by the author with Al Lineberry, December, 1974, Walter Johnson, December, 1978, and with Sieber, Bluethenthal, and Evans.
4   For a full discussion of the conflict at Dudley High School and A & T, see Chafe, *Civilities and Civil Rights*, 242–86. See also reports in the Greensboro *Daily News*, Greensboro *Record*, and *Carolina Peacemaker*, May through July,

As awareness seeped in of how destructive further civil strife would be, established leaders of both races started to explore ways to prevent additional polarization. Business interests in particular groped for a program of conciliation. Their search was informed by the tactical insight that concessions on issues of primary concern to blacks offered the best hope of defusing black radicalism. Acting on this intuition, Greensboro's white leaders sought an accommodation with the black middle class on political representation, jobs, and school desegregation. They hoped in the process both to refurbish the city's progressive image and to drive a wedge between black radicals and reformers. Thus the stage was set for the first real attempt by business leaders to promote substantive school desegregation.

Just one day after violence began at Dudley High, a committee of the Greensboro Chamber of Commerce convened hearings on the confrontation. Within a week the committee proposed that Dudley students decide for themselves whether they wished Claude Barnes excluded from the ballot. The Chamber of Commerce report was important, not because it transformed the immediate situation, but because it represented the first time that a powerful white organization had clearly sided with black insurgents. For the moment little happened as a result of the hearings. But they represented a significant move by at least part of Greensboro's white elite away from polarization and toward a framework for building a new interracial alliance.[5]

The Chamber's response in the late 1960s reflected in large part the work of Hal Sieber. A German-American who had suffered prejudice himself during World War II because of his ethnic origins, Sieber had gone to college at the University of North Carolina where he imbibed the liberal gospel of Frank Porter Graham, UNC's president, and then had gone to work for Senators Ernest Gruening and John F. Kennedy in Washington. Later he served as public relations director of the North Carolina Heart Association.

1969; "Trouble in Greensboro," report of North Carolina Advisory Committee on Civil Rights, in Greensboro Chamber of Commerce office; and interviews by the author with Nelson Johnson, November, 1978, Lewis Brandon, October, 1978, Nell Coley, July, 1974, Jack Elam, November, 1978, and S. N. Ford, April, 1979, and with Sieber, Bishop and Hairston.

5   Greensboro *Daily News*, May 29–31, 1969; *Carolina Peacemaker*, May 31, June 6, 1969; interviews with Sieber and Lineberry.

Within weeks after Sieber's appointment to the public relations post with the Greensboro Chamber of Commerce in 1966, he began to reshape the Chamber's priorities. Though Sieber claimed not to have race on his mind, he operated in such a manner that the issue could not long remain off the Chamber's agenda. Sieber genuinely believed in Greensboro's progressive reputation. But "that didn't mean it didn't have a damn long way to go." Thus whenever Sieber wrote a speech for a Chamber official, he emphasized how much still remained to be done. Words by themselves, Sieber believed, exerted little impact on people's actions. But they could establish standards and expectations that then could lead to substantive action. "When you have a chance to write the speeches as well as to manage the way that things get into the press," Sieber noted, "you start seeing some results." Unabashedly, Sieber insinuated new symbols and concepts into the public realm—symbols that soon carried a political message. Thus after creating the cartoon character Nate Green to represent the city's namesake, Sieber had the cartoon figure alternately appear in a black and a white skin.[6]

Sieber built his approach around having people discover for themselves how central race was to their lives. The public relations director initiated conversations throughout the community, supposedly to discover the major problems in the city. As different issues surfaced, it quickly became clear that most were related to race. Sieber skillfully applied the same techniques in small "cell" group meetings. There, he would repeat back to community representatives, with uncanny skill, the essence of what they had just described as pressing problems, in the process underlining the "race-relatedness" of the issue. Throughout, Sieber appeared to be totally neutral, simply a facilitator of dialogue. In addition, he earned praise for his powers of recall, reassuring people that they were receiving a fair hearing. By the end of the meeting, participants shared a sense of having arrived at a new insight about the importance of race in their community.

The theme of "total community" provided the vehicle through which Sieber injected non-Chamber issues onto the Chamber's

6   Interviews by the author with William Little, July, 1974, and Michael Weaver, July, 1977, and with Sieber and Bishop; issues of *Greensboro Business*, the Chamber of Commerce magazine edited by Sieber, 1966–73.

official agenda. "If you are involved in a total community approach," Sieber noted:

you are sooner or later going to be involved with people who have a lot
of bottled-up reactions to . . . the established way of doing things . . .
and you are going to be exposed to the very intense feelings that have
developed over a period of time among the white poor, the black poor,
the Indian poor . . . and if you are exposed to those things you are
going to be exposed in human terms rather than statistical or paternal-
istic terms and you are probably going to be more responsive than you
might be if you had never opened up that Pandora's box.

By tying the Chamber to such a community approach, issues
like housing, political representation, and school desegregation
became legitimate Chamber concerns.[7]

Nevertheless, the Chamber experienced difficulty in gaining
credibility with many blacks. Lawyers, doctors, and university
officials were ready to join once they sensed a welcome environment. But others viewed both Sieber and the Chamber with suspicion. NAACP leader Dr. George Simkins, for example, kept a
careful distance from the Chamber, anxious to preserve his independence and leverage even after the Chamber later presented
him with an award for his leadership. Sensitive to this suspicion, Sieber moved to win over blacks he perceived as most influential. Thus, he early recruited David Morehead of the Hayes-
Taylor YMCA, Rev. Otis Hairston and Rev. Cecil Bishop, two
prominent activist ministers, and John Marshall Stevenson, editor of the *Carolina Peacemaker*. Still, many other black community leaders—less prestigious and more radical in white
terms—shunned what they perceived as a devious effort by the
white establishment to co-opt them.

In response to such opposition Sieber encouraged the Chamber to form the Community Unity Division. Established in 1968
after the death of Martin Luther King, Jr., the CUD represented
the institutional embodiment of Sieber's outreach strategy. Although an official committee of the Chamber, the CUD was to

7   Interviews by the author with Lewis Dowdy, January, 1975, and John Marshall Stevenson (now Kilimanjaro), November, 1972, and with Sieber, Little,
Weaver, and Hairston. See also Greensboro *Daily News*, April 5, 1968; "One Community: Some Background on Race Relations-Related Activity of the Greensboro
Chamber of Commerce," a Chamber of Commerce document; *Congressional Record*, May 28, 1970.

consist primarily of "average" community people who were encouraged to maintain their independence. The King assassination highlighted how little real communication existed between whites and blacks and how widespread was the disaffection of the black community from existing white leadership. The CUD represented an explicit attempt to overcome that disaffection and expose white Chamber leaders to black community sentiments.

The CUD earned its spurs in 1969 during the tragedy at Dudley and A & T. At a time when other community organizations proved unable to mediate, the CUD heard testimony from all sides and offered specific recommendations. In addition to proposing a referendum where Dudley students could decide if they wanted new elections, the CUD also recommended reinstatement of suspended students, a review of the high school constitution, and measures to establish more meaningful communication between students and administrators. "We heard no evidence from any source," the CUD declared, "that Claude Barnes was a person of other than good character and citizenship." Given Barnes's past record, the Chamber committee called "debatable" the school's decision to exclude him from the election. Thus, the CUD had acted decisively on an issue of extreme volatility. Grudgingly, even leaders of the Greensboro Association of Poor People praised the CUD report. A school spokesman, by contrast, declared that education officials would treat the document as they would any other report from an organization such as HEW or the NAACP.

The CUD hearings in late spring of 1969 represented a public "coming out" of the Sieber strategy. Prior to that time, most of his organizing activities were hidden from outside view. Although the analogy of undercover intelligence is not exact, there was a sub rosa quality to the Chamber's shifting political orientation. Intentionally, Sieber disguised his approaches to black community leaders with the rhetoric of traditional Chamber concerns for business and membership. Neither Sieber nor the Chamber had actively opposed the position of city leaders on school desegregation, preferring to work behind the scenes to change people's assumptions and perceptions. Nor were they involved in decisions over the use of force against black protesters. Now, however, the potential impact of the Chamber's activities upon traditional patterns of race relations became dramatically visible. Not only was a Chamber committee intervening; it was siding with the "radicals."[8]

In this context, the most decisive aspect of the CUD action was the support given it by Chamber executives. The CUD, almost by definition, consisted of people sympathetic to the black community. By standards of white power, therefore, what mattered was how the Chamber's executive committee reacted. Most of its members agreed with the Greensboro *Daily News*, which mockingly praised the CUD for its "pure heart" but declared that "no concessions . . . ought to be made to gratify unruly and disruptive tactics." Chamber president Al Lineberry, however, had listened carefully to the testimony on the school crisis as an ex officio member of the CUD. (Lineberry was also on the school board.) If a mistake had been made, he believed, the only answer was to acknowledge it. In the end, Lineberry decided that school officials had committed a tragic error at Dudley. "After Al took such a strong stand," a black minister recalled, "a lot of executive committee members changed their minds," even if only out of personal loyalty. Caught in a difficult position, the Chamber president had followed his conscience, knowing that his position would alienate the Chamber's business constituency. But in doing so, the Chamber won an incalculable increase of respect from blacks who saw for the first time a prestigious white organization willing to risk controversy on an issue of social justice.[9]

With the CUD victory behind him, Sieber and his allies moved overtly to attack institutional racism. Testifying before the North Carolina Advisory Committee on Civil Rights, Sieber declared that all the problems at Dudley High were "related to a community's inflexibility during a time for change." For too long, he said, Greensboro had been victimized by "cultural taboos and institutionalized responses" that had failed to deal with underlying issues of racial oppression and cultural miscommunication. The white ghetto, Sieber declared, was just as trag-

8 Interviews with Hairston, Bishop, Nelson Johnson, Brandon, Stevenson, Dowdy, Sieber, and Lineberry. See also Greensboro *Daily News*, May 29–31, 1969; and *Carolina Peacemaker*, May 21, June 6, 1969.
9 Interviews with Lineberry, Sieber, and Hairston; Greensboro *Daily News*, May 29–31, 1969.

ically separated from the "total community" as the black ghetto. Hence, both had to learn about the other, not with the goal of "making milquetoasts out of militants" or "Amy Vanderbilts out of bigots," but with the intention of confronting directly the legacies of centuries of racism. To implement such a goal, the Chamber began in the summer of 1969 to sponsor sensitivity training institutes and human relations workshops where fifty or more people—half black and half white, half male and half female—would explore each other's perceptions of race and become better able to work with others to overcome discrimination.[10]

Through all of this, Sieber inevitably became a figure of controversy himself. In the beginning, he had moved behind the scenes, almost invisible as he worked to alter Chamber policies. "Hal had a way of getting across varying viewpoints and getting other people to champion a cause," one of his friends recalled. "I felt like I was watching a maestro." As Sieber's politics became more visible, however, dissension increased. White conservatives attacked him as a subversive trying to destroy the Chamber as a business institution. Some white liberals, in turn, criticized the Chamber for behaving as though it had invented civil rights. A few white radicals ended up on both sides. "When I first met you about three years ago," one activist white minister wrote, "I thought of you as a smooth talking con-man trying to divert the community's attention from the real issues of community change. . . . I now realize that you were in the forefront of community change."

Black perceptions of Sieber were equally mixed. Many welcomed his commitment to social justice. "I don't think anybody will ever know," a black college president said, "how many things were prevented from occurring because of [Hal] getting us together." On the other hand the same qualities generated suspicion. "Sieber was a snake in the grass," one young black declared. "He used people in the community to get information. . . . In some quarters black people thought he was the greatest thing that ever existed because he was doing favors.

10 Greensboro *Record*, October 10, 1969; "Trouble in Greensboro," report of the North Carolina Advisory Committee on Civil Rights; *Carolina Peacemaker*, July 9, 1969; interviews by the author with Eula Hudgens, December, 1974, and with Sieber and Lineberry.

But he was out to destroy us." From the perspective of some black radicals, Sieber represented the ultimate example of paternalism, using flattery or the offer of jobs and political help to win allies.[11]

Whatever the verdict on Sieber personally, there could be little question that by 1970 the Chamber of Commerce had become a central presence in Greensboro's racial situation. Through its emphasis on "total community," the creation of cell groups, the recruitment of more than three hundred black members, and the activities of the CUD, the Chamber had moved from being only a booster of big business to serving also as an advocate of racial reconciliation. Chamber leaders had recognized, Al Lineberry noted, that "as long as you've got that tall dry grass growing there is always a danger of fire; and when you break that ground and turn that grass under, the fire dangers are much less. So the Chamber was breaking new ground." With the aid of men like Lineberry, Sieber had persuaded Chamber leaders, for the moment at least, that change in the racial status quo would serve Greensboro's best interests. Chamber of Commerce identification with that proposition, in turn, provided important legitimacy for those supporting a shift in the racial status quo. "For the first time," one businessman observed, "a lot of people changed a part of their mind and said . . . maybe it is socially acceptable to allow some integration." Clearly, Sieber had brought the Chamber of Commerce a long distance in four years. Whether for purposes of subtle social control or radical social change, the organization was destined to play a pivotal role in Greensboro's future racial politics.[12]

The issue that would provide the crucial test of the Chamber's new policy was school desegregation. In 1971 Greensboro was one of only five North Carolina school systems still not in compliance with federal civil rights guidelines. As a result federal funds had already been deferred, including money to sensitize teachers about the different cultural backgrounds of their stu-

11 Interviews by the author with Warren Ashby, September, 1974, John R. Taylor, July, 1973, Thomas Bailey, July, 1977, Linda Bragg, July, 1974, and Carolyn Mark, October, 1974, and with Lineberry, Bluethenthal, Weaver, Little, Bishop, Hudgens, Brandon, Nelson Johnson, Dowdy, Hairston, and confidential sources. See also Jim Clark to Hal Sieber, March 2, 1973, in Hal Sieber Papers, a private collection made available to the author.
12 Interviews with Lineberry, Weaver, Little, and Dowdy.

dents. Judicial action, meanwhile, continued to undercut Greensboro's legal position. In the aftermath of the *New Kent County* case, district courts ordered local communities in North Carolina and elsewhere to adopt HEW-suggested methods to achieve desegregation.

Against this background George Simkins and ten other black parents filed suit demanding the immediate desegregation of Greensboro's schools. The plaintiffs charged the board of education with intentionally perpetuating a racially discriminatory school system and providing unequal educational facilities and opportunities for black students, solely on the basis of race. School board attorneys responded that the school board had already accomplished, "as rapidly as practicable, the complete elimination of any and all discrimination."

On April 30, 1971, Judge Edward Stanley rejected, once and for all, Greensboro's contention that "freedom of choice" was a legal means of pursuing desegregation. In light of the *Swann* decision upholding busing as a means to integrate schools, Stanley ordered the Greensboro school board to produce a plan providing for complete desegregation by June 18, with implementation to occur the following school year. Everyone recognized that large-scale busing and a universal ratio of black to white in each school would be necessary components of any acceptable plan. On the day of the decision, twenty-seven schools in Greensboro were more than 95 percent white or black. Although more than 10,000 students were bused daily, only 115 were transported from the black section of the community to predominantly white schools. For more than a decade, the school board had argued that such a situation amounted to elimination of a dual school system. Now, the city had less than five months to compensate for the failures of past policies. As the city moved to confront the crisis, two questions dominated the scene: would a school board that had said "No!" for so long respond affirmatively to the desegregation challenge? And would the white and black communities of Greensboro be able to accept what amounted to a transformation of the city's school system?[13]

13 Greensboro *Record*, February 25, April 11, 29, 1970; Greensboro *Daily News*, February 27, 1970, May 1, 1971; interviews with Lineberry, Walter Johnson, and Sieber.

The answer to the first question revealed how quickly a strategic elite could reverse field and effectively implement a policy that for so long had been resisted. Almost immediately, it became clear that the time for naysaying was past. Just as the city's economic and political leaders had responded in the aftermath of the Dudley crisis with some concessions, school officials now chose to comply without hesitation with complete school desegregation.

The process was aided by the rise to leadership of a new generation of school board officials. During the preceding two years, three of the men most closely identified with "freedom of choice" had died. A different position by any of the three might have altered school board policy earlier. Now, all were gone. At the same time, three new men joined the board, including Walter Johnson, a widely respected black attorney, and Rev. Otis Hairston, the author of black desegregation demands in the early 1960s. The third newcomer was Carson Bain, a former mayor, and a tough, result-oriented businessman.

Presiding over the reconstituted school board was Al Lineberry, a former president of the Chamber of Commerce and owner of one of the city's largest funeral homes. Elected to the chairmanship the same week as the *Swann* decision, Lineberry was the white leader most capable of forging a creative, compassionate alliance with community groups interested in desegregation. "The first thing to know about Lineberry," one black leader noted, "is that he is a Christian." Deeply committed to acting on his faith twenty-four hours a day, Lineberry saw reconciliation as a religious mission. Lineberry defended the school board's actions during the late 1960s, believing that its members, including himself, had acted in pursuit of the best educational policies. But Lineberry's own views had been altered during the CUD hearings on the Dudley crisis. That involvement, Hal Sieber later noted, was probably the "single most sensitizing experience" that Lineberry could have had in preparation for being school board chairman.

When Lineberry took the chair for the first time shortly after Judge Stanley's decision, he charted a firm course. "We're going to comply," he told the board. "We're not going to fight the court, we're going to satisfy the court." From that point forward, complete cooperation—not resistance—marked the school board's posture toward desegregation. The NAACP plaintiffs submitted their desegregation plan to Judge Stanley on June 2. The Greensboro school board presented its proposal on May 26. The two plans were similar in outline, except that under the school board proposal five schools would remain all-white and three would have remained predominantly black. The NAACP, by contrast, insisted that all schools should have the same racial proportions. Judge Stanley—with the school board's acquiescence—supported the NAACP and the issue was decided. In a little less than two months, the school board had accomplished, on paper at least, what for almost twenty years it had said would be educationally impossible.[14]

School board action meant little, however, without community acquiescence. To that end, white-led citizen groups had begun to mobilize citizen support for desegregation even before the case was decided in court. For more than three years the Chamber of Commerce's Community Unity Division had been building a framework where white and black citizens could confront and resolve their problems. In addition, a small group of Greensboro women decided in the winter of 1969–1970 to study the issue of social change in education for their "Great Decisions Club." The activities of both groups created a structure within which popular support for desegregation could be rallied once the decision was handed down.

The three-person "Great Decisions" team was headed by Joan Bluethenthal, a Philadelphia native who had moved to Greensboro in 1950 and become involved in a variety of activities including public housing, day care, and the Council of Jewish Women. Impatient at the superficiality of many "Great Decisions" discussions, Bluethenthal and her compatriots set out to examine the unmet needs of the school system. Not surprisingly, the group concluded that human relations represented the number one problem of the schools. Everybody talked about

14   Interviews with Bluethenthal, Lineberry, Dowdy, Hairston, Bishop, Sieber, and Walter Johnson. See also notes from "Great Decisions Club" file, Joan Bluethenthal Papers, a private collection made available to the author. Bluethenthal and her friends had conducted extensive interviews with school board members, teachers, administrators, and community leaders. Through such interviews they had arrived at a keen assessment of the personality factors involved in the desegregation controversy.

the issue, but no one was prepared to do anything about it. "In spite of the fact that the *Brown* decision . . . was over fifteen years old," Bluethenthal later wrote, "we had no plans." If only money were available, Doris Hutchinson, director of school staff development told the group, teachers, parents, and students could be brought together to look down the road and make those plans.

When Bluethenthal and her friends delivered their findings to the Great Decisions Club in January, 1971, they had completed their assignment. But at almost the same time Bluethenthal attended a conference at A & T entitled "Getting To Know You." There, Dr. Dorothy Williams of Shaw University presented a poem on the dilemmas of racism.

> Prejudice is cancerous to mind
> It eats and eats at soul 'til blind
> Blind and weak the soul is pained
> All is lost—nothing is gained
> The prejudiced soul must now take heed
> Or it is doomed to hell with all deliberate speed.
> Prejudice, what is it?

The conference, together with Bluethenthal's own instinct for action, convinced her that more than study was needed. "The time was ripe," she later wrote. "Responsible, caring people wanted to do something and we just happened upon a course of action—positive action—and . . . offered anyone who wanted it a chance to participate."[15]

Bluethenthal and Doris Hutchinson of the school system worked out a four-stage human relations program, beginning with a series of weekend retreats for students, parents, teachers, and administrators in the spring of 1971. Each retreat sought to find ways to avoid racism in the schools and promote justice and communication between blacks and whites. To implement the plan, Bluethenthal raised twenty-five thousand dollars—half from United Community Services, and half from the Chamber of Commerce. The first retreat was already scheduled when the Supreme Court handed down its *Swann* ruling.

The so-called "Chinqua-Penn retreats" became the training

15 Notes from "Great Decisions Club" file and miscellaneous notes, Bluethenthal Papers; interviews with Bluethenthal, Mark, Sieber, Lineberry, and Bishop.

ground for hundreds of Greensboro residents who subsequently worked on behalf of the transition to integration. Held in an old mansion surrounded by grassy slopes, each of the three retreats involved two hundred people. Those attending represented a cross-section of the community—black and white students, parents, teachers, and administrators. With the assistance of psychologists, the participants learned to interact closely with someone of the other race, often for the first time in their lives. Those attending spoke candidly about their fears, the stereotypes they harbored, and the specific problems the community faced in preparing for desegregation. Parents learned that principals were human, and administrators heard, perhaps for the first time in depth, a student and parent perspective on education. "Most of us," Bluethenthal recalled, "experienced a oneness as we struggled with feelings and challenges which we all shared and of which we were all a part. We left knowing we had to do something." If nothing else, the retreats created cadres of individuals, who through their experience together, found a common commitment to make desegregation work.[16]

Like Lineberry, Bluethenthal occupied a position of maximum responsibility at a critical time. Many talented women, a friend wrote her, spent their lives searching for an identity and purpose without ever finding it. "[That is why] I envy you three girls," the friend continued. "You're where the world is at. As I weed my vegetable garden, I am well aware that this is temporarily what I need, but . . . it's just a pacifier when the world is on fire. It's really exciting to see someone in the right place at the right time. . . . It's almost as if you had been preparing for this moment." In fact Bluethenthal had been "preparing" for nearly a year, and as the spring turned into summer, she, as much as anyone, shaped the nature of citizen response to desegregation.[17]

In the meantime, the Chamber of Commerce pursued its own program. Hal Sieber had admired the efforts of the three women, especially their ability to communicate with the con-

16   Notes from "Great Decisions Club" file and miscellaneous notes, Bluethenthal Papers; interviews with Bluethenthal, Mark, Sieber, Lineberry, and Bishop. See also "Human Relations Retreat—Concerned Citizens," a file of evaluations and firsthand reports on the Chinqua-Penn retreats, Bluethenthal Papers.
17   Private correspondence, Bluethenthal Papers.

servative community. In his own work he sought a similar base of operations. "I felt the day of reckoning would come," he commented, "and when it did come there was a need for a coalition of community leaders to say that we in Greensboro are going to comply with the law . . . that we support the public schools, and that we believe in improved human relations." In order to establish such a coalition, Sieber recognized the need to avoid debate on issues such as busing. Rather, he emphasized the importance of committing people to obey the law of the land, however the court might interpret it. Through such a device, individuals of different persuasions could maintain their own points of view even as they joined in an alliance dedicated to upholding the law. During the winter of 1970–1971 the CUD established a subcommittee to build the alliance that Sieber envisioned. Significantly, the new organization was to be called Concerned Citizens for Schools (CCS), a name consciously chosen to preempt the "concerned citizens" label that White Citizens Councils had so often used in the past to oppose desegregation.

In the months prior to the *Swann* decision, the CCS operated as an extension of the Community Unity Division. While the staff compiled a mailing list of 1,700 influential community leaders to be contacted when a court decision was handed down, informal discussion continued with the aim of building a broad base of support for the public schools, regardless of which way the court decided. While some staff people planned publicity, others discussed such issues as how to control rumors. Most of the Chamber's energy went into a continuation of the human relations workshops and cell groups that since 1968 had been an integral part of the CUD program. Meeting on a weekly basis, the cell groups involved anywhere from 5 to 150 people discussing a broad range of community problems. The human relations workshops, on the other hand, were one-time events designed to bring together representatives from all segments of the community to focus specifically upon race relations. Like the Chinqua-Penn retreats, the human relations workshops were intense experiences. "You're taking a close look at yourself, and other people are criticizing [you]," one participant recalled, "and that's the part most people can't accept. . . . you feel like you're being exposed." Yet those who joined such sessions inevitably gained a deeper understanding of the racial dynamics at work in themselves and the community. From 1968 through 1971, more than 2,400 Greensboro citizens took part in these Chamber-sponsored sessions.[18]

At the end of May, the CCS went public. Inviting a representative segment of the community, the Chamber of Commerce convened the first official meeting of the CCS "to foster community cooperation with Greensboro's school system in order to assure quality and equality education as designed and required by law." Although no final judicial decision had been handed down, the CCS emphasized, "[our] organization is concerned about one thing—to make sure that all of us do our best to make a necessary school assignment transition as educationally helpful, productive, and dignified as possible." By the end of June, the CCS had elected Rev. Cecil Bishop, a black, and Rev. Robert Mayer, a white, as cochairmen. By July more than one thousand members were enrolled.[19]

The Bluethenthal group, in the meantime, persuaded the board of education to establish its own Human Relations Advisory Committee. Chaired by Bluethenthal, the Lay-Professional Advisory Committee (LPAC) was divided equally between blacks and whites, and drew upon many of the people who had emerged as leaders during the Chinqua-Penn retreats. Like the CCS, the LPAC attempted to mobilize all the forces it could. "We weren't fighting [others]," Bluethenthal noted; "we're just saying, if it's going to happen anyway, [let's do it right]." The major difference between the two groups was that the CCS dealt primarily with the larger community, while the LPAC concentrated on solving problems inside the schools.

During the early part of the summer, the coalition created task forces to deal with crises that would arise when desegregation began. One group worked on publicity, another on setting up a rumor control center where parents could call to verify

18   Interviews with Sieber, Lineberry, Walter Johnson, Bishop, Hudgens, Mark, Bluethenthal, Little, and Hairston. See also "A Review of the Programs and Activities of Concerned Citizens for Schools," prepared by the Greensboro Chamber of Commerce; "It's Not Over in the South," a report prepared by the Southern Regional Council and five other civil rights organizations, in Greensboro Public Library; *Greensboro Business*, January, 1970–December, 1973.
19   CCS to Joan Bluethenthal, June 9, 1971, in Bluethenthal Papers; Greensboro *Daily News,* May 28, June 25, 1971; Greensboro *Record*, May 22, June 25, 1971.

or report news of trouble. Desegregation supporters identified parent and student leaders who could develop a positive atmosphere in the new schools. The LPAC focused especially on student council representatives and PTA officers from the old schools who might provide a leadership core in the new schools until elections could be held. Another task force, called the Problem Solving Group, brought together students from different geographical and cultural backgrounds to discuss common fears and concerns.

To parallel these efforts, school administrators moved to facilitate the transition. Under pressure from Carson Bain and Walter Johnson, the superintendent appointed blacks to a series of high-level positions. Mel Swann, a black named to be assistant superintendent of schools for student affairs, became a pivotal figure, working as coordinator with the LPAC, establishing a liaison with each school in the community, and communicating directly with parent and student groups. Under Swann's leadership, new assistant principals were named for each high school to work primarily with student affairs. Each high school appointed a black head coach in at least one major sport. Schools also introduced new courses on black history and culture. In addition, new black principals were named, and the school board avoided demoting or dismissing principals or assistant principals affected by the transition.

At the same time school administrators implemented their own four-stage human relations program devised in conjunction with the Bluethenthal group. An outside expert conducted an eight-day workshop for principals on the importance of providing for the individual needs of the students. Later in the summer, the supervisory staff met to develop strategies for dealing with interpersonal problems. School board officials, meanwhile, did their part to overcome the communication barriers that had existed in the past. Al Lineberry spoke to 111 meetings and was constantly available for consultation. "Whoever calls," he told his wife, "they've got a problem and somebody needs to listen to them."[20]

20   Interviews with Bluethenthal, Bishop, Sieber, Lineberry, Walter Johnson, Mark, Hudgens, and Hairston. See also folder entitled "Lay-Professional Human Relations Advisory Committee," in Bluethenthal Papers; Greensboro *Daily News*, August 1–6, 1971. Each committee and subcommittee of LPAC had equal participation of blacks and whites.

The primary burden for communicating with the outside community, however, rested with the CCS. With precision and imagination, the CCS set out to combat the greatest obstacles facing desegregation—ignorance and fear—and to make known as much of the unknown as possible. To cope with parent fears about busing, the CCS published statistics on how safe school buses were. For those concerned that children might be unruly on the bus, the Chamber advertised the presence of adult bus monitors. Perhaps most important, the CCS mounted an intensive advertising campaign designed to create a positive community attitude toward the transition. IT CAN WORK was the message delivered by thousands of bumper stickers and billboards. Community service television programs, radio talk shows, and frequent newspaper stories provided an ongoing forum for CCS representatives to drive home the theme that Greensboro could make desegregation a positive experience. A six-page brochure depicted the back of a school bus, with black and white faces in the window, headlining the slogan, "Maybe We'll All Learn Something." Brimming with information, the pamphlet answered every conceivable question that parents might ask: how PTAs would be reorganized, what the white/black ratio would be in different schools, how teachers were being prepared for the transition, where parents might call for imformation, how long was the longest bus ride (forty-five minutes), and whether there was any difference at all in the facilities available in the formerly black and formerly white schools. As the summer wore on, there was hardly a person in the entire Greensboro area who did not see or hear each day the CCS message that desegregation could work for the benefit of everyone.[21]

None of this, of course, occurred without significant opposition. Whites who were angered at the prospect of "forced busing" organized two groups, one called Positive Leadership for Educational Action (PLEA), the other Americans Concerned about Today (ACT). Each campaigned for a constitutional amendment that would prohibit compulsory school assignments for teachers and students, and recruited support for al-

21 Interviews with Hudgens, Lineberry, Sieber, Bishop, and Walter Johnson. See also "Maybe We'll All Learn Something," Chamber of Commerce brochure; Boston *Globe*, September 4, 1973; annual report of Human Relations Commission, August 24, 1971, in Greensboro Public Library; Greensboro *Daily News*, August 1–6, 1971.

ternatives to the existing school system such as "Christian academies." At times, as many as two hundred people attended meetings of PLEA. Resistance also appeared among some people who attended CCS meetings. Why should whites be made to feel guilty about race, one woman asked Joan Bluethenthal. Blacks already had their "quota of jobs assured under federal legislation."

But the greatest opposition came from within the black community. As early as April, a group of blacks mobilized to oppose "mass forced integration, particularly busing." With integration, these parents believed, black children would be made to feel inferior. Black culture and leadership would be de-emphasized, and Negro pupils would lose the positive sense of identity associated with schools such as Dudley and Lincoln. Some blacks perceived the integration order as "a calculated plan to keep our people down" through the destruction of black pride and institutions. At an early meeting of one black PTA group, a majority voted to oppose the integration plan. "The 1954 decision," one activist told the audience, "was based on aspirations for quality education. Integration was only a tactic. Today black pride has led to cohesiveness; therefore the whites want to integrate in order to break this down and control our schools." In the view of some black activists, attending school with whites ensured neither quality nor equal education. Rather, integration was being substituted as a panacea to divert attention from real issues like jobs and housing. Ironically, many adopted the position taken earlier by foes of the *Brown* decision. Racism, they said, could not be legislated out of existence. According to this point of view, freedom of choice represented the only viable alternative.[22]

Through the weeks and months after the court decision, debate over the issue raged inside the black community. Many black parents insisted that some schools should retain a black majority, both for purposes of cultural identity and because it seemed advisable to keep control over at least some institutions.

22 Greensboro *Daily News*, August 7, 24, 25, 27, September 1, 1971; miscellaneous notes, Bluethenthal Papers; interviews with Nelson Johnson, Bailey, Brandon, Bishop, Stevenson, Hairston, and Walter Johnson; Greensboro *Record*, April 30, May 20, 1971; *Carolina Peacemaker*, May 29, June 5, 12, 19, 26, July 3, August 7, 14, 1971.

White parents would not want their children to be a minority in other schools, these black parents argued; both races legitimately feared that their independence would be compromised in a school dominated by the other.

Yet the plaintiffs in the Greensboro court case all had been black. It was they who insisted on a seventy-thirty ratio in *every* school within the system. Speaking for those who had long struggled against segregation, John Marshall Stevenson of the *Carolina Peacemaker* asked editorially: "Are we are doomed to re-live our past?" Eloquently, Stevenson asked his readers to remember black teachers who had been fired from their jobs for fighting on behalf of integration. He recalled the common laborers who had stood guard over homes assaulted by white opponents of desegregation. It was true, he acknowledged, that white leadership had shown a massive capacity for duplicity and exploitation; it was also important that Black Power advocates should continue to free the minds and bodies of blacks. But, he concluded, "Time has run out on freedom of choice. What a sad commentary for black citizens who now stand on the brink of true freedom for the first time, to be willing to run back into the dark forest of segregation, of second-class citizenship."[23]

As the internal struggle continued, the prointegration point of view gradually gained the upper hand, at least publicly. Most black leaders had been identified with the fight for school desegregation too long to abandon it now. Rev. Cecil Bishop was cochairman of the CCS. Rev. Otis Hairston served on the school board. Rev. Julius Douglas and Dr. George Simkins both had devoted their lives to the cause of integration. Even though some established blacks wished privately that a few schools could retain a black identity, they were unable to say so because of the precedent of their own past actions. In addition, the school board's selection of blacks for prominent administrative positions provided important ammunition for those supporting desegregation. "The sun do move," a *Peacemaker* gossip columnist declared after the rash of black appointments. Instead of being "dragged screaming into the 21st century, the school board [is] walking into the new day with pride and dignity."

As a result, black community leaders eventually came down

23 *Carolina Peacemaker*, May 29, June 5, 19, 26, 1971.

on the side of busing. To have done otherwise would have precipitated a devasting internecine war. Not only had blacks initiated the desegregation suit; prominent members of the black community were involved at every level of the effort. In effect, they were taking the calculated risk that "if we go along with [whites] we'll get where we ought to be—eventually." Some younger blacks justifiably perceived the school board plan as a threat to their hopes for Black Power and community development. But compromise on this issue—unlike others—could not be reached because the underlying principles were too basic. Once it became clear that Black Power advocates could not carry their fight without creating permanent divisions within the community, the younger leaders down-played their hostility to the desegregation plan. "Our base was really not that strong to survive without [the older leaders,]" one younger leader recalled, "and it became more and more apparent to us that that was the case." Particularly devastating was support for desegregation by men like Hairston. "It was hard to criticize Otis," Walter Johnson noted, "because [he] was out in front of all the others. He was taking risks when it wasn't [fashionable]. . . . Everything they were talking about doing, he'd already done." By midsummer even those who still led the black opposition had adopted a flexible position. Cecil Rouson, a black activist who was a member of PLEA, announced that even though his supporters opposed forced pupil assignment, they supported obedience to the law. Intentionally or unintentionally, white leaders had finally found an issue on which they could defeat black radicals, even while creating divisions of class and ideology in the black community.[24]

As August began, supporters of desegregation mounted their final mobilization drive. "The sand bags are all in place," one supporter wrote Mel Swann. "Everyone seems outwardly relaxed [even if] inwardly braced for whatever." In order to prepare for "whatever," the CCS and LPAC coordinated a blitzkrieg of activity. The LPAC and school board sponsored a four-day period of parent hearings where individuals could receive answers

24 Interviews with Bailey, Nelson Johnson, Hairston, Walter Johnson, and Brandon. See also Greensboro *Daily News*, August 7, 1971; and *Carolina Peacemaker*, June 12, 19, 26, July 3, August 7, 14, 1971.

to their questions. More than 1,500 people attended one meeting. The CCS, meanwhile, intensified its cell discussions, with more than one hundred meetings held in local neighborhoods. Such discussions not only brought people of different backgrounds together; they also created a new reserve of leaders who, as a result of their experiences, developed an investment in making desegregation work. Parents could remain indifferent as long as their own children were not involved, but once the issue struck home, many began to work actively for the cause.

In its most ambitious effort, the school desegregation coalition declared August 15 "Public School Sunday." Ministers emphasized the importance of "beginning to learn how to live with each other in an open community," urging Greensboro's citizens to be gentle and kind, honest and open, and prepared to answer for past mistakes. The next Sunday, rhetoric was translated into action. Knowing that fear of the bus ride represented the greatest concern of parents, desegregation supporters sponsored a mass visitation of parents and students to the schools. Along with the pupil assignment letters sent to parents, the school board issued invitations for an open house to be held on Sunday, August 22. Parents rode on the buses their children would take. They were met by teachers, students, and administrators who conducted guided tours of the new schools. In each place, core members of the new PTAs served refreshments as teachers answered parent's questions. More than thirty thousand parents visited Greensboro's schools on Open House Day, with a thousand greeted at Dudley High School alone during one forty five-minute period. Each parent was handed a copy of the CCS brochure, "Maybe We Will All Learn Something," as well as school bus schedules and a sheet giving parents advice on how to prepare their children for the transition.[25]

By the time "Public School Sunday" occurred, practically every contingency had been dealt with. Each day for more than a week the local newspapers had presented lengthy descriptions of each school, featuring pictures of libraries, cafeterias, and

25   "A Review of the Program and Activities of Concerned Citizens for Schools," Chamber of Commerce document; *Greensboro Business*, November–December, 1971; annual report of Human Relations Commission, August 24, 1971; miscellaneous notes, Bluethenthal Papers; Greensboro *Daily News*, August 1–7, 21–23, 1971.

recreation facilities. School personnel, together with numerous volunteers, had moved more than twelve thousand pieces of furniture and seventy thousand library books into their new facilities. More than one thousand adults had been recruited to serve as bus monitors, guaranteeing that on each trip to and from school the bus would be accompanied by adults and met at the school gate by a parent volunteer. Sixty more adults had been trained to handle the telephone at the rumor control center. So thorough was the preparation that CCS officials invited members of PLEA and ACT to bring their case to the final meeting of the CCS so that each side might have the opportunity to air its point of view. When the meeting occurred, Cecil Rouson, a black executive committee member of PLEA, criticized plans to boycott city schools. It was time, he told the meeting, for the opposition to "open their eyes and learn from the positive attitude and constructive spirit which characterized Greensboro here on the eve of school opening."

When the day for desegregation of Greensboro's schools finally arrived, the battle had already been won. Two buses got lost. A few children ended up going to the wrong school. But, most observers agreed, it would have been difficult to imagine a smoother transition. Three months earlier there had been twenty-seven schools in the city that were nearly all white or all black and only five that could reasonably be called integrated. Now, the entire system had been transformed. Within days a new world of busing, integrated PTAs and biracial student governments had become routine. A local journalist who served as a "bus father" concluded that "the slogan 'it will work' can be changed to 'it is working'. . . . The people of Greensboro have every reason to be proud of themselves and even more of their children." Although all the underlying problems of race and discrimination remained, Greensboro had reached a milestone. "I feel so proud to say that I'm from Greensboro," Dr. George Simkins declared.

Within a few months, experts were citing Greensboro as proof that blacks and whites could work together to make desegregation work. In a survey of forty-three school districts in the South, the NAACP Legal Defense Fund and four other organizations concluded that Greensboro's desegregation was "probably superior to that of almost any other city in the south."

The Chamber of Commerce was especially singled out for its role in "stepping into the leadership vacuum which is often filled by vocal opponents of desegregation." Two years later, beset by a desegregation crisis in its own city, the Boston *Globe* called Greensboro "a model" for the others to emulate. "Desegregation in Greensboro was not an accident," the paper said. "It was a case of community leaders setting a goal and capitalizing on community pride, respect for law, and a recognition that children should have the same educational opportunity." [26]

Thus seventeen years after leading the nation in declaring it would comply with the *Brown* decision, Greensboro was once again in the headlines as an example of racial progress. As observers from other communities took note of the city's desegregation procedures, local leaders boasted of their "feeling of pride that Greensboro was different from other cities, that it was a city interested in improving human relations." Yet, if it was important to ask how Greensboro had accomplished so smoothly the transition to integration, it was also important to ponder why the process had taken so long. As Joan Bluethenthal told a meeting in August, 1971, "We are the ones who always believed in E-Quality education, we always wanted to live by the law of the land. . . . We always wanted to, but what did we do about it?"

Looking back at Greensboro's history after 1969, the one theme that stands out above all others is the speed, efficiency, and skill with which white leaders implemented a radical change in policy. Clearly, the use of force at Dudley and A & T had gone too far. Not only did it provoke an angry response from blacks that could not be tolerated on a long-term basis; it also shattered Greensboro's reputation for racial enlightenment. "We had been through 1969," one observer remarked. "Were we going to do it all over again. The answer [was] no. We're going to do what's good for business. Which is the reason we settled in 1963. It's a question of economics." Yet, if a progressive image was to be retrieved and made creditable, a new tack was necessary. [27]

26   Greensboro *Daily News*, August 27, September 1, 4, 1971; Greensboro *Record*, August 27–29, 1971, May 23, 1972; Boston *Globe*, September 4, 1973; "It's Not Over in the South."
27   Statement by Joan Bluethenthal to CCS, August 17, 1971, Bluethenthal Papers; interviews with Sieber, Walter Johnson, and Hairston.

Much of the groundwork for the new strategy was laid through the subtle organizing skills of Hal Sieber. But once his purpose became visible, figures in the white business and political community aligned themselves on Sieber's side, even if reluctantly. Through an effort notable for its sheer intensity, new forums for interracial communication were established, long-standing black grievances were redressed, and a framework was created for middle-class cooperation across racial lines. The desegregation drive in 1971 simply culminated the campaign, crystallizing strategic developments that had been evolving over the previous two years. Almost overnight, the city accomplished what for ten, fifteen, and twenty years white leaders had described as impossible to attain.

In the face of this effort, black activists displayed a remarkable degree of unity in working toward common objectives. Black power advocates participated in NAACP voter registration drives, worked for the election of blacks to city office, and cooperated with the leadership agenda set forth by black ministers and businessmen. More traditional leaders, in turn, provided substantial support for most of the radical organizing activities championed by the "young turks." Because of their unity, blacks achieved more victories in the years after 1969 than ever before. In addition, the black community pulsated with political energy as different groups debated how to defeat slumlords, whether to work within "the system," and when to resort to strikes or boycotts. Yet this solidarity and dynamism could continue only by avoiding issues that evoked deep-seated conflicts over black separatism and political radicalism.

When school desegregation became the primary focus of attention, it was inevitable that the unity would break down. For most young radicals, going to school with whites had never occupied the same symbolic or substantive importance that an older generation attached to the issue. School desegregation represented a priority of another era. From a radical point of view, the issues were class and race oppression, creation of distinctively "black" values, and the development of independent community institutions. Older black leaders, however, had sacrificed too much for desegregation to dismiss it now as secondary. For most of them, integration still exemplified what the struggle was all about. They believed in it, they had bled for it, and they would not move to new priorities—at least not until that victory had been won. For such individuals, giving up the goal that had driven them for so long would be tantamount to rejecting a segment of their lives. Clearly such a step was impossible. Both for reasons of ideological conviction and psychic integrity, they needed to see the battle through—even if the price was a break with the younger generation of more radical activists.

There were two ways of viewing these developments. From one perspective, Greensboro had achieved a new maturity of race relations. For the first time in their history, city leaders had operated straightforwardly in an interracial coalition to bring about significant change in the racial status quo. More than at any time in the past, the alliance had been based upon a recognition that the contribution of each side was indispensable for success. With skill, imagination, and above all dedication, black and white leaders had worked together to move Greensboro in the direction of racial equality, in the process burying traditional modes of paternalism and white supremacy.

From another perspective, however, the older forms of control had simply taken on a new appearance. Through black political appointments and capitulation on issues like school desegregation, white leaders had successfully "co-opted" members of the black middle class, giving them an investment in the prevailing system of political and economic authority. Yet had power really changed hands? Were blacks any more in control of their own fate? Was not the primary achievement of the post-1969 period the polishing of Greensboro's progressive image and the isolation of her young black radicals? In short, did not the victories of the post-1969 years simply reflect paternalism raised to a new level of shrewdness and sophistication? In the end, there may be no definitive answers to such questions. But they remain the crucial issues for Greensboro in the 1980s—joining the history of those decades to the history of all the generations that have gone before.

PAUL S. LOFTON, JR.

CALM AND EXEMPLARY

DESEGREGATION IN COLUMBIA, SOUTH CAROLINA

Columbia, South Carolina, is a professional town, proud of its history and concerned with its image. Located in the geographic center of South Carolina, the city not only serves as the capital of the state but also as a distribution center and as state and regional headquarters for numerous business concerns, private nonprofit organizations, and government agencies. Cotton textiles are the single largest industry, but they in no way dominate the economic and cultural life as they do many cities and towns of the Carolina Piedmont. The city can in no way match the aristocratic hauteur of Charleston, but several other factors combine to make Columbia the best educated, most heterogeneous city in the state. Highly influential in forming the city's character are the myriad of state government employees, soldiers from nearby Fort Jackson, and students at the University of South Carolina and five private colleges. Enough old families are present to preserve valued traditions and counterbalance the many new faces that constantly arrive from around the state and beyond.

The downtown business community consists of department stores, men's and women's specialty shops, variety stores, jewelry stores, movie theaters, pawnshops, restaurants, and book-stores—in short, the same conglomeration that one might expect to find in almost any American city.

In 1960, on the eve of the civil rights revolution, Columbia's population was 97,433, of which 29,488, or just over 30 percent, was black.[1] Race relations were about "normal" for a city of this size, complexity, and location. Good will and harmony, which usually prevailed, depended on everyone's adhering to the roles that custom had long dictated. Yet by no means was cordiality as all-pervading as some like to think that it was, as from time to time certain black spokesmen freely used the news media to speak out against forms of discrimination that seemed to them particularly abhorrent. At the same time local black leaders were notoriously divided, a fact evidenced in numerous organizational squabbles through the years.[2] This divided leadership contributed to a relative lack of militancy on the part of the black community.

Columbia has always been jealous of its image as a peaceful, progressive community, and nothing typifies that outlook more clearly than the city's perennial quest in the 1950s and 1960s for the *Look* magazine All-America City Award. In 1951 Columbia made the select circle of eleven winning cities, and in 1962 the judges named it a runner-up. It was a winner again in 1964 and was runner-up again in 1968 and 1969. Such fascination with this kind of national recognition made city fathers extremely anxious to avoid at all cost any kind of appearance of disorder or disruption that might smear the good name of Columbia. Thus, by the time that the civil rights movement clearly was forcing southern communities into decisions either to move toward desegregation of public facilities or to risk the consequences related to continued segregation, Columbia's choice was clear. At the same time it would be an oversimplification to

1   U.S. Bureau of the Census, *U.S. Census of the Population: 1960, Vol. I, Characteristics of the Population*, Part 42, South Carolina (Washington, D.C.: Government Printing Office, 1963), 51.
2   South Carolina Council on Human Relations [SCCHR], Quarterly Report for December, 1958–February, 1959 (mimeograph copy in South Caroliniana Library, University of South Carolina, Columbia). See also contrasting letters to the editor of the Columbia *State*, March 11, 1960, Sec. A, p. 9, and March 15, 1960, Sec. A, p. 10.

imply that the local Chamber of Commerce's desire to keep order and maintain a proper image above all else was the sole or overriding reason for the city's decision to move ahead peacefully with integration. That it was extremely important cannot be denied, but at the same time both subtle and overt pressures from the black community along with behind-the-scenes negotiations involving a number of responsible parties had been in progress for years so that no single issue, group, individual, or interest could claim exclusive credit for a calm and almost exemplary end to segregation. Even the federal government's role was minimal.

The most important of the negotiators was South Carolina's branch of the Atlanta-based Southern Regional Council. The local organization had its origins in 1919 as the South Carolina Committee of the Commission on Interracial Cooperation and went through several name changes before becoming the South Carolina Council on Human Relations in 1954. Its approach was to appeal to the traditional virtues of courtesy and decency in trying to solve the state's racial problems. (An old adage around South Carolina has long been that if you can't appeal to a man's morals, then appeal to his manners.) By the 1960s in Columbia the SCCHR had worked tirelessly and effectively to bring together various kinds of groups for biracial dialogues. One of its primary purposes was to motivate blacks to be aware of and to be more involved in civil rights activities. It was particularly active in its work with the several denominational centers near the campus of the University of South Carolina and with local ministerial associations. Conservative parents and congregations did not always approve of its activities, and naturally it was the target of occasional criticism. Still, the SCCHR was not a pressure group, although militant segregationists and often the press called it worse names than that. Through the years it did much to keep lines of communication open so that when other, stronger forces began eventually to confront each other, everyone could be thankful for the few seeds of good will sown earlier by the SCCHR.

The local chapter of the National Association for the Advancement of Colored People, like its national counterpart, had worked through the courts and legislative processes to change existing laws and write new legislation affecting the welfare of the black population. Since the early 1940s the South Carolina NAACP had been quite effective in initiating suits that had challenged successfully such bastions of white supremacy as the white Democratic primary in 1947, public school segregation in 1954, and even closer to home for Columbians, segregated seating on Columbia's city buses in 1956.[3]

The most active pressure group, even more active than the local NAACP, was the Richland County Citizens Committee. Founded in 1944 as an organization to work through political action to help meet problems facing blacks of that day, it had since the mid-1950s emphasized "the respect and observance of all laws—national, state, and local. We would have it clearly understood," read one of its statements, "that we include the Supreme Court Decision of May 7, 1954."[4] This committee rendered its greatest service through its radio program and periodic newsletters which kept the black community informed on all matters relating to civil rights. The great bulk of the committee's activities resulted from the ideas and labors of one individual, Modjeska Simkins, a person of remarkable integrity, fortitude, and enthusiasm. Mrs. Simkins had been quite visible around Columbia and South Carolina since the mid-1930s when her adamant insistence and vigorous personality forced the local WPA office to make jobs available to blacks above the level of manual labor.[5] She had served as state secretary of the NAACP for twenty years and had long been in the forefront of all the struggles in the state to nibble away at the worst features of segregation. In a sense she relished her role as gadfly and was somewhat scornful of those whom she considered compromisers. Partly for this reason and partly because she was the most outspoken black leader on the scene, even the northern press labeled her a "militant,"[6] a term hardly deserved considering her respect for law and the moderate nature of her demands.

Mrs. Simkins' chief antagonist was the white mayor, Lester L. Bates, another figure who loomed large in the race relations

3   Interview with Modjeska Simkins by the author, April 22, 1978; Columbia *Record*, April 23, 1956, Sec. A, p. 1.
4   Columbia *Record*, November 10, 1955, Sec. B, p. 1.
5   Edwin D. Hoffman, "Genesis of the Modern Movement for Equal Rights in South Carolina, 1930–1939," *Journal of Negro History*, XLIV (1959), 361–62.
6   "Weep No More Columbia," *Newsweek*, May 3, 1965, p. 33.

picture of early 1960s Columbia. Bates had his origins in the Hell Hole Swamp area of Berkeley County and despite a limited formal education had risen to become a highly successful insurance executive. Bates knew people and in his way counted himself a friend of blacks. When he won the mayoral office in 1958 by fourteen votes, he received so much support from black neighborhoods that some had accused blacks of bloc voting. In predominately black Ward Nine, for example, Bates received 690 of 735 votes cast.[7] Mrs. Simkins considered him a sellout and a defender of the status quo. But this assessment was as unfair to Bates as was his label of her as a "radical." Bates most of all was a shrewd politician. Besides courting blacks, he was also a staunch ally of the white business community, and his ten-point program for a better Columbia meshed almost exactly with the Chamber of Commerce's own ideas for growth and progress.[8]

Before assuming the leadership of South Carolina's capital city, Bates had already run for governor twice, and whatever his political aspirations may have been by 1960, he was certain to do nothing that would bring embarrassment to the name of Lester Bates or to the city of Columbia. Determined to project an image as a man in charge, Bates believed that Columbia had to make the first move before it was faced with a situation in which it might react with more vigor than was necessary. He was equally determined that no outsiders should come into Columbia to force anything on the city.

Bates was at his political best when he worked behind the scenes, enlisting those he considered to be local experts for informal consultations and securing their approval before making his moves. Early in his mayoralty he had met sporadically with selected black leaders, although often those "experts" were all of the same mind and agreed with the mayor from the beginning. Thus, some charged that the blacks with whom he met were all accommodationists and appeasers. Bates did refuse to meet with anyone whom he considered to be representing any sort of militant or pressure group, which meant that he turned away delegations of students and of the Richland County Citizens Committee.

7   SCCHR Report for January–May, 1958; interview with Lester Bates by the author, April 25, 1978.
8   Bates interview; "Weep No More," 33.

Into this milieu in the spring of 1960 came the student sit-in movement, a movement that in Columbia was late, timid, and short-lived. Demonstrations came earlier and were considerably more turbulent and disruptive in other parts of South Carolina—Rock Hill, Sumter, and Orangeburg. The sit-ins first came to South Carolina in Rock Hill, a community where blacks had more experience with protests and discrimination than most other areas of the state. In 1958 black leaders there had organized a city bus boycott that eventually forced the bus company out of business.[9]

At noon on Wednesday, March 2, 1960, almost a full month after the first sit-in in Greensboro, North Carolina, some fifty black students from Allen University and Benedict College, Columbia's two black institutions of higher learning, sat for eight minutes at the lunch counter at the F. W. Woolworth Company. There were no disturbances, no arrests, and no service. The students then moved on to S. H. Kress, where they found seats either occupied by whites or roped off. The demonstrators had notified the local press ahead of time so that a fair number of reporters and two state legislators were present for the event. The local police were also in evidence, but they did no more than join other curious spectators. The next day some two hundred students sat at lunch counters for two hours in ten downtown establishments, again without incident. But that evening the city manager's office issued a lengthy statement to the effect that the demonstrations would not again be tolerated. In the face of an expected showdown on Friday the students released a statement themselves saying that they had made their point.[10]

A week later when the students announced a planned march to the statehouse "to pray and sing songs of freedom," Governor Ernest F. Hollings warned that any such assemblage would result in arrests. Again, the students backed down. Declaring that the governor was "the victim of an acute tension attack," the students also claimed that they were law-abiding and did not want to provoke a show of force.[11]

The first arrests in connection with Columbia's sit-ins came

9 I. A. Newby, *Black Carolinians: A History of Blacks in South Carolina from 1895 to 1968* (Columbia, S.C.: University of South Carolina Press, 1973), 317.
10 Columbia *State*, March 3, 1960, Sec. A, pp. 1, 9, March 4, 1960, Sec. A, pp. 1, 9, March 6, 1960, Sec. A, p. 2.
11 *Ibid.*, March 11, 1960, Sec. A, p. 1, March 12, 1960, Sec. A, p. 6.

on March 14 when two black youths at Eckerd's Drugs ignored police warnings to leave the lunch counter. Five others went to jail the next day after sitting-in at the Taylor Street Pharmacy. Willis Johnson, a black funeral director, posted bail for the demonstrators. Both the SCCHR and the Richland County Citizens Committee issued statements supporting the actions of the students, but with the coming of spring holidays and the approach of final examinations at the black colleges, the sit-in movement faded in Columbia. In comparison, on the same day as the arrests in Columbia, police in Orangeburg, home of black South Carolina State College, jailed 425 protestors and used tear gas and fire hoses to disperse marching demonstrators.[12]

Present at every Columbia demonstration had been adult observers from the SCCHR to serve as objective witnesses in case incidents or abuses occurred. Most of the stores where the sit-ins took place were national chain stores whose managers were men who had lived in other parts of the country and who consequently were not apt to act rashly when blacks first appeared at their lunch counters.[13]

Only one major protest of civil disobedience occurred in the capital city, and that not until a year later when 189 marchers, mostly students, went to jail for demonstrating on the statehouse grounds. This was the largest and final protest of this kind to be made in Columbia, and at the time it involved one of the largest groups to be arrested in connection with a civil rights demonstration in the South.[14] But as other protests in other southern cities became more frequent and turned into disruptions and even violence, Mayor Bates and responsible persons all over town were forced to contemplate the consequences of continuing to resist what was surely inevitable—the acceptance of black citizens on an equal basis with white citizens in the collective, public life of the community. Not to be overlooked at this time was the fact that once again the All-American City Award was almost within grasp. *Look* named Columbia a runner-up in the contest in 1962, and the Chamber of Commerce

12   *Ibid.*, March 15, 1960, Sec. A, p. 1, March 16, 1960, Sec. A, pp. 1, 5; Simkins interview.
13   Interview with Alice Spearman Wright by the author, December 3, 1978. During the 1950s and 1960s Mrs. Wright was the moving force in the SCCHR.
14   Columbia *State*, March 3, 1961, Sec. D, p. 1.

was determined that the city should receive no adverse national publicity.

Bates continued clandestine meetings with selected black leaders but still refused to have an audience with anyone who was publicly vocal. By the spring of 1963, after the news media had given national exposure to turmoil and disorder in Birmingham, Alabama, the mayor decided that the time had come to move beyond talk. In July he called together eighty-seven prominent business figures in Columbia and told them that trouble was surely in store if the city's leaders did not prevent it. The meeting was stormy, as opinions varied greatly over what and how much should be done; even one father and son found themselves in heated debate. Most finally agreed, however, that in spite of long-standing traditions, an honest and realistic assessment of the present situation dictated that nothing positive would result from continued adherence to segregation policies in public accommodations.[15]

Out of the meeting came an informal committee of some fifteen of the most venerable figures in Columbia's business community, a group that began immediately a quiet drive to persuade their fellow businessmen that the time had come to try a new approach in race relations. These men worked without publicity and almost in secret, meeting individually with their neighbors to urge good will and restraint in a time of inevitable change. With such respected citizens as William G. Lyles, head of the prestigious architectural firm Lyles, Bissett, Carlisle & Wolff, and esteemed attorney R. Beverly Herbert calling for change, lesser figures found a posture of resistance difficult to maintain.

More in the public eye was another committee that Bates appointed at the same time, a biracial committee composed of twenty-five blacks and twenty-five whites that was designed to act as a kind of liaison between the black and white communities, to promote interracial understanding and harmony, and to make a smooth transition toward desegregation. One immediate

15   Bates interview; interview with Milton Kimpson by the author, May 19, 1978. Kimpson, one of those blacks with whom Mayor Bates was early communicating, later became director of the Greater Columbia Community Relations Council.

criticism of this very visible committee was that at least in the beginning the black and white members met separately with only the mayor as liaison. To some blacks this arrangement appeared to be merely a perpetuation of segregation, but on the other hand, this was the only way some whites would agree to cooperate. Other critics said that the racial composition of the committee should reflect the racial composition of the population and that blacks should make up only about one-third of the committee's membership. But the mayor reasoned that such an arrangement would not work as blacks would feel outnumbered and defeated from the beginning.[16]

Only those blacks whom the white community regarded as "responsible" were on the committee, causing Mrs. Simkins to claim that the whole thing was a fraud. "They all hop when the mayor says 'frog'" was her summation of the proceedings. She herself would not have accepted a position on the committee had she been invited, as she would not be a party to what she considered compromise. Also, by sitting down with the mayor she would automatically become a part of the establishment and would no longer be free to criticize in the manner to which she had long been accustomed. But by no means was the black contingent of the committee composed of hat-in-hand appeasers. James M. Hinton, long-time president of the South Carolina NAACP, was cochairman. Funeral director A. P. Williams spoke out early against the policy of the divided meetings. Attorney Lincoln C. Jenkins, Jr., a partner in the firm that represented those students arrested in sit-ins in South Carolina, was another member. (Within that partnership Matthew J. Perry was the better known; some would say, fairly or not, that Perry did the talking and received the publicity while Jenkins did the work.)[17]

By this time television's almost nightly airing of civil rights demonstrations throughout the segregated South was enough to give pause to even the most adamant standpatter in Columbia. And all the while in the background was the Richland County Citizens Committee, whose very existence caused a great deal of negotiating. When the Citizens Committee hinted at a boycott of downtown stores, most merchants realized that the talk coming

16   Bates interview.
17   Simkins interview; Kimpson interview.

from the mayor's office was making sense. The approach of those who were working quietly for change was in no way acrimonious, but one fact was increasingly clear to the business community: Columbia could no longer afford the risk of disorder that would surely come if business establishments continued to insist on policies of segregation in their public accommodations. These men made no threats, as merely a calm and realistic look at the situation was in itself convincing. When Lincoln Jenkins spoke of the sensibleness of avoiding litigation, responsible citizens listened, remembering the NAACP's success before the courts over the past two decades.

Main Street merchants soon were ready to move, and most businessmen quickly fell in line so that by the end of the summer discrimination in public facilities had come to an end in Columbia. It all happened so quickly and quietly that many were surprised by the lack of commotion and by the ease with which whites accepted the changes. The first symbols of segregation to go were the separate or "white only" rest rooms and drinking fountains, including the ones at city hall. With leaders urging restraint on all sides, many other discriminatory practices soon disappeared. By October the mayor's committee could report that all signs indicating race or color had been removed from water fountains, rest rooms, and dressing or fitting rooms; that merchandise in department stores was available for customers to try on without regard to race; that all customers were being treated with the same courtesies and appreciation, and were being addressed by appropriate titles; and that the city had adopted an official policy of nondiscrimination in all city employment.[18]

In the first several weeks of integration, some establishments found that enough of their old white customers were staying away so that their businesses had declined somewhat; especially hurt were variety store lunch counters and movie theaters. The SCCHR at this point moved to help those places that had gone ahead with integration by urging all its members to patronize complying establishments as much as possible until a degree of business normalcy could return.[19]

18   SCCHR Report for October, 1963.
19   Wright interview.

That summer blacks also gained admission to the University of South Carolina for the first time since Reconstruction. No one protested that move, as the crisis in desegregating higher education in the state had come earlier, in January, 1963, when Clemson College (later Clemson University) admitted its first black student, Harvey Gantt, without even the slightest disturbance. The peaceful integration of Clemson was more than a lucky happenstance, however. In the several weeks before Gantt's matriculation a small cadre of influential industrialists, educators, and business leaders had persuaded the state's potential troublemakers that law and order in South Carolina must be preserved at all cost.[20]

Desegregation of Columbia's public schools came in the following year. For the school year 1964–1965 the Columbia city school board decided unanimously to move ahead voluntarily with integration as it saw the folly of involving itself in lengthy litigation. In the fall twenty-two black pupils enrolled in six previously all-white schools. On opening day no significant numbers of outside spectators gathered and no policemen were on duty at the schools.[21]

With the end of the worst features of de facto segregation, the mayor's biracial committee turned to the next pressing need, decent jobs for blacks. In the summer of 1963 the committee created a guidance center where black and white professional counselors screened and coached black applicants to prepare them for employment in heretofore "white only" positions. Using all the same arguments they had used earlier for quiet desegregation, members of the committee approached local merchants with a plan that would put selected blacks in visible, responsible jobs. Some businessmen balked at first, but enough agreed with the plan that a beginning was made. Modest in comparison with later advances, this plan was a major step forward at the time. The guidance center developed into a permanent organization, listening to complaints from employers and requiring periodic counseling sessions with black employees placed in

20   For details of desegregation at Clemson, see George McMillan, "Integration with Dignity," *Saturday Evening Post*, March 16, 1963, pp. 15–21.
21   *Southern School News*, September, 1964, p. 12; Columbia *State*, September 1, 1964, Sec. A, p. 1.

new positions. The committee itself eventually became an established Columbia institution, expanding its activities over the years and continuing today as the Greater Columbia Community Relations Council.

Progress in race relations was one of the major points Columbia used to win the All-America City Award in 1964. *Look's* laudatory assessment of the city's leaders was that they "haven't mistaken racial quiet for progress. If they keep on, this Deep South city might show the North the way to brotherhood."[22]

22 "All-America Cities," *Look*, May 4, 1965, p. 96. In 1969 when Columbia was again competing for the *Look* award, the Richland County Citizens Committee made a vigorous protest to the judges, pointing out that the city's claim to progress in race relations was a sham, as so-called urban-renewal programs had ruthlessly displaced black families "without even to this day the provisions of one new low-rent unit." Richland County Citizens Committee to *Look*, November 9, 1969, in Richland County Citizens Committee file, South Caroliniana Library, University of South Carolina. *Look* awarded Columbia the runner-up position that year.

MORTON INGER

THE NEW ORLEANS SCHOOL CRISIS OF 1960

New Orleans, which seemingly was ready to be a leader in racial matters, became instead a center of resistance to school integration.[1] When four Negro first graders entered two previously all-white schools on November 14, 1960, the reaction of the city's extremists was so intense and went unchecked for so long that the city suffered a near catastrophe. White children boycotted the two schools for a year, and for months—while the nation watched on television—an unruly crowd cursed, stoned, and spat upon the few children who continued to pursue an education despite the presence of blacks in their midst.

Behind these events lay the city's most serious problem—a

[1] This essay is excerpted from Morton Inger, *Politics and Reality in an American City: The New Orleans School Crisis of 1960* (New York: Center for Urban Education, 1969). Portions of this article have appeared in Robert L. Crain, *The Politics of School Desegregation* (Chicago: Aldine, 1968). This account is based primarily on personal interviews with many of the principal actors in the events related here. In many instances, these people also made their personal papers available. Understandably, they were all promised anonymity. The only footnote citations, therefore, are to matters that are in the public record. The research was conducted under the direction of Peter H. Rossi and Robert L. Crain at the National Opinion Research Center.

lack of leadership. Not one of New Orleans' political and business leaders had even attempted to prepare the community for desegregation. As late as the fall of 1960—three years after Little Rock—they all believed that the New Orleans schools would never have to be desegregated. All of them were stunned when the federal judge handed down the order to desegregate. Even then, the leaders did nothing to prepare the community for a peaceful transition. Yet all this took place, not in some landlocked Bible Belt country town, but in the nation's second largest port and one of America's most cosmopolitan cities—cultured, civilized, heterogeneous New Orleans—the home of liberal French Catholicism, a city that was thronged with tourists and businessmen from all over the world, a city that had had racially integrated residential neighborhoods for three hundred years.

An article in the *New Republic* in February, 1959, first reported the surprising news that no support for peaceful school desegregation had yet emerged in New Orleans. "There is no organized effort," it reported, "as in Atlanta—to encourage people to think in advance of what the loss of the public schools would mean to them and to make their views known." Still, the article saw hope for the city in the enlightened self-interest of the city's "power structures": "The 'power structure' of New Orleans business and finance . . . have no congregations or clients to consult or fear, and their main preoccupation is to keep New Orleans the flourishing center of a growing state. The forward-looking 'reform' mayor, deLesseps S. Morrison, whom they have kept in office for 13 years, looks coldly on anything that might sully the image of the modern progressive city he has helped create."[2]

Chep Morrison had been hailed as one of the new breed of southern politicians concerned with attracting industry and shrugging off the old stereotype of the sleepy, prejudiced South. He was first elected mayor in 1946 when a group of women—who became known as the "Girls"—worked hard and led him to an upset victory over Robert Maestri, who had been mayor since 1936. In his first years in office, Morrison launched a campaign

2 Hellen Fuller, "New Orleans Knows Better," *New Republic*, February 16, 1959, p. 16.

to attract industry to the city. By 1948, New Orleans, whose port had ranked sixteenth in the country in dollar volume and exports after World War I, had become the nation's second busiest port. In 1951, more than $200 million worth of industry moved into the area, and in 1952, another $150 million moved in.

Morrison was reelected in 1950, 1954 and again in 1958. By the late 1950s, however, Morrison was finding city government too confining, and the businessmen seemed to have lost interest in the rejuvenation of their city. Some major companies were leaving the area, and New Orleans was regaining its reputation as one of America's sleepier cities. In 1958, 1959, and 1960, not one major company moved to the New Orleans area. In 1961, Morrison resigned office to take a position in John Kennedy's administration.

Despite Morrison's long tenure and despite the zeal and organization of the Girls, reform never became institutionalized, except in one area of the city's life. Encouraged by their success in electing Morrison in 1946, the Girls went to work on the public schools, which had been weakened and were deteriorating because of a corrupt administration. In 1948, a position opened on the school board, but the Girls could not find a man willing to run for it.[3] Many civic leaders said that their businesses were too sensitive to allow them to take part in controversial issues. So one of the Girls made the race, and won.

By 1956, the Girls' candidates held all five seats on the school board. These five—Ted Shepard, Emile Wagner, Matt Sutherland, Louis Riecke, and Lloyd Rittiner—young, honest, civic-minded, nonpolitical businessmen or professionals, but not of the community's elite—constituted the school board during the desegregation crisis of 1960. One of them was one of the city's leading segregationists. The other four believed in segregation but were much more moderate.

The series of events that rocked New Orleans in 1959 and 1960 was set in motion in September, 1952, when the NAACP filed a suit against the Orleans Parish School Board.[4] At first the

3   The board is composed of five members serving staggered six-year terms. Every two years, the voters elect one or two members depending on whether terms of one or two expire at that time.
4   In Louisiana, the parish is the area known as the county in most other American states. Geographically, Orleans Parish and the city of New Orleans are

case lay dormant while the local NAACP awaited a signal from the national office. The signal did not come for four years—until after the second *Brown* decision in 1955.[5] On February 15, 1956, Judge J. Skelly Wright of the federal district court in New Orleans delivered the first court decision in the case (known as *Bush* v. *Orleans Parish School Board*). Among other things, Wright's decision enjoined the Orleans school board from requiring and permitting racial segregation and directed the board to "make arrangements for admission of children . . . on a racially nondiscriminatory basis with all deliberate speed."[6] The school board made no such arrangements and instead resisted Judge Wright's decision, appealing his rulings through the federal court system. The Fifth Circuit Court of Appeals and the United States Supreme Court affirmed the decisions of the district court.[7]

Throughout this period from 1956 to 1959, neither the school board nor the city government made any efforts to prepare for integration. Finally, in 1959, the Negro plaintiffs urged further action by the court. Accordingly, on July 15, 1959, more than three years after he had directed the board to begin making arrangements, Judge Wright ordered it to file a desegregation plan by March 1, 1960.[8] Wright later changed this date to May 16, 1960, at the request of the school board.

Meanwhile, the state government, led by Governor Jimmie Davis, was determined to preserve segregation even if the only way to do so was to close the New Orleans schools. Louisiana's attorney general, Jack P. F. Gremillion, went into the state courts to block the federal desegregation order. In March, 1960, the Louisiana Court of Appeals ruled that the Orleans Parish

---

identical; historically, the two units developed with different political functions, and though the two were consolidated in 1870, some functions are still distinct. The school board is a parish board responsible directly to the state, not to the city.

5 *Brown* v. *Board of Education of Topeka*, 349 U.S. 294 (1955)

6 *Bush* v. *Orleans Parish School Board*, 138 F. Supp. 337, 342 (1956).

7 *Orleans Parish School Board* v. *Bush*, 242 F. 2nd 156 (affirmed, March 1, 1957), 354 U.S. 921 (cert. denied, June 17, 1957), 252 F. 2nd 253 (affirmed, Feb. 13, 1958), 356 U.S. 969 (cert. denied, May 26, 1958).

8 *Orleans Parish School Board* v. *Bush*, United States District Court, Eastern District, Louisiana, Civil Action No. 3630, in *Race Relations Law Reporter*, IV (Nashville: Vanderbilt University School of Law, 1959), 583.

School Board no longer had power to "classify" (as white or Negro) its schools.[9]

On May 16, 1960, the date by which Judge Wright had ordered the Orleans Parish School Board to produce its desegregation plan, the school board told the court that it had developed no such plan. Judge Wright responded by ordering the desegregation of all first grades at the opening of school in September.[10] Though great attention had been directed to school desegregation in many cities, particularly in Little Rock, and though the city had been on notice for ten months that it had to come up with a desegregation plan, board members and civic leaders said that they were "stunned" by this order. In part they were stunned because all of the community's institutions had either taken a stand opposing integration or else had retreated and maintained a frightened silence. Not one white moderate group in New Orleans was publicly supporting school desegregation. Throughout this period, the community's business leaders remained silent. They were "out" to anyone who wanted to talk to them about the schools.

Removed from politics, the school board had to make a political decision without the support of any major institution in the city. Isolation made the four moderate board members desperate. Two of them considered resigning. On June 20, 1960, the board passed a resolution asking Governor Davis to interpose the sovereignty of the state to prevent integration. Board member Theodore Shepard saw it as the only way to keep the schools open on a segregated basis. The board was at the end of its rope.

At this low point, a new development changed the entire picture. A group of native New Orleanians who had never before favored integration formed the Committee for Public Education (CPE) and urged publicly that the schools be kept open even if that meant integration. The very existence of CPE apparently emboldened some of the older institutions for very shortly the Episcopal clergy of New Orleans, the clergy of the United Church of Christ, and the pastors and elders from the Methodist churches came out for open schools.

9 *State of Louisiana* v. *Orleans Parish School Board*, 118 So. 2nd 471 (1960).
10 *Bush* v. *Orleans Parish School Board*, United States District Court, Eastern District, Louisiana, Civil Action No. 3630, in *Race Relations Law Reporter*, V (Nashville: Vanderbilt University School of Law, 1960), 378.

Throughout the summer of 1960, the federal courts and the State of Louisiana fought a running battle. On August 17, Governor Davis notified the city's superintendent of schools, James Redmond, that the governor was now running the public schools of New Orleans; he also ordered Redmond to open the schools on September 7 on a segregated basis. The same day, thirty white parents who feared the state would close the schools filed a new suit (*Williams* v. *Davis*) asking for a temporary injunction to restrain the governor and other state officials from obeying the state court injunction and the state statutes with regard to segregation. Because the *Williams* and *Bush* suits sought essentially the same relief against the same parties, the court consolidated the cases.[11] On August 27, the federal district court, awarding judgment for the Negro and white parents in both cases, struck down as unconstitutional all of the acts of the legislature that would directly require segregation of the races in the public schools, nullified the seizure of the school board by the governor, and ordered the board to get on with the desegregation of the schools.[12]

The filing of the *Williams* case was a vital move. Prior to this suit, one was either pro-Negro and prointegration or prowhite and prosegregation. Now, moderates could opt for a third choice—keeping the schools open. Thus, a move for "open schools," not a move to desegregate them, was the avenue upon which moderates, including the four members of the school board, finally entered the controversy. The formation of CPE, the suit by the white parents, and Judge Wright's unyielding position eased the course for the four moderate members of the school board. These four and the board's lawyer, Sam Rosenberg, met privately with Judge Wright and told him they had made no plans to desegregate but were now ready to comply with his orders.

School was scheduled to open on September 7, little more than a week away, so the board asked Wright to delay desegre-

11   The joining of the *Williams* and *Bush* cases in no way signified cooperation between the Negro and white plaintiffs—even though the two suits ostensibly sought the same relief. At no time did white moderates work with or for Negroes to desegregate the schools; the white efforts were strictly to keep the schools open.
12   *Bush* v. *Orleans Parish School Board*, *Williams* v. *Davis*, 187 F. Supp. 42 (1960).

gation until November 14 to give the board time to devise a de-segregation plan. A delay would also mean that school would open on a segregated basis, and the difficulty of transferring would reduce the number of Negro pupils in white schools. The fewer the Negroes, the board members believed, the easier would be the transition. Furthermore, with a delay, desegregation would not occur until after the November 8 election for the school board position held by Matthew Sutherland, one of the moderates. Judge Wright agreed to postpone the start of desegregation until November 14.[13]

In drawing up a plan the board refused to use the community support it now had. Against the advice of friends, the board members steadfastly refused to consider such political considerations as who would support what plan, where support would most likely arise, and where the opposition would be concentrated. Trying to arrive at a legally acceptable way to limit the number of Negroes who would be entering the white schools, the board and the superintendent adopted a lengthy administrative process. Negro applicants were reviewed by psychologists, psychometrists, the acting director of guidance and testing, and an administrative review team composed of the superintendent, the first assistant superintendent, the acting superintendent for instruction, and the school system's medical director.

The choice of the white schools to be integrated was to be determined by finding a school whose first-grade median achievement scores matched the scores of the Negro applicants. Some people (both inside and outside the school system) urged Redmond and the board, instead, to select schools where the white parents and children would accept Negro pupils. The PTAs of two schools asked the board to send Negro children to them. These schools, Wilson and Lusher, were in middle- and upper-class neighborhoods, and Negro children were living right across the street from one of the two schools. But Redmond and the board would not accept what they regarded as subjective criteria.

The practical result of the board's policy was that it chose to

13 Bush v. Orleans Parish School Board, Williams v. Davis, United States District Court, Eastern District, Louisiana, in Race Relations Law Reporter, V (Nashville: Vanderbilt University School of Law, 1960), 669; motion to vacate denied, 364 U.S. 803 (1960).

desegregate the worst possible schools. In the first place, two schools were chosen in the same neighborhood, thus enabling the segregationists to concentrate their fire. Moreover, these schools were in the most neglected section of the city, the ninth ward. The ninth ward had been the last to get streetlights, the last to get paved streets—and now it was the first to be integrated! Even the moderates in the ward were furious.

While the school board and the staff were developing their screening procedure, the open schools campaign focused on the reelection of Matthew Sutherland. The Independent Women's Organization (IWO), an important element of the Girls, came out publicly for open schools on August 3 and joined forces with the women of the Committee for Public Education (CPE) in asking the community's influential people to support Sutherland. Having largely held themselves aloof from the reform movement and from the city's politics, the city's business leaders were not easily moved by these appeals. Moreover, Morrison refused to endorse either Judge Wright's order or the board's decision to comply with it.

On October 27, the school board announced that it had granted transfer permits to five Negro girls, and the next day Governor Davis called the legislature into the first of several special sessions, to begin on November 4. Rumors swept the city that the governor was going to close the schools, and this threat finally forced the city's business leaders to act. On November 1, for instance, in a front-page editorial, the *Times-Picayune* endorsed the candidacy of Matthew Sutherland and called attention to his opposition to forced integration. On November 4, the first day of Governor Davis' special session, a committee of one hundred important business and professional men, headed by an executive committee of eighteen of the city's most influential citizens, at last endorsed Matt Sutherland. The endorsement, "for the future of our children and for the continued growth of New Orleans as a major industrial center in the South," made no mention of the desegregation issue except for an indirect reference to the closing of the schools: "Our struggle with the Soviet Union . . . makes it imperative that the education of our children not be stopped or interrupted."[14] The day before the election, this committee ran a three-quarter page ad in the *Times-*

14   New Orleans *Times-Picayune*, November 4, 1960, sec. 2, p. 7.

Picayune listing ninety-eight names and signed "Business and Professional Men's Committee for Sutherland." Though the only message on the page was, "We believe that we and our children will all have a better future if Matt Sutherland is elected to the School Board," the "best people" in the city were now at least advocating Sutherland's election and contributing money to his campaign.

Within five days all of Davis' bills had passed both houses of the state legislature and were signed into law. The federal court that reviewed these laws at the end of the month summarized their function:

In order to forestall any effective integration order for this school year, present enrollment on a segregated basis is "frozen" and transfers are forbidden (Act 26); but, for the future, any school under an order to desegregate is immediately closed (Act 22), whereupon the local school board ceases to exist (Act 21); to carry out these directives . . . the state police are given additional powers and placed under the orders of the Legislature (Act 16), and if demonstrators are needed, they may now be recruited among the students who are no longer compelled to go to school (Act 27); to assure that an integrated school does close, the new legislation provides that if it continues to operate it shall enjoy no accreditation (Act 20), teachers shall lose their certificates (Act 23), and the students themselves shall receive no promotion or graduation credits (Act 24).[15]

The school board members pledged their full cooperation if the governor succeeded. "The only thing I am against," one said, "is the closing of schools. As an elected official I feel it is my duty to provide public education, if possible on a segregated basis but, if not, on an integrated basis."[16]

On election day, the "moderate" Matt Sutherland won by a wide margin. Sutherland's victory suggested that the community was ready to accept token integration. From that moment, the school board members dropped their passive role and became actors bent on achieving peaceful desegregation. Nonetheless, time was running out. On the morning of November 10, four members of the legislature, accompanied by three armed state police, arrived at the New Orleans board of education

15   *Bush* v. *Orleans Parish School Board, Williams* v. *Davis, United States* v. *Louisiana,* 188 F. Supp. 916, 928 (November 30, 1960).
16   New Orleans *Times-Picayune,* November 5, 1960, p. 19.

building and stripped the school board of its authority. A few hours later, Judge Wright, acting at the request of the white parents in the *Williams* case, issued orders temporarily forbidding state intervention. At 6 P.M., Sam Rosenberg told the board members they were back in control of New Orleans' public schools. With this assurance, the board formally authorized the transfer of the five Negro girls into two all-white schools.

That night Governor Davis called his second special session. On Saturday, November 12, state education superintendent Shelby Jackson declared a state holiday for the fourteenth, but on Sunday morning the thirteenth Judge Wright issued restraining orders against the holiday. On Sunday the legislature also fired Redmond and Rosenberg and placed the entire legislature in charge of the New Orleans schools. No judge had ever enjoined an entire legislature, but that evening, at the request of the New Orleans school board, Judge Wright signed preliminary restraining orders against Governor Davis and all members of the legislature.

Unfortunately, the school board's integration plan was so poorly conceived that the gains so laboriously achieved by the formation of CPE, the filing of the *Williams* case, and Sutherland's decisive victory were all but thrown away. Support had been created uptown, but the schools were being integrated downtown. The board had been kept out of politics; the price for this triumph of reform principles was to be a breakdown of social controls in the city.

On November 14, 1960, four frightened Negro girls (the fifth had withdrawn her application), three at McDonogh 19 and one at Frantz, became the first of their race in the Deep South since the end of Reconstruction to attend classes with whites below the college level. That morning, many white parents came to take their children home. By the end of the week, every white child was withdrawn from McDonogh 19, and all but two white children were withdrawn from Frantz. Except for one brief period in January, 1961, no white pupil returned to McDonogh 19 during that school year. Walgreen's fired the father of the children who temporarily broke the boycott at McDonogh 19, and he was forced to leave town when no one else would hire him. At Frantz, a few more parents allowed their children to return, and the boycott at that school was never complete.

On Tuesday, November 15, the day after school opened, roving packs of teenagers tried to break into the two desegregated schools, but they were turned back by police. That night, Willie Rainach, Leander Perez, and other segregationist leaders spoke to a rally of five thousand at the municipal auditorium. The next day, a mob variously estimated at between one and three thousand swept through the New Orleans civic center and into city hall and then marched on the federal courts and the board of education. Police turned the mob away from the board of education, but the unruly assemblage continued to roam through the business district throwing bottles and stones at Negroes.

Mayor Morrison appealed for an end to the violence. His talk stressed the damage that could be done to the "image" of New Orleans "as a thriving center of commerce and industry" if the "ugly irresponsible incidents such as took place today" continued. At the same time, he said, "I should like to repeat that the New Orleans police department has not and is not enforcing the federal court order relative to school integration."[17] Morrison's close friends in the good government movement were aghast at his failure to call for support of the school board. That evening, after Morrison's talk, black teenagers went out on the streets seeking revenge for the stonings. One Negro boy was knifed, three white men were shot, and many other whites were beaten. That night, police made 250 arrests, mainly of blacks.

The next day, the mayor called an urgent closed-door meeting of leading citizens to discuss the crisis. One hundred and sixty business and professional leaders attended the meeting and issued a statement calling on citizens to do their part to preserve peace and order. The statement, signed by many of the city's most influential men, commended the mayor, the police, and the city council for preserving law and order, but made no mention of the school board.[18] Two days earlier, the Young Men's Business Club had also spoken out against the demonstrations, but it, too, failed to support the school board, expressly tabling a resolution to do so.[19]

At McDonogh 19 and especially at Frantz a huge crowd

17   *Ibid.*, November 17, 1960, sec. 2, p. 11.

18   Since the unruly demonstrations by whites were continuing, this praise of the city officials made no sense—except that the praise came the day after the police moved swiftly to stop the *Negro* outbursts.

19   New Orleans *Times-Picayune*, November 16, 1960, p. 31.

gathered every morning to taunt, shove, heckle, threaten, and spit at the Negro girls and the few white children who dared go to school in violation of the boycott. On November 29, the police permitted a mob of four hundred to follow one white woman and her daughter all the way home from school and swarm over them, shouting obscenities, and smashing windows in their house.

In the second special session of the state legislature, which began on November 15, the state legislators declared illegal all acts of the "now defunct New Orleans School Board" and warned all banks and businesses not to do business with or honor checks of or make loans to the "old" school board. They also directed that the funds of the Orleans school board be transferred to the legislature and provided for a system of education expense grants for children attending nonprofit, nonsectarian, nonpublic schools. The state bond and tax board refused to authorize the school board's request for a loan to meet its November 23 payroll, and one bank, the Whitney National, which continued to cash the school board's checks, was removed as fiscal agent for the state.[20]

On November 30, the federal court in New Orleans announced its decision on all the matters that had come before it during the month. Once again, the court enjoined over seven hundred state and city officials from interfering with what the federal court called "the school board's proposal" to admit Negroes to previously all-white schools. In addition, the court turned down the school board's request to delay desegregation.[21] On December 12, the United States Supreme Court upheld the district court's decision.[22] The November 30 decision of the district court, though by no means the last decision in the case, was nevertheless the climax to the legal battle.

Perhaps because legislative interposition had failed and integration had thus succeeded, the street disturbances in New Orleans grew more intense after November 30. The street battle

20   Louisiana State Advisory Committee to the United States Commission on Civil Rights, *The New Orleans School Crisis* (Washington, D.C.: Government Printing Office, 1961), p. 23. The teachers at McDonogh 19 and Frantz were not paid until after Christmas.
21   *Bush* v. *Orleans Parish School Board, Williams* v. *Davis, U.S.* v. *State of Louisiana*, 188 F. Supp. 916 (1960).
22   *Ibid.*, 364 U.S. 500 (1960).

focused on perfecting the white boycott. Given some sense of safety by a carlift, a number of parents had begun to send their children back to Frantz; by December 6, a total of twenty-three white children attended Frantz, but a new wave of threats, stonings, and other harassments quickly reduced the number of white students to eight. On December 8, the White Citizens Council distributed a list of all the volunteer drivers, describing their cars and disclosing their telephone numbers. This stopped the carlift. On December 9, federal marshals began transporting white children who wanted to attend Frantz, but by this time the parents were too frightened. The number of whites attending Frantz was kept at ten or fewer for the remainder of the school year. The New Orleans crisis now became an international spectacle, with a huge press and television corps covering the street battle. Many national journals and papers carried a running box score on the number of whites attending Frantz.

The publicity hurt the city. A page-one story in the New York *Times* was headlined "New Orleans Rift Takes Trade Toll."[23] Business leaders privately estimated hotel and restaurant trade to be about 20 percent off the customary rate. There were also sharp declines in department store sales. Business leaders were greatly disturbed but "reluctant to make any public attempt to resolve the problem apparently out of fear that this might bring economic sanctions from the Citizens' Councils."[24]

But the businessmen could not remain silent forever. On December 14, a total of 105 business and professional men of New Orleans ran a three-quarter page advertisement in the newspaper appealing for an end to threats and street demonstrations and for support of the school board. Significantly, the ad contained the name of a man who was generally believed to be at the pinnacle of the social and business life of the city. However, he was the only member of what was considered the inner circle of influence to sign the ad. This advertisement, distributed throughout the nation in an effort to counteract the bad publicity, signaled the beginning of the end of the business leaders' passivity.

Meanwhile, the school board's problems mounted. On December 22, the legislature had adjourned without releasing

23 New York *Times*, December 6, 1960, p. 1.
24 *Ibid.*, November 28, 1960, p. 1.

funds for the salaries of four thousand teachers and other employees of the Orleans school system. With the state loan board still refusing to sanction loans in anticipation of local taxes, Mayor Morrison appealed in January to property owners to pay their taxes in advance. Leading businesses, including the city's public utilities and the newspapers, did pay in advance, thus providing funds for school personnel who had not been paid for two months.

Throughout the troubled months, the women in CPE, IWO, and the League of Women Voters had worked unceasingly to involve influential businessmen. The women had obtained the signatures for the ad endorsing Sutherland and for the December 14 ad, and on January 30, 1961, their efforts culminated in a huge testimonial dinner at the Roosevelt Hotel for the four board members and the superintendent. To understand the significance of this public dinner, one must recall that during the height of the crisis, the board members were not only reviled by their opponents, but, in many cases, shunned by their friends.

One of the organizers of the dinner said in his address that a recent New York *Times* editorial had asked, "Where are the Southern moderates?" This gathering, said the speaker, is our answer. "We are at the Roosevelt Hotel." When the main speaker, Harry Kelleher, a prominent attorney, was introduced, the master of ceremonies said: "If the face of the mob . . . is our worst face, our speaker tonight represents our best face—the aspect with which we would like to face the nation and world at this time." Citing the "gallant" fight the board put up to resist desegregation, Kelleher said, "It behooves all of us to support these four honorable men. . . . We owe them our everlasting gratitude."[25] Although the boycott continued, and although the school system's finances took another year to recover, the school board and the superintendent felt that the problems were now manageable. Events of the remainder of the school year and of the following year proved the school leaders were justified in their confidence. The crisis was over.

In July, 1961, Morrison resigned as mayor to become the United States Ambassador to the Organization of American States, and the city council appointed Victor Schiro to succeed him. Schiro

25   New Orleans *Times-Picayune*, January 31, 1961, p. 2.

was precisely the kind of politician reformers despise. Many derided him as "just a party hack." Yet Schiro led the city to its successful desegregation of the schools in 1961. Determined to avoid another economic setback, Schiro told the public: "I am putting all on notice that law and order will be maintained at any cost."[26] Schiro, of course, was not acting alone. His strong statements appeared simultaneously with a series of moves and statements by the city's business and professional leaders. On August 22, the Chamber of Commerce, which had been notably silent in 1960, stated: "Business climate greatly affects the economic development of our area. . . . New Orleans . . . has been subjected to adverse publicity regarding incidents that involve friction between the races." The Chamber went on to ask for "the assistance and support of all citizens in the maintenance of law and order and in the avoidance of all situations and incidents that could be magnified and publicized in a manner that would create an unfavorable image of our city."[27]

At the end of August, 315 civic and business leaders ran a full-page advertisement in the *Times-Picayune* that, for the first time, called for peaceful desegregation of the schools. The ad carried three times the number of signatures and went much further than the ad of December, 1960. The opening sentence said that "public education . . . must be preserved . . . and the dignity of our city upheld." "Preservation of law and order in Louisiana," the statement continued, "requires compliance with the final decisions of the United States Supreme Court; any other course would result in chaos."[28]

In September, 1961, the school board, with the mayor and other community leaders behind it, selected four additional schools to receive Negroes, including the two schools, Wilson and Lusher, whose PTAs had requested Negro pupils in 1960. Desegregation that fall went smoothly and peacefully. Schiro instructed the police not to allow any crowds to form around the schools. At each of the six schools, police barricaded an area extending one block in each direction from the schools. At the end of the first day, Mayor Schiro thanked the people of New Orleans

26   *Time*, August 25, 1961, p. 40.
27   *Southern School News*, September, 1961, p. 10.
28   New Orleans *Times-Picayune*, August 31, 1961, p. 13.

"for the manner in which they accepted this mandate of our federal government and courts."[29]

"We were the first in the Deep South, so how could we prepare for it?" In slightly altered form, this question was raised in defense of the city's behavior by several New Orleanians. But New Orleans' political and business leaders had refuse to learn from the mistakes and solutions of other southern cities—notably Little Rock. In contrast, the mayor of Atlanta had a study of Little Rock prepared and distributed to the city's business leaders. Furthermore, Atlanta's business leaders had already been preparing for desegregation for two years when New Orleans' schools were desegregated. Thus, those who say Atlanta had the opportunity to learn from New Orleans' mistakes miss the point. Atlanta learned from Little Rock's mistakes and set to work immediately to avoid them. New Orleans could have learned from Little Rock's mistakes and Atlanta's two years of preparation, but chose not to.

This account, focusing on a dramatic series of events in the late 1950s and early 1960s, does not purport to give the complete history of race relations in New Orleans. Nonetheless, these events constituted a critical turning point. Prior to the school crisis of 1960, business leaders in New Orleans felt that they could isolate themselves and ignore public issues. The crisis had its origins in this head-in-the-sands attitude; it ended when business leaders got involved. Though race relations problems were not completely solved in New Orleans, they have never again reached such crisis proportions. In fact, there has been considerable improvement. Clearly, the New Orleans story is not a fairy tale where everyone lives happily ever after and problems magically disappear. It is a story of a city learning to grapple with problems instead of ignoring them. That change took place in the 1960 school crisis.

29 *Southern School News*, October, 1961, p. 2.

CARL ABBOTT

THE NORFOLK BUSINESS COMMUNITY

THE CRISIS OF MASSIVE RESISTANCE

The pivotal scene in the drama of Norfolk school integration opened on January 25, 1959, with the jangle of a telephone. Mayor Fred Duckworth sat behind his desk at city hall, sorting through the stacks of paper which besiege even a part-time chief executive. He jerked the phone from its cradle and barked a sharp hello, for the mayor was a man with a "bulldozer" approach to city problems. He listened intently, but with growing anger.

The caller was J. Pretlow Darden. Elected to Norfolk's city council in 1946 as a member of a businessmen's reform ticket, Darden had served as mayor from 1948 to 1950 before returning to semiprivate life to manage his business interests and serve on the board of the Norfolk Redevelopment and Housing Authority. He had also taken the lead in arranging an advertisement which was to appear on January 26 in the morning *Virginian-Pilot* and the evening *Ledger Dispatch*. When Darden finished reading the copy over the phone, Duckworth ended the conversation with a cry of dismay. "Oh my God," he shouted before slamming down the receiver, "you've stabbed me in the back!"[1]

1 Interview with J. Pretlow Darden by the author, April 4, 1978.

As published the following day over the names of one hundred leading business and professional men, the short statement offered strong support for the preservation of Norfolk public schools.

While we would strongly prefer to have segregated schools, it is evident from the recent court decisions that our public schools must be either integrated to the extent legally required or abandoned. The abandonment of our public school system is, in our opinion, unthinkable, as it would mean the denial of an adequate education to a majority of our children. Moreover, the consequences would be most damaging to our community. We, therefore, urge the City Council to do everything within its power to open all public schools as promptly as possible.

In an accompanying editorial, the previously segregationist *Ledger Dispatch* commented on the "tremendous weight" carried by the advertisement. The next morning, the more liberal *Virginian-Pilot* rejoiced that "a new clear voice speaks in Norfolk." The editors hoped that the action of "an impressive group of men of large responsibilities and of effective leadership in their own fields" would encourage other moderates to speak out on the city's desegregation problems.[2]

It was not only the daily newspapers which applauded the action of the "Committee of 100." The historical mythology of Norfolk credits them with the decisive voice in resolving a crisis which deeply divided the city and disrupted public education for half a year. Except among those who were active advocates of public schools, local memories tend to skip quickly from the school closings in September to their reopening with limited integration in February. Even Fred Duckworth showed where he placed the responsibility by framing the Committee of 100 advertisement in black and hanging it on the back of the closet door in his city hall office.[3]

The first section of the present essay describes the evolution

2   Norfolk *Ledger Dispatch*, January 26, 1959; Norfolk *Virginian-Pilot*, January 26, 27, 1959.
3   Norfolk *Virginian-Pilot*, July 25, 1961; Lenoir Chambers, *Salt Water and Printer's Ink: Norfolk and Its Newspapers, 1865–1965* (Chapel Hill: University of North Carolina Press, 1967), 387; John J. Brewbaker, "Desegregation in the Norfolk Public Schools" (Typescript dated July, 1960, in J. L. Blair Buck Papers, Alderman Library, University of Virginia, Charlottesville); interview with Roy Martin by the author, April 10, 1978.

of school integration policy in Norfolk and identifies the groups and interests in the community which played major roles in determining the outcome of the massive resistance crisis. Between 1956 and 1958, the focus of the decision process on integration moved from the Virginia General Assembly to the National Association for the Advancement of Colored People to the Norfolk School Board and City Council. During the tumultuous fall of 1958, public positions were also established by white liberals in the Norfolk Committee for Public Schools, by black leaders, and by segregationists organized as the Defenders of State Sovereignty. The crisis ended in January, 1959, when separate actions by state and federal courts overturned the Virginia legislation and the Committee of 100 emerged to ratify the judicial results. The second section of the essay turns more directly to more detailed discussion of the role of the business community in the development and resolution of the school crisis. In order to evaluate the basis of Norfolk's historical consensus, it analyzes the character of the membership of the Committee of 100, their shared ideology, and their relationship to the statewide Virginia establishment. The concluding section briefly weighs the long-range impact of massive resistance on Norfolk politics and on business influence during the 1960s.

In summary, the essay finds that no single group or interest in Norfolk controlled the outcome of the school-closing crisis, but that a large number of groups and interests contributed to the result. In particular, the Norfolk business leadership played an important part by helping to ratify or make acceptable the January court decisions. However, they were no more the determining factor than were a number of other participants. Members of the Committee of 100 themselves have acknowledged the roles of the liberal minority who kept the issue of open schools on the public agenda and of the judges who handed down the crucial decisions. One could also cite the parents who filed several court challenges to the massive resistance laws, the teachers who refrained from cooperation with alternative private schools, the journalists and Navy Department bureaucrats who kept up outside pressure, and the city council members who made the cause of school segregation increasingly ridiculous.

Perhaps the most useful model for understanding the pattern of decision making in Norfolk is that developed for the comparably sized city of Syracuse, New York. In a study published in 1961, Frank Munger distinguished between a Syracuse "mythology" which included a belief in a centralized and monolithic power structure and a reality in which there were "many kinds of community power, with one differing from another in . . . fundamental ways." Decisions eventuate from "a flow of choices" involving a long sequence of discrete actions taken by a series of actors who are all necessary to the process but no one of whom is sufficient to carry a decision on public policy. In short, "power roles are not competitive, but complementary; they are links in a chain." As this essay indicates, the same metaphor is also applicable to Norfolk in 1958 and 1959. The business community during the school crisis functioned as one link in the chain of decision-makers who brought about the peaceful reopening of public schools. Indeed, the image of a mobilized business leadership which could take the city's problems in hand was a sophisticated form of boosterism as much as it was a description of political realities.[4]

Certainly there was reason for Mayor Duckworth's temper to be frayed by the fifth month of Norfolk's encounter with massive resistance. The previous August, Judge Walter Hoffman of the U.S. district court had required the admission of seventeen black students to three senior and three junior high schools. On September 27, after the Fourth Circuit Court of Appeals had denied the state's protests of Hoffman's order, Governor Lindsay Almond had officially assumed state control of the affected schools and had ordered their closure. The action locked out of their classrooms the 9,950 white students and 17 black students who had been scheduled to attend the six schools. The racially segregated education of 21,000 other white students and 15,000 other black students continued in the other city schools which had not been subject to desegregation orders.[5]

4   Roscoe Martin, et al., Decisions in Syracuse (Bloomington: Indiana University Press, 1961), 305–306, 311–19.
5   School was also suspended that fall for high school students in Warren County and for students in two Charlottesville schools. Accessible accounts of massive resistance as a statewide issue are Benjamin Muse, Virginia's Massive Resistance (Bloomington: Indiana University Press, 1961) and James W. Ely, Jr., The Crisis of Conservative Virginia: The Byrd Organization and the Politics of Massive Resistance (Knoxville: University of Tennessee Press, 1976). Accessible

The dispatch of Almond's telegram to the Norfolk School Board climaxed three years of Virginia effort to develop a program of state resistance to school integration. In 1956, the Virginia General Assembly had responded to the wishes of Senator Harry F. Byrd by rejecting a local-option plan which had been developed by a legislative study commission and approved in part by statewide referendum. Instead the legislators adopted a set of laws designed to block any effort to desegregate Virginia schools. A statewide Pupil Placement Board was established to allow delays through the application of administrative remedies. Once the final integration order was issued by the federal courts, the governor was required to take control of any affected school, close it, and attempt to reopen it on a segregated basis. State funds were to be denied any schools operated locally on an integrated basis and tuition grants were to be provided for private school students in affected areas. A modification of the plan in 1958 required the local school board and local governing body to petition the state jointly if the community wished to operate its schools under local control. Essentially, the laws were designed to delay integration by placing state law in direct confrontation with the federal courts and thereby forcing additional time-consuming litigation. Under the ideal scenario envisioned by determined resisters, the governor was to risk jail and martyrdom by refusing all cooperation with federal authorities after he seized an integrated school.[6]

The obstructionist actions of the general assembly provided the backdrop for legal action by 233 black parents who filed suit in federal court asking admission of their children to all-white Norfolk schools in May, 1956. A year of legal maneuvering between the school board and NAACP attorneys brought a federal injunction in 1957 forbidding the school board to use race as a basis for pupil assignment. In response, Norfolk school officials

summaries of the Norfolk crisis are found in Forrest P. White, "Will Norfolk's Schools Stay Open?" *Atlantic*, September, 1959, pp. 29–33; Luther J. Carter, "Desegregation in Norfolk," *South Atlantic Quarterly*, LVIII (Autumn, 1959), 507–20; and Thomas J. Wertenbaker and Marvin Schlegel, *Norfolk: Historic Southern Port* (Durham, N.C.: Duke University Press, 1962), 387–94.

6   Ely, *The Crisis of Conservative Virginia*, 45, 71; James J. Kilpatrick to M. H. Sass, November 12, 1958, in James J. Kilpatrick Papers, Alderman Library, University of Virginia; Darden interview.

devised six "nonracial" assignment criteria including scholastic tests and personal interviews. Eighty-eight of the 151 black children who had applied for admission to white schools submitted to the full selection process, only to be denied on the basis of the newly established standards. On appeal by the rejected students, Judge Hoffman at the end of August upheld the applications of 17 students who had been refused admission because they had applied to schools in areas of "racial tension" or because they would be isolated individuals in otherwise all-white schools.[7]

The Norfolk School Board members found themselves caught between a distaste for integration and a commitment to public education. Their freedom of action was also limited by their status as administrators rather than politicians, for members were appointed by the city council and depended on the council for the school budget. Between Hoffman's preliminary ruling at the end of August and his formal order on September 18, the board agreed to accept the expected decision. The inevitable result, as the school board realized, would be confrontation between the state and federal governments.[8]

Through the summer of 1958, few residents of Norfolk apart from the school board took the threat of school closure seriously. The fast-breaking events of September, however, forced the city's population to define their opinions on the conflicting values of public education and racial segregation. The strongest opposition to massive resistance came from the Norfolk Committee for Public Schools (NCPS). After tentative discussions with city officials in the spring, a dozen or so organizers attempted to recruit members during July and August. At the urging of community leaders who privately applauded the committee's efforts but who withheld their own names, the group waited until September 16 to elect a board and executive committee and until September 19 to issue a statement favoring limited desegregation. The group followed on September 24–25 with a large newspaper advertisement which included a clip-off membership coupon. With perhaps a hundred supporters can-

7   Paul Puryear, "The Implementation of the Desegregation Decision in the Federal Courts of Virginia: A Case Study of Legal Resistance to Federal Authority" (Ph.D. dissertation, University of Chicago, 1960), 142–53, 206–322.
8   Interview with Francis Crenshaw by the author, March 31, 1978.

vassing door to door and at shopping centers, the NCPS gathered 6,190 names for a petition presented to Lindsay Almond in a one-hour meeting on October 22.[9]

The immediate efforts of the Norfolk Committee for Public Schools had little impact at city hall or the capitol. Much of the problem resulted from the makeup of the committee itself, whose members were "respectable, but [carried] no great weight in the community." NCPS supporters as indicated by the September 24 advertisement were solidly middle-class, with roughly equal numbers of doctors, teachers, small businessmen, and white-collar wage earners. The residential property assessment for the twenty-one homeowners among the executive board averaged $9,547 with a median of $7,100, compared with a $4,364 average for all property owners in the city.[10] The leaders of the group were a college professor, a Unitarian minister, a teacher, two physicians, an artist, two real estate men (one with a reputation for radicalism), a navy wife, and two other members from the local Women's Interracial Council. In the eyes of many established Virginians, most of the activists were also suspect for previous work on behalf of Francis P. Miller's unsuccessful campaign against Senator Byrd in 1952 and in opposition to the local option plan in 1956.[11]

Within the context of mid-century Virginia, the public school advocates were a liberal fringe. Proschool statements by the NCPS, the Norfolk Education Association, the League of Women Voters, and several PTAs were easily counterbalanced by mass meetings of the Defenders of State Sovereignty and Individual Liberties, whose loud support helped elected officials in city and state claim a willingness to accept a limited educational system as the alternative to desegregation. Seeking a more effective avenue for action, the NCPS turned to the federal courts and assumed an obligation for the expenses of a suit on behalf

9   Jane Reif, *Crisis in Norfolk* (Richmond: Virginia Council on Human Relations, 1959), 4–6; interview with Forrest P. White by the author, March 30, 1978; interview with Mary Thrasher by the author, April 10, 1978.
10   City of Norfolk Land Book, 1958, City Hall, Norfolk, Virginia.
11   Forrest P. White to Edward L. Breeden, Jr., November 25, 1955, and flyers from Norfolk Branch of Virginia Society for the Preservation of Public Schools, all in Forrest P. White Papers, Old Dominion University Archives, Norfolk, Virginia; Norfolk *Virginian-Pilot*, January 5, 1956.

of twenty-six white students and parents. Filing on October 22, the plaintiffs in *James et al.* v. *Almond* argued that the Virginia statutes denied them equal protection under the Fourteenth Amendment by blocking access to public schools that were available to others in their class. Several weeks before, questions about the massive resistance laws had also surfaced within the state administration. Attorney General Albertis Harrison had therefore filed a suit before the Virginia Supreme Court of Appeals (*Harrison* v. *Day*) to clarify their compatibility with the state constitution.[12]

In filing *James* v. *Almond*, the public school advocates in Norfolk had been eager to preempt the NAACP. They believed that a successful strategy to preserve public schools required that Norfolk's desegregation crisis be defined as a *white* problem. Both the NCPS and the Virginia Committee for Public Schools (organized in December and January by Norfolk, Arlington, and Charlottesville groups) explicitly excluded black members in order to broaden their appeal to white families and to maintain open schools rather than integration as the central issue. News reports from Norfolk in 1958 focused on "The Lost Class of '59." Picture spreads in *Life* on November 3 and November 10 showed white teenagers—boys hanging around a drugstore, student leaders in prayer, girls preparing to marry early, cheerleaders practicing on the sidewalk in front of Norview High, participants in *James* v. *Almond* standing before the locked doors of Maury High. The *New York Times Magazine* on January 4 showed white students in a variety of improvised classrooms. Almost every national article during the long fall described the alternatives available to the nine thousand "lost" students—night classes in the adjacent city of South Norfolk, informal tutoring in church basements, enrollment in other cities, private schools operated by the racist Tidewater Educational Foundation, or no schools at all.[13]

For the black community in Norfolk, the fall of 1958 was

12   Purycar, "Implementation of the Desegregation Decision," 329–30.
13   William M. Lightsey, "Organizing to Save Public Schools" (Typescript dated 1959, in Papers of Virginia Committee for Public Schools, Alderman Library, University of Virginia); "The Lost Class of 1959," *Life*, November 3, 1958, pp. 21–27; Wilma Dykeman and James Stokely, "Report on 'The Lost Class of '59,'" *New York Times Magazine*, January 4, 1959, pp. 54–55.

thus a time for quiet concern rather than direct action. The weekly *Journal and Guide* advised the black community "to remain calm and prayerful and to look to the judicial and executive branches of government to restore order where there is now confusion." Through the fall, the *Journal and Guide* carefully reported proschool activities and followed the NCPS lead in emphasizing the central issue of the availability of public education.[14] Recognizing the limitations of their political influence, black leaders advocated the rights of the seventeen students in the face of repeated demands for withdrawal of their applications but otherwise kept a low profile as white Norfolkians argued among themselves.[15]

The seven members of the Norfolk City Council were responsible for explicitly introducing the themes of racial prejudice during Norfolk's troubled autumn. At a regular Monday council meeting on September 30, the mayor responded to a proschool statement presented by the interracial Norfolk Ministers' Association with an antiblack tirade. "We know the colored here pay less than five per cent of the taxes and make up seventy-five per cent of the jail population," he told an astonished audience. "The City of Norfolk has done more for its Negroes, within its limits, than any other city of the South. . . . We thought if we cleared up the slums we could have a better environment and better citizens." Long-time Councilman George Abbott seconded Duckworth in placing the blame on blacks: "We've got seventeen Negro children who are keeping 10,000 white children out of school."[16]

Norfolk's city council clearly represented the views of Harry Byrd. The senator's Norfolk viceroy was Clerk of Courts William L. Prieur, Jr., who had long worked to advance the careers of

14 Norfolk *Journal and Guide*, September 20, 1958, November 22 and 29, 1958.
15 Carter, "Desegregation in Norfolk," 512–14; Norfolk *Journal and Guide*, December 13 and 20, 1958, January 24 and 31, 1959. Norfolk blacks in 1958 totaled 28 percent of the city's population but only 18 percent of its registered voters, and black candidates had been consistently unsuccessful in city races. See Dan Wakefield, "Lost Class of '59," *Nation*, November 22, 1958, pp. 372–76; Andrew Buni, *The Negro in Virginia Politics, 1902–1965* (Charlottesville: University Press of Virginia, 1967), 149–52, 158, 167, 206.
16 Norfolk *Ledger Dispatch*, September 30 and October 1, 1958; Norfolk *Virginian-Pilot*, October 1, 1958.

George Abbott and Fred Duckworth and who had shared private meetings with the school board as the crisis developed. During the summer and fall, Prieur regularly described to the senator the evolution of "our" plans to implement massive resistance. Prieur and Duckworth also held meetings with Almond and with Byrd to discuss the Norfolk situation. In turn, Duckworth's loyalty to the segregationist cause earned him visits to the senator's favorite retreat at Skyland in Shenandoah National Park and letters grouping him among Byrd's close friends.[17]

City council members continued their support of massive resistance through the entire crisis. After allowing the Defenders of State Sovereignty to use school buildings for evening meetings, Duckworth denied the same privilege to the NCPS and refused to be interviewed by CBS television reporters.[18] The council also refused to agree to a school board request in October that it join in petitioning Almond to return the closed schools to local authorities. Avoiding a direct commitment, the council scheduled an advisory referendum for November 18 and ordered school board members to "stay out of politics as far as the school situation is concerned." The ballot question read as follows: "Shall the Council of the City of Norfolk, Pursuant to State Law, Petition the Governor to Return to the City Control of Schools, Now Closed, to be Opened by the City on an Integrated Basis as Required by the Federal Court?" Below the direct question was a statement "for information only": "In the Event the Closed Schools Are Returned to the City of Norfolk, And Are Re-Opened Integrated By the City, It Will Be Necessary Because of The Loss of State Funds, For Every Family Having A Child or Children In Public Schools From Which State Funds Are Withheld, To Pay To The City A Substantial Tuition For Each Child In or Entering Such Public School."[19]

17   William Prieur to Harry Byrd, June 24, 1958, and June 15, 1960, William Prieur to Harry Byrd, Jr., November 26, 1958, Harry Byrd to William Prieur, October 20, 1959, Harry Byrd to Fred Duckworth, October 22, 1959, and October 20, 1960, all in Harry Byrd Papers, Alderman Library, University of Virginia; "Remarks of Henry Howell, Jr., Delegate, on June 9, 1961," in Henry Howell, Jr., Papers, Old Dominion University Archives.
18   "President's Report to Norfolk Committee for Public Schools, May 26, 1960" (Typescript in White Papers).
19   Norfolk *Virginian-Pilot*, October 22, 1958; Puryear, "Implementation of the Desegregation Decision," 343, 348–49.

The NCPS campaigned for a favorable vote during November and even the segregationist *Ledger Dispatch* dropped its editorial pummeling of the NAACP to question the wording of the informational paragraph, but Norfolk voters took their cue from the city council. Black precincts voted yes overwhelmingly, lower-income white precincts voted no by nine to one, and affluent white precincts split down the middle. The totals were 8,712 for a petition to Richmond and 12,340 for continued resistance, with a positive majority in only two white districts.[20] Although proschool spokesmen argued that the low turnout of 21,000 out of 39,325 registered voters invalidated the referendum, the level of voting was twice that in recent council and general assembly elections. The greatest weakness in the advisory vote was less the rate of participation among registered voters than Virginia's poll tax and other electoral restrictions which excluded many blacks and short-term residents. In Norfolk in 1958, the median age for registered voters was over fifty while that for all adults was thirty-eight. A survey in January found that the registered voters who stayed home on November 18 were more liberal on racial issues than those who went to the polls and that nonregistered adults and navy families were more liberal than registered voters as a group. Since roughly 60 percent of the nonvoters claimed that they would have cast a positive ballot, the city as a whole presumably favored open schools by a margin of 55 to 45 percent, an opinion shared privately by Mayor Duckworth.[21]

The advisory referendum, a series of interviews and meetings for CBS cameras, and arguments on *James* v. *Almond* and *Harrison* v. *Day* all preceded a six-week lull. Again, it was Fred Duckworth and the city council who focused attention on the underlying question of racial prejudice. Acting under provisions of the Virginia statutes which allowed a month-by-month appropriation for school costs, the city council on January 13 resolved to stop funding for *all* classes above the sixth grade at

20   Norfolk *Ledger Dispatch*, October 23, 1958; "Meeting of People Throughout the State of Virginia for Open Public Schools" (Typescript of minutes, December 6, 1958, in Papers of Virginia Committee for Public Schools).

21   Ernest Campbell, *When a City Closes Its Schools* (Chapel Hill: Institute for Research in Social Science, University of North Carolina, 1960), 81–87; Mary Thrasher, quoted in transcript of meeting of Women's Council for Interracial Cooperation, Norfolk, February 25, 1959, in White Papers.

the end of the month. The action affected four additional schools with an enrollment of 1,914 white students and 5,259 black students. Only future mayor Roy Martin refused to join the other councilmen in the effort to spread the burdens of massive resistance to black families.[22]

At the same time that council actions reinvigorated the NCPS and other supporting groups, state and federal courts moved to overturn the state legislation. On January 19 Judge Walter Hoffman agreed with the plaintiffs in *James* v. *Almond* that Norfolk could not maintain a partial school system with revenues collected city-wide. The Virginia Supreme Court on the same day ruled that statutes requiring the closure of schools and the denial of funds violated the state's constitutional injunction to maintain "efficient" public schools. After listening to an emotional segregationist outburst by Lindsay Almond over a statewide radio network on January 20, Norfolk residents switched on their televisions at 8 P.M. the next night to watch Edward R. Murrow's analysis of the "Lost Class of '59" on "CBS Reports."

The Norfolk school crisis reached its climax with Darden's call to Duckworth and the publication of the Committee of 100 statement on January 26. A day later, Judge Hoffman invalidated the council's vindictive fund cutoff in a ruling on *James et al.* v. *Duckworth* and the council immediately reversed its position. The school board on January 29 dispatched a telegram to one member who had escaped the continuing pressures with a Florida vacation. "Western Union?" said board president Paul Schweitzer as he placed his call. "Take this wire: 'Barring further instructions from the apple orchard we will be back in business on Monday.'"[23] On Monday, February 2, fifty outside newsmen and scores of local residents watched seventeen black teenagers walk through the unlocked doors of six previously segregated schools.

Most participants in the school crisis revealed their motives and goals through long months of public involvement. The motiva-

22   The retaliatory strategy was discussed during the fall among Byrd and such strong supporters as Prieur and Mills Godwin. Ely, *The Crisis of Conservative Virginia*, 82.

23   Norfolk School Board members to Ben Willis, January 29, 1959, in Paul Schweitzer Papers, Old Dominion University Archives.

tions of the Committee of 100, however, remained a mystery. Indeed, one of the most intriguing questions about desegregation in Norfolk is why the business establishment delayed in taking an active part. On the one hand, many of the city's leaders congratulated themselves on intervening decisively to resolve the city's crisis. On the other hand, many of these same community leaders had adamantly refused to offer leadership through the long summer and fall, repeatedly rejecting pleas from the Norfolk Committee for Public Schools that they make their influence felt. To proschool stalwarts, they were not so much community leaders as followers who had kept their own counsel until the crisis was actually decided.[24]

The Committee of 100 unquestionably represented the Norfolk establishment. The statement of January 26 was written jointly by three directors of the National Bank of Commerce, the city's leading financial institution. Charles Kaufman, as general counsel for both daily papers and as chairman of the Norfolk Redevelopment and Housing Authority, was a key figure in numerous local decisions. Pretlow Darden had business, political, and family ties throughout the state. In particular, his brother had served as congressman and governor and was president of the University of Virginia during the 1950s. Frank Batten was the publisher of the two metropolitan dailies and vice-president of the city's largest broadcasting company. During the months of massive resistance, Batten and three other participants in the Committee of 100 also worked with an informal group of Virginia businessmen organized by Richmond attorney Lewis Powell and Norfolk and Western Railroad executive Stuart Saunders. Along with manufacturer Ralph Douglas, Chamber of Commerce president H. C. Hofheimer II, and Bank of Commerce chairman John Alfriend, he worked to alert Lindsay Almond to the negative impact of massive resistance on the state economy.[25]

After working through independent drafts, the three orga-

24   Reif, *Crisis in Norfolk*, 31; Carter, "Desegregation in Norfolk," 518; White, "Will Norfolk's Schools Stay Open?" 30; Norfolk *Journal and Guide*, January 31, 1959; Peyton Williams to Colgate Darden, October 29, 1958, in Papers of the Presidents, University of Virginia, Alderman Library, University of Virginia.
25   Lewis Powell to Stuart T. Saunders, March 5, 1959, in Samuel F. Bemiss Papers, Virginia Historical Society, Richmond; Carter, "Desegregation in Norfolk," 511; Darden interview.

nizers had parceled out the list of potential participants. As a group, the ninety-seven other community leaders whom they recruited to urge the reopening of the public schools are best described as "respected citizens." The newspapers made much of the fact that the list contained two former mayors (and one future mayor) and nine men who had been honored as "first citizen" of Norfolk. At the same time, most members were men of means and position but not men of extraordinary wealth. Seventy-five of the one hundred lived in the city's three stable and established upper-middle-class neighborhoods, eight elsewhere in the city, and seventeen in suburban Princess Anne County. The average 1958 residential property assessment for the sixty-nine Norfolk homeowners in the group was $17,529 and the median was $12,810, three times the city average. By another measure, the median value of owner-occupied houses in the metropolitan area was $11,500 in 1960. Thirty-nine of the businessmen lived in census tracts with median house values of over $25,000, six in tracts in the range $20,000 to $25,000, forty-two in tracts in the range $15,000 to $20,000, and nineteen in tracts with median house values under $15,000.[26]

Most of the businesses represented on the Committee of 100 shared a "Chamber of Commerce" orientation toward Norfolk markets. There were only six men from important manufacturing firms—Royster (chemicals and fertilizer), Smith-Douglas (fertilizer), and Norfolk Shipbuilding and Dry Dock Company. Eight participants served as chairman, president, or officer of a bank or savings and loan. Seven others were involved in the operation of the port through shipping and railroads. The remaining members of the committee, however, worked with local business and professional concerns. Ten were physicians, ten were lawyers, seventeen sold insurance, stocks, or real estate, and sixteen owned or managed retail firms. Twenty-three worked in the broad area of local business support services including the wholesaling or manufacturing of food products, machinery, paper and marine supplies, construction, transportation and business services, and mass communications.[27]

26   City of Norfolk Land Book, 1958, City Hall, Norfolk, Virginia; Princess Anne County Land Book, 1958, and City of Virginia Beach Land Book, 1958, both in City Hall, Virginia Beach, Virginia.
27   To make the characteristics of the Committee of 100 more vivid, we can take

The profile of the Committee of 100 accurately reflected Norfolk's character as a "second city" whose important decisions were made in Pentagon offices, legislative committee rooms, and the halls of Richmond's Commonwealth Club. The leading families in Norfolk owned considerable wealth but none were aristocrats of industry and real estate to match the Dukes of Durham or the Reynoldses of Richmond. At the bottom of the scale, Norfolk's large military population and unskilled labor force pulled the city's income levels below regional and state averages. At the 1960 census, the median family income in Norfolk ($4,894) was 83 percent of the figure for urban Virginia and 86 percent of the national figure. Norfolk similarly ranked below urban Virginia as a whole in median years of education for adults (10.8 compared to 11.5) and in proportion of employment in professional and managerial jobs (19.0 percent compared to 26.9 percent).

For the two previous decades, the central aim of many of the men who participated in the Committee of 100 had been to rescue Norfolk from its limited economic base. Local newspapers traced the origins of concerted business efforts to revitalize the city to the organization of a new Community Fund drive in 1939 and the establishment of the Norfolk Housing Authority in 1940. The same leaders had recruited and backed the successful "People's Ticket" which swept the 1946 city council election on a platform of vice control, slum clearance, and economic development. With an expanded Norfolk Redevelopment and Housing Authority, the city became the first to execute a loan and grant under the urban renewal provisions of the Housing Act of 1949. In 1950, Norfolk's reformers had negotiated a compro-

---

J. Warren White as a typical member. White was a resident in 1958 of the established old-line neighborhood of West Ghent and owned a house valued at $12,500. He was president of the Old Dominion Paper Company, a major wholesale distributor in the Norfolk area. Educated at a Virginia college and a World War II veteran, he was active in charitable organizations and belonged to the standard Norfolk social clubs. Although not yet a public figure, he had been active in Democratic party politics since 1946 (since 1962 he has served in the Virginia House of Delegates). In retrospect, he argues that almost no one in Norfolk expected massive resistance to involve more than a short, symbolic school shutdown. When it became clear that the school closings promised economic disaster to the city, he willingly followed the lead of Pretlow Darden in joining the Committee of 100. Interview with J. Warren White by Katie Keeton, June 20, 1978.

mise with William Prieur and the city's political professionals. The reform leaders agreed to destroy their precinct voter card files and to remain neutral in legislative and state elections. In return, they retained a voice in the selection of city council candidates and received a favorable climate for economic development and renewal under the direction of Fred Duckworth. During the 1950s, local newspapers and business leaders were intensely proud of "the benevolent contagion of redevelopment and its renewal of spirit in Tidewater."[28] New housing, new business investment, a new airport, new building and zoning regulations, new highways, new tunnels to Hampton and Portsmouth—all promised to obliterate sour wartime memories with the shining steel and solid concrete of a "new Norfolk."

Norfolk's business and political leaders had expected 1958 to be a particularly good year. The city's major downtown urban renewal project had been unveiled in 1956 and approved in 1957 to city-wide applause. The sleazy sailor bars of Norfolk's world-famous East Main Street had begun to crumble before the grunting bulldozers of the redevelopment authority in the summer of 1958. Redevelopment plans called for a civic center and public library, new bank buildings and office towers to make Norfolk an important financial center for the south Atlantic coast. Even if they doubted the consultant who predicted that urban renewal would transform Norfolk into "the Manhattan of the South," the city's businessmen viewed downtown renewal as the crucial turning point in Norfolk's economic life.[29]

Members of the business community feared that the destruction of Norfolk's public schools would halt the civic renaissance. Without bothering to gather specific evidence, many residents assumed that the school closure would scare off new industry and trigger moves out of the city.[30] The Norfolk Committee for Public Schools similarly argued that a complete school system was "vital to the . . . economic life of Norfolk."

28 Henry Howell to Calvin Childress, April 1, 1961, in Howell Papers; Norfolk *Virginian-Pilot*, July 23, 1961.

29 Norfolk *Virginian-Pilot*, August 14, 1956, July 31, 1957, January 11, 1958; Norfolk *Ledger Dispatch*, August 14, 1956.

30 In January, 1959, the rate of agreement with the two propositions was respectively 85 percent and 77 percent. See Campbell, *When a City Closes Its Schools*, 164.

During the fall, reporters for *Business Week* and the New York *Times* had no difficulty in finding businessmen to express anonymous concern about falling real estate prices, the loss of new companies, and the phase-out of navy operations. A general analysis of the impacts of massive resistance by University of Virginia professor Lorin Thompson drew statewide attention with its warnings of long-range problems if Virginia made itself unattractive to outside companies and failed to provide a trained labor force.[31]

By January, the economic dangers of the school crisis had become a staple of public discussion in Norfolk itself. Every day brought new rumors or new worries about navy plans to relocate major operations, to reassign warships to Charleston or Philadelphia, or to establish its own school system. The *Virginian-Pilot* deplored the council's decision to cut off funds as a serious threat to the city's port development and urban renewal programs. Roy Martin echoed the same sentiments in voting against the cutoff, as did a group of thirty-five young businessmen. Editorial writers and public school partisans both attributed the action of the Committee of 100 to "the growing conviction among businessmen that the school closings militate increasingly against this city's economic life" or to the "onslaught of economic law."[32]

If concern for the local economy urged members of the Committee of 100 to act in support of public schools, fears of retaliation by state officials pressured them to hold the line for massive resistance. Because of the relatively cosmopolitan population brought by the military, Norfolk was viewed elsewhere in the state as a liberal island in the conservative sea of southside Virginia. In recent years its legislative delegation and the *Virginian-Pilot* had made enemies in Richmond by opposing the

31   Norfolk *Ledger Dispatch*, October 28 and December 16, 1958; "What 'Massive Resistance' Costs Norfolk and Its Businessmen," *Business Week*, October 4, 1958, pp. 32–34; Dykeman and Stokely, "Lost Class of '59"; Lorin Thompson, "Some Economic Aspects of Virginia's Current Educational Crisis," *New South* (February, 1959); Louis T. Rader, "Public Schools and the Economy of Virginia" (Typescript dated 1959, in Buck Papers).
32   Louise McWharter to Paul Schweitzer, January 23, 1959, in Schweitzer Papers; Norfolk *Journal and Guide*, December 29, 1958; Norfolk *Ledger Dispatch*, January 22 and 26, 1958; Norfolk *Virginian-Pilot*, January 16 and 28, 1958; Reif, *Crisis in Norfolk*, 14; Warren White interview.

adoption of the massive resistance laws and the city's voters had given only narrow approval in the 1956 referendum. The city had also been a center of anti-Byrd feeling in 1952 when Francis Miller had run against the senator. Six years later, in the midst of the school crisis, 40 percent of Norfolk voters had favored independent challenger Louise Wensel over Byrd as opposed to 28 percent statewide. To a stalwart of the party organization like Congressman William Tuck, there seemed little question that Norfolk was foreign territory that should be forced to "go along" if necessary.[33]

Pulled by conflicting pressures, the Norfolk business establishment convinced itself to wait for the strategic moment at which to oppose the city and state party organization on the issue of schools without upsetting the somewhat uneasy alliance for economic development. As Frank Batten wrote to Paul Schweitzer after a private meeting of businessmen and school board members, "the business leaders of the community should join together to plan the action they should take at the proper time to help Norfolk and the school board."[34] In the ensuing action, the Committee of 100 served as a rear guard rather than as pioneers. The percentage of Norfolk residents favoring the reopening of schools with limited integration had climbed from 58 percent in September to 67 percent by the time of the January statement, and the city council's proposed shutdown of black schools had already brought an outpouring of opposition from civic groups and previously uncommitted citizens.[35] Few Virginians held the federal judiciary in high regard, but the Virginia Supreme Court ruling in *Harrison* v. *Day* helped to convince uncertain minds. It also provided an occasion for action with which even hard-core resisters found it difficult to argue.[36]

33 William Prieur to Harry Byrd, May 28 and June 4, 1957, in Byrd Papers; Carter, "Desegregation in Norfolk," 510, 518; Buni, *Negro in Virginia Politics*, 181–83, 199; Norfolk *Virginian-Pilot*, November 16, 1958.

34 Frank Batten to Paul Schweitzer, October 28, 1958, J. Rives Worsham to Paul Schweitzer, October 29, 1958, and W. McC. Paxton to Paul Schweitzer, October 30, 1958, all in Schweitzer Papers.

35 Campbell, *When a City Closes Its Schools*, 49–51, indicates that 71 percent of Norfolk residents who held an opinion opposed the council action.

36 Darden interview; Carter, "Desegregation in Norfolk," 518. On October 18, 1958, Colgate Darden wrote Phillip P. Burks of Norfolk that "it would be well to have the advantage of the decision of the Supreme Court of Virginia on the pres-

The months of massive resistance had lingering effects on Norfolk politics. There was certainly justification for fears that integration would bring retaliation. Once the relatively liberal city of Norfolk was picked to bear the burden of the Virginia cause, it was hard to satisfy radical resisters that its children had suffered their full share. The attitude of many militant segregationists was captured by James Kilpatrick, who could ignore the city's sacrifices to argue in February that "there simply was not the slightest community will to resist." In June, Prieur refused to help in the state senate reelection campaign of Edward Breeden because Breeden had spoken out for open schools. During the 1960 session of the general assembly, Norfolk representatives found themselves assigned to dead-end committees. They were also unable to find allies to fight legislation which simplified procedures for city-county consolidation. As a result, Norfolk's annexation plans were blocked the following year by governmental consolidations which transformed Princess Anne County into the supersuburb of Virginia Beach and Norfolk County into the new city of Chesapeake.[37]

During the same years, the forces mobilized by the school crisis helped to reaffirm the local alliance of Norfolk businessmen and professional politicians, who shared a mutual distaste for Henry Howell. A liberal activist since the early fifties, Howell capitalized on Norfolk's unsettled political scene to run in the June, 1959, Democratic primary for the House of Delegates. Although he had stayed in the background during the school fight itself, Howell and his running mate Calvin Childress drew much of their backing in a successful campaign from the Norfolk Committee for Public Schools and the Norfolk Education Association. The next spring, Howell and the NCPS leadership cooperated in a new effort which replaced a conservative incumbent on the city council with a liberal.[38]

---

ent school legislation before making an effort to suggest a course to be followed." Papers of the Presidents, University of Virginia.

37   Ely, *The Crisis of Conservative Virginia*, 75; Carter, "Desegregation in Norfolk," 508–10; Mary Thrasher, speech to Community Democratic Club, Norfolk, May 24, 1961 (Typescript in Howell Papers); David Temple, *Merger Politics: Local Government Consolidation in Tidewater Virginia* (Charlottesville: University Press of Virginia, 1972), 100–102.

38   Henry Howell to Margaret White, April 30, 1959, Henry Howell to Robert

The showdown came in the Democratic primary of July, 1961, when Howell stood for renomination and Childress challenged Prieur's thirty-six-year tenure as clerk of courts. Howell organized a Committee for Democratic Government, which again drew on NCPS activists and old-line backers of Francis Miller. Prieur and the party regulars worried about the unreliable voters who had been brought into political activity for the first time by the school crisis.[39] Business leaders feared Howell as an economic reformer who had targeted high utility rates. As spokesmen for the business community, Norfolk newspapers therefore defended Prieur against charges of bossism and went so far as to deny that he had favored massive resistance. Howell and Childress took ten-to-one margins in black precincts and did well in recently annexed neighborhoods that had not yet been organized by Prieur's workers. The establishment candidates, however, were able to win with 60 to 80 percent margins in the genteel West Side precincts which housed the core support for the old "People's Ticket" and most members of the Committee of 100.[40]

A veteran political reporter for the *Virginian-Pilot* summarized the outcome of the 1961 election: "For the organization, it was a back-to-normal sweep after the ranks had been split by dissension over the desegregation of Norfolk's schools. For the Committee for Democratic Government, it was the end—for the moment—of a payoff parlay of antiorganization labor, liberal and Negro votes." Two weeks later, the same newspaper published a ten-thousand-word series of retrospective articles which argued in detail that "the business core of the city has been the key force in the making of the new Norfolk. It has acted with

---

Kennedy, November 10, 1960, both in Howell Papers; "President's Report to Norfolk Committee for Public Schools, May 26, 1960," in White Papers; Virginia Committee for Public Schools, Minutes of Executive Board meetings on October 26, 1959, and January 23, 1960 (Typescript in Virginia Committee for Public Schools Papers).

39   The total vote in city council elections rose from 3,300 in 1956 and 8,000 in 1958 to over 20,000 in 1960, 1962, and 1964. The total vote in the Democratic legislative primary rose from 10,731 in 1957 to 22,329 in 1959 and 25,115 in 1961.

40   Citizens for Democratic Government, Minutes of meeting on November 21, 1960 (Typescript in Howell Papers); Norfolk *Virginian-Pilot*, November 16, 1960, July 7 and 13, 1961; Norfolk *Ledger Dispatch*, July 12, 1961.

cohesion, direction, and remarkable unanimity."[41] In the gentle-
manly style of Virginia politics, respectable moderates and respectable resisters had turned back the new forces mobilized by
the school crisis in order to proceed with the important matters
of economic development.

Certainly for the remainder of the 1960s and the early
1970s, the reunited business leadership in Norfolk acted vigorously to regain the urban renewal momentum of the middle
1950s. The administration of Mayor Roy Martin (1962–1974)
worked to fill in downtown renewal land with the typical inven-
tory of coliseum, auditorium, bank buildings, and public offices
and undertook additional projects which leveled an entire black
neighborhood. As it had before the embarrassment of the school
crisis, Norfolk tried to follow the prescriptions of boosterism. In
one telling example, Martin reversed a school board decision
and refused to allow CBS to use school property in filming a
follow-up to their 1959 documentary on the grounds that old
disputes were better left unremembered. Despite the election of
one black member to the seven-member city council in 1968,
Norfolk's black residents retained the status of guests whose living space was subject to constant amendment by the Norfolk
Redevelopment and Housing Authority. In particular, several
land clearance and public housing projects during the 1960s
were designed to assure continued segregation in neighborhood
schools by isolating and concentrating black families. Just as
the 1950s had ended with token desegregation under federal
court order, in consequence, the 1970s opened with court-ordered busing within the city for fuller racial integration of public schools.[42]

The Norfolk business community did not determine the city's
choice to accept or resist school integration. In spite of the ac-
claim they received in 1959 and the common assumption among
local writers since then, their public action in fact came after
the decision had been made. Partly because of the NCPS and
other public school advocates, opinion in the city had already

41   Norfolk *Virginian-Pilot*, July 13 and 25, 1961.
42   *Ibid.*, May 9, 1964, September 11, 1968; Norfolk *Journal and Guide*, December 2, 1967.

swung toward acceptance of limited desegregation by the winter of 1959. The federal and state courts directly decided the issue by declaring the closure of the Norfolk schools unconstitutional and providing the school board with the opportunity to meet public desires and reopen the six schools.

If the participants in the Committee of 100 did not serve as the major force for change in Norfolk, they did assure a peaceful process of desegregation. By openly ratifying the inevitable, the city's business leaders helped to make desegregation respectable. Between January 26 and February 2, they worked behind the scenes to make sure that the initial desegregation itself would take place without violence. By stating the basic issue in terms of public education and economic growth rather than racial relations, they made it easier for conservative residents to accept a basic alteration in their way of life. Norfolk's historical mythology, which passes quickly over the painful autumn of 1958 and elevates the final week of the crisis as a demonstration of civic unity under the guidance of the Committee of 100, has been itself part of the process by which the city's economic elite tried to minimize the memories of internal conflict in order to continue with their program of economic growth.

ALTON HORNSBY, JR.

A CITY THAT WAS TOO BUSY TO HATE

ATLANTA BUSINESSMEN AND DESEGREGATION

On August 30, 1961, nine black children entered four previously all-white high schools in Atlanta, Georgia. Atlanta police watched nervously, as did an entire city, but at the end of the day the first public school desegregation in Georgia below the college level had been achieved without violence.[1] The peaceful desegregation of Atlanta's schools marked a turning point in the heretofore tumultuous annual fall ritual of trying to eliminate dual education in the South. The nation took notice and generally applauded the accomplishment. President John F. Kennedy sent personal congratulations to Atlanta leaders and pointed out the example to the rest of the South. *Newsweek* applauded "a proud city." The *Reporter* saw in it "hope for us all"; the journal also complimented parents who "were able to enlist business leaders and elected officials," and Mayor William B. Hartsfield, who had made famous his slogan "Atlanta is 'a city too busy to hate.'" *U.S. News and World Report* saw a "New Mood in the South on Mixed Schools." For the next several days, Atlantans

1 Atlanta *Constitution*, August 31, September 1, 1961; Atlanta *Journal*, August 30, 1961.

were patting themselves on the back, as the future of their town looked very good indeed.[2]

In order to understand fully how Atlantans succeeded when so many other cities had failed, one must begin with the six institutions of black higher education known as the Atlanta University Center. These schools and their products furnished the city with an unusually large group of educated middle-income blacks who joined with the masses to become, by 1948, an influential political force in the city. Additionally these blacks generated a substantial part of the city's expendable income. On the one hand they were, because of their income and education, restless under the caste system, but on the other they were secure enough in their own right to be cautious and patient. This attitude, as much as anything else, delayed desegregation in Atlanta until 1961. The delay was perhaps fortunate, for had the crisis come in 1954 or 1957, chances of success would have been measurably diminished.

It was fortunate for Atlanta that for at least twenty-five years prior to desegregation, Atlanta's political leadership had had very close ties to the city's business community. In fact Mayor William B. Hartsfield, who, in his last days in office, presided over the desegregation process, came out of that community, as did his successor, former Chamber of Commerce president Ivan Allen, Jr. The politicians and the businessmen, then, were often of one mind when it came to city policies.

Finally, the fact that Atlanta was becoming the industrial, commercial, and transportation center of the South influenced its businessmen to follow the course of moderation on the question of desegregation. Business would not locate or stay in places where there was turmoil or disruption of education. Violence in the streets would deter customers from shopping. It was, then, good business to be "too busy to hate."

As every student of southern history knows, "the railroads made Atlanta" the bustling metropolis it became. The railroads which brought Yankee goods and Yankee entrepreneurs to and through Atlanta were also soon to bring increasing numbers of

2   Atlanta *Constitution*, August 31, September 1, 1961; *Newsweek*, September 11, 1961, p. 31; *Reporter*, September 15, 1961, p. 14; *U.S. News and World Report*, September 11, 1961, p. 72.

unskilled blacks from rural Georgia and other parts of the agricultural South into the city. Equally important, however, they brought northern white educators into the city to found black colleges and universities for the freedmen and to serve as teachers in these institutions. Within a generation of the Civil War's end, highly trained blacks were also coming into the city to take their places as teachers and administrators in black schools. These developments proved to be of monumental significance for black Atlanta and, indeed, for black America. For by 1929, when the six black colleges and universities began a program of affiliation, Atlanta had become the largest and best-known center for the higher education of blacks in the world.[3]

The combination of the black academic elite, augmented by grammar school teachers and principals, preachers, a few other professional people, and black businessmen had produced a highly visible black upper stratum in Atlanta even by 1900. By 1930, Atlanta had achieved national notoriety as a social and business capital for American blacks. These realities did not, however, loom very large in the minds of white Atlantans. White Atlantans, like most southerners, believed in the inferiority of blacks, no matter how well educated or how wealthy, and believed in the sanctity of the caste system.[4]

While white Atlanta, for the most part, could and did remain smug under the protection of the caste system and in the knowledge that "a nigger is a nigger," black Atlantans, particularly educated middle-income ones, continuously chafed under southern apartheid. The inhumanity and illogic of the system

3   C. Vann Woodward, *Origins of the New South, 1877–1913* (Baton Rouge: Louisiana State University Press, 1951), 7, 34, 108, 144, *passim*; Alton Hornsby, Jr., "The Negro in Atlanta Politics," *Atlanta Historical Bulletin*, XXI (Spring, 1977), 7–8; C. T. Wright, "The Development of Public Schools for Blacks in Atlanta, 1872–1900," *Atlanta Historical Bulletin*, XXI (Spring, 1977), 115–28; Myron W. Adams, *A History of Atlanta University* (Atlanta: Atlanta University Press, 1930), 1–38, *passim*; Willard Range, *The Rise and Progress of Negro Colleges in Georgia, 1865–1949* (Athens, Ga: University of Georgia Press, 1951), 23–26, 193–97, 224–27.
4   Alexa Benson Henderson, "Alonzo F. Herndon and Black Insurance in Atlanta, 1904–1915," *Atlanta Historical Bulletin*, XXI (Spring, 1977), 34–47; Robert C. Vowels, "Atlanta Negro Business and the New Black Bourgeoisie," *Atlanta Historical Bulletin*, XXI (Spring, 1977), 48–63; August Meier and David Lewis, "History of the Negro Upper Class in Atlanta, Georgia, 1890–1958," *Journal of Negro Education*, XXVIII (Spring, 1959), 128–39.

was particularly acute for them as they daily dwelled in a community which taught freedom of the mind, yet they themselves were virtually imprisoned in that community. From time to time this group would dare to speak out against the injustices which surrounded them. More often they would organize politically and urge their fellow blacks of every station to follow them in their quest to use the ballot to break down the racial barriers.[5]

Despite an occasional victory, however, the existence of Georgia's white primary virtually assured minimal black influence in Atlanta politics. Only after the outlawing of that all-important primary by the U.S. Supreme Court, in *Chapman* v. *King* in 1946, could blacks begin to hope for effective participation in Atlanta politics. The opening of primary, as well as general and special elections, to blacks was the foundation on which the black leadership of Atlanta eventually built a citadel of political influence. Seizing quickly upon the new freedom and opportunity, Atlanta's black elite influenced the city's black masses to flock to the registrar's booth and later, quadrennially, to the polls. By 1948, the potential impact of the black vote was revealed in the growing number of registrants and particularly in its relative proximity to white voting strength (there were twenty-one thousand black voters, about 40 percent of the total). Although the black vote alone, even if solidly cast, could make or break no one, it could constitute an important balance between the competing interests of white voters and white candidates. This fact was not lost upon the incumbent mayor, William B. Hartsfield, when, in 1948, he succumbed to several years of pressure by blacks and appointed the first black policemen in Atlanta.[6]

In the mayoral election of 1949, a solidly cast black vote influenced the outcome of a municipal primary or general election for the first time in Atlanta's history. Analyses of the results of that election revealed that the winning candidate, incumbent Mayor Hartsfield, secured victory on the strength of the black

5   Hornsby, "The Negro in Atlanta Politics," 7–11.
6   Floyd Hunter, *Community Power Structure: A Study of Decision Makers* (Chapel Hill: University of North Carolina Press, 1953), 113–68; Jack Walker, "Negro Voting in Atlanta: 1853–1961," *Phylon*, XXIV (Winter, 1963), 379–87; Clarence A. Bacote, "The Negro in Atlanta Politics," *Phylon*, XVI (Winter, 1955), 331–51; Hornsby, "The Negro in Atlanta Politics," 8–9.

vote and ballots cast by affluent white Atlantans. This unstruc-tured coalition of black bloc votes and upper-income white votes became invincible, and no person could expect to be elected mayor of Atlanta in the years following 1949 without its sup-port.[7]

The group of black Atlanta preachers, professors, lawyers, and businessmen who organized the black vote came to control it through an organization known as the Atlanta Negro Voters League. The cochairman of the bipartisan group, an attorney known as "Colonel" A. T. Walden, became the New South's first black political boss as he wheeled and dealed in the councils of white leadership. The Walden-led cadre of leaders bargained with white politicians, offering black votes in exchange for a favorable climate of race relations. Largely because of this bro-kering, together with the desire of Atlanta businessmen to avoid conditions adverse to high profits, Atlanta developed a reputa-tion as an "oasis of tolerance" in southern race relations.[8]

Although by 1954, the year of *Brown* v. *the Board of Edu-cation*, Atlanta's blacks could boast that the middle class was spared most of the brutalities experienced by blacks elsewhere, that the city had had black policemen (who patrolled only in black communities) for six years, that their leaders had an *entrée* into city hall, and that their city was nationally recog-nized for its racial tolerance, the fact of the matter was that the city was rigidly segregated and there was widespread discrimi-nation. Even by 1960, six years after *Brown*, desegregation had come only to the golf courses and to the buses. But circum-stances and events inside as well as outside of the city were pro-pelling Atlanta to its testing time—a time when she could no longer hide behind sanctimonious and patronizing slogans, but would have to show whether in deed as well as word she was truly "an oasis of tolerance" and "a city that was too busy to hate."[9]

The first desegregation of a facility for public education in Georgia had actually been ordered two years earlier at the Geor-

7   Hunter, *Community Power Structure*, 113–68; Walker, "Negro Voting in At-lanta"; Hornsby, "The Negro in Atlanta Politics," 8–9.
8   Hornsby, "The Negro in Atlanta Politics," 9.
9   Lester A. Sobel (ed.), *News Dictionary* for 1959 and 1960 (New York: Facts on File, 1959, 1960), *passim*; Atlanta *Constitution*, 1957–60, *passim*.

gia State School of Business Administration in Atlanta. But the plaintiffs had been found educationally unfit and, thus, the crucial moment had been delayed. Everyone expected that 1961 would be the year and that the Atlanta public schools would be the site. At the inaugural meeting of the Atlanta Chamber of Commerce in January, 1960, the group adopted a program of projected progress for the decade, in which was included a statement that "open schools" must be maintained. The clear implication was that this was to be done, even with some desegregation. Then on January 5, 1961, the Atlanta *Constitution* recognized that the city's "critical year" was at hand. The *Constitution*'s editors expressed the hope "that the schools can be preserved and the children spared such experiences as we've witnessed in New Orleans." The newspaper also quoted Atlanta Mayor William B. Hartsfield as calling for "cool-headedness and common sense to solve our problems and to preserve the city's reputation." The alternative, he said, "to permitting Atlanta and other communities to handle their own problems is a bitter power struggle between federal and state authority with the children as pawns. In such a struggle the outcome is certain, as proved in Virginia, Little Rock and now New Orleans. Mobs, lawlessness, and terror won't change the courts." Similarly, Atlanta Board of Education president A. C. "Pete" Latimer said, "We are hopeful that the General Assembly will let us do what we have to do and that we will be able to go about it in an orderly, peaceful manner."[10]

These appeals for calm and statements of hope were made amid the acceptance by a federal district court, on January 4, 1961, of an Atlanta plan for the "token integration" of the schools, and a campaign promise by Georgia governor S. Ernest Vandiver to preserve segregation forever. The matter was also slated for priority consideration before the overwhelmingly segregationist Georgia General Assembly, which was then convening in Atlanta. The general assembly was slated to receive a report from its commission on schools (commonly called the Sibley commission), which had found a surprising degree of sentiment in the state for organized open schools, even with de-

10   Interview with Ivan Allen, Jr., by Marcellus C. Barksdale, September 25, 1979; Atlanta *Constitution*, January 5, 1961.

segregation, but was to report that Georgians by a three-to-two majority still opposed the changing of their laws and customs on race.[11]

As Atlantans and other Georgians remained tense in the early days of the new year, thunder and lightning struck from a somewhat unexpected quarter. The question of desegregation at the state's revered university, the University of Georgia at Athens, had been decided more quickly than had been expected. On January 6, 1961, U.S. District Court Judge William A. Bootle in Macon ordered two young blacks admitted to the university. But Bootle, on January 9, granted a stay of his desegregation order pending an appeal by State Attorney General Eugene Cook to the Fifth U.S. Circuit Court of Appeals. This stay interrupted the plans of the blacks to register at the school immediately. The next day, at the request of the students' attorneys, Chief Judge Elbert P. Tuttle of the court of appeals set aside the stay. On January 10, the two blacks, Charlayne Hunter and Hamilton Holmes, enrolled at the University of Georgia—the first desegregation in public education in the state's history.[12]

State laws already existed that prohibited appropriations to desegregated schools, and Governor S. Ernest Vandiver was now faced with the prospect of backing up his campaign promise that "no, not one" black would enter a white school in Georgia. As Vandiver remained noncommittal in the first hours of the desegregation, key legislators voiced their opposition to closing the University of Georgia. House floor leader Frank Twitty said, "I for one am not in favor of closing the University of Georgia under any circumstances." Senate president pro tempore Carl Sanders said it would be "a calamity" to close the school and asserted, "I believe that the General Assembly will do everything possible to keep the university open." And Lieutenant Governor Garland T. Byrd dismissed outright closing, but cautioned that "it poses a grave problem and most certainly calls for serious consideration by the General Assembly."[13]

At the same time, however, the federal courts were to aid

11   The Sibley commission received its name from its chairman, John Sibley, a venerable Atlanta lawyer who, as a board member of several businesses, had strong ties to the business community. Allen interview.
12   Atlanta *Constitution*, January 7–11, 1961.
13   *Ibid.*, January 9, 10, 1961; Atlanta *Journal*, January 10, 1961.

Georgia in its dilemma. Judge Bootle, in his original desegregation order on January 12, had issued a permanent injunction prohibiting Vandiver and other state officials from implementing the state law that denied the payment of state funds to desegregated schools. All knew that this clash between the state and the federal government over the University of Georgia would settle the legal and political status of desegregation of Atlanta's public schools. Understandably, then, Atlanta Mayor Hartsfield said, "Atlanta will watch this situation with great interest." Others were later to say that "the University of Georgia Crisis" saved the Atlanta public schools.[14]

Once Governor Vandiver decided to speak on the issue he appeared, at first, to make contradictory declarations. At the opening session of the general assembly on January 9, the governor had said that "we cannot abandon public education" and insisted that he had not halted any state aid for the University of Georgia. But on January 11 Vandiver said that he would deny state funds to any school that desegregated. He called on blacks and the National Association for the Advancement of Colored People to end legal actions to gain admission to white schools in order to avert a "head-on collision between federal and state sovereignty" and the probable closing of the schools. "But if they [blacks] persist," he warned, "we are going to resist . . . again and again. We are going to exhaust every legal means and remedy available to us."[15]

Meanwhile, sentiment both inside and outside of the legislature was growing for a preservation of the University of Georgia and of public education generally, even if desegregated. House floor leader Frank Twitty summed up a feeling of many legislators when he declared that there was "too much money and too many lives at stake to think of closing the University. The people I've come in contact with endorse almost unanimously the idea of keeping the University open." Lieutenant Governor Garland Byrd had also said, at the opening session of the legislature, that the state must "seek ways and means of continuing public education." At the same time representatives

14 Atlanta *Constitution*, January 7, 13, 1961; Atlanta *Journal*, January 7, 14, 1961.
15 Atlanta *Constitution*, January 10, 12, 1961; Atlanta *Journal*, January 10, 12, 1961.

and senators from sixteen of the smaller counties of the state proposed a repeal of the segregation laws and an adoption of local option plans.[16]

On January 9, a petition was also adopted by the east and west districts of the Atlanta Methodist Church which favored a "continued uninterrupted operation of the University System and the public schools of Georgia." All of the 175 Greater Atlanta Methodist ministers who were present voted for the petition. A total of 200 delegates representing more than 60 Methodist churches in the Decatur-Oxford district unanimously adopted a similar resolution asking Governor Vandiver and the state legislature to keep Georgia's schools open. Meanwhile, the Athens Ministerial Association called upon Governor Vandiver and the general assembly to enact such laws as would make possible the uninterrupted operation of all Georgia schools. And in Brunswick, the Glynn County Protestant Ministerial Association wired Governor Vandiver and other state legislative leaders urging them to keep the University of Georgia and other schools open despite the desegregation orders. Also, at his installation as president of the Greater Atlanta Council of Churches, Dr. Arthur Vann Gibson, pastor of the city's Morningside Presbyterian Church, said that the role of ministers is "not promoting integration or segregation but creating an atmosphere in which men may think straight. . . . The educational system must be preserved, and in doing so Christians must exercise great patience and love."[17]

Governor Vandiver sent his annual budget to the legislature on January 16. It was very significant that the appropriations bill left out the sections in the last appropriations act which provided that no funds could be spent on schools where the courts had ordered desegregation. This action came just one day after the United Churchwomen of Georgia, representing all faiths, adopted a resolution in Atlanta asking political leaders to keep the schools open by "making whatever changes necessary in the laws of Georgia."

One day after Vandiver's action James S. Peters, chairman

16   Atlanta *Constitution*, January 9–11, 1961; Atlanta *Journal*, January 9–11, 1961.
17   Atlanta *Constitution*, January 10, 12, 1961; Atlanta *Journal*, January 10, 12, 1961.

of the state board of education, wrote in a letter published in the Atlanta *Journal-Constitution* that "some form of integration is inevitable, and the only question . . . is whether integration will be under the control of friends of segregation or the proponents of integration." He suggested that segregationist leaders should meet and seek a solution or face "defeat and the loss of our power and influence" in Georgia's state government. Peters warned fellow supporters of Senator Herman Talmadge, a rabid segregationist, that unless they compromised on segregation, Talmadge might be defeated in his upcoming bid for reelection and the state's next governor might be former governor Ellis Arnall, who had said that if the schools were closed, he would campaign for high office on a pledge to reopen them. The practical wisdom of "Mr. Jim" Peters, especially as it reflected the views of those close to Senator Talmadge, was a compelling call to end massive resistance to desegregation in Georgia.

Until the "University Crisis," a group of moderate Atlanta professionals and housewives called HOPE (Help Our Public Education), had been the most vocal white organization openly supporting public education even if desegregated. The Sibley commission, in its hearings throughout Georgia, had discovered a sizable minority of other such group and individual voices; but not until the crisis was at hand did powerful political, educational, and religious figures in Georgia face up to the realities of the situation. Once this was done change was imminent.[18]

On Wednesday night, January 18, Governor Vandiver went before an unusual joint session of the legislature and, in effect, asked the state to abandon its resistance to some desegregation. He called his program a formula designed to keep the schools open and in the hands of local officials. He emphasized that new laws were necessary to keep federal courts from seizing the schools. The four-point program included a pupil protection amendment which would write into the state constitution a provision that no child would be required to attend an integrated school; a tuition grant program which would authorize the issuance of funds to parents who wanted their children to attend private schools rather than public schools; a local referendum

18   Atlanta *Constitution*, January 16–18, 1961.

provision under which each community could vote to close its schools or to keep them open in the event they were ordered integrated; and a classification of the system under which appeals could be made from local schools to the state board of education. Immediately after the governor spoke, legislative leaders predicted passage of the bills "within a week." Vandiver himself had said the opposition would come from only "a few" who would favor "unreconcilable conflict with superior armed forces." That conflict could end only in "abject defeat," he added.[19]

In Atlanta, where the threat of school desegregation was looming for the fall, Vandiver's speech was generally greeted with praise and relief. In an Atlanta *Constitution* poll immediately following the address, sentiments included: "I liked it very much" and "What he said was exactly what we feel." Other comments were: "I'm with him 100 percent. I just hope his program can be carried out"; and "We thought it was wonderful." Almost all of the residents polled lived in all-white neighborhoods in Greater Atlanta.[20]

Two days after Vandiver introduced his "save the schools" package to the Georgia General Assembly, James S. Peters, the chairman of the state board of education and an elder statesman of Georgia politics, said the plan was "fair to all parties." "It is now up to the local units to operate their schools with or without integration," he added. Following this lead, State School Superintendent Claude Purcell wrote local school officials to enlist their help in asking legislators to support the school bills. In Dalton, the Whitfield County Grand Jury praised its local legislators for supporting the open schools bills. The grand jury said: "We support the position of local state legislators (Jack Boyett and Virgil T. Smith) in their announced views favoring continuation of the public school system in Georgia and recommend that they support legislation to abolish existing segregation laws and enact laws for a pupil-placement plan." Meanwhile, the executive committee of the Atlanta Chamber of Commerce, at this point the only major business group in the state openly in favor of public education with desegregation, wired Vandiver congratulating him on his "excellent proposals."[21]

19   *Ibid.*, January 18, 19, 1961.
20   *Ibid.*, January 19, 1961.
21   *Ibid.*, January 21, 1961.

The Chamber of Commerce telegram may have served to break a long official silence on the desegregation question by the rest of Georgia businesspersons. To be sure, men and women in business had expressed individual views on the school question. Some had served on the Sibley commission and others had testified before the body in support of "open schools." Although it was widely rumored at the time that several of the state's business leaders had practically ordered Vandiver to take the action he announced on January 18, warning him of the catastrophic consequences for Georgia's industry and trade if massive resistance continued, there is no available evidence to support the contention. In fact, Atlanta Chamber of Commerce president Ivan Allen, Jr., said he knew of no such pressure on the governor. But the Chamber's wire of January 20 was an open, group pronouncement which, when extended several days later, would place the business community squarely behind the movement for change in the midst of the crisis. In fact, the Atlanta Chamber pledged to the governor their "full cooperation in moving toward these new goals." The telegram was signed by Chamber President Ivan Allen, Jr., Vice-Presidents E. D. Smith, Rawson Haverty, and Ben S. Gilmer, Treasurer Mills B. Lane, Jr., and immediate past president Edgar J. Forio. Allen was a multimillionaire office furniture dealer and would soon be mayor of Atlanta; Smith and Lane were the presidents of the two largest banks in Georgia; Haverty was a wealthy furniture dealer; and Gilmer was president of one of the state's largest utilities. Some of the most influential men in the state, thus, had endorsed limited desegregation on behalf of themselves and their colleagues.[22]

Immediately following the Atlanta Chamber's call for "open schools," the businessmen of Georgia made their strongest and most forthright statement ever on desegregated education in the state. On Sunday, January 22, nearly a thousand Georgia businessmen called on Governor Ernest Vandiver and state legislators to keep the schools open, even with some desegregation. Some of the biggest names in the state's business community

22 Atlanta *Constitution*, January 21, 23, 1961; Allen interview. Mayor Allen insists that no behind-the-scenes maneuvering took place between influentials in Georgia and the governor. The university crisis was the decisive factor in the governor's decisions.

signed a five-paragraph resolution which said that "disruption of our public school system would have a calamitous effect on the economic climate of Georgia." The businessmen announced their support of "such legislation in the 1961 General Assembly as may be necessary to effect the uninterrupted operation" of Georgia's public schools. They stressed that "immediate legislative action is urgently needed." They voiced confidence that the governor and legislature would act "to avoid the tragedy and unrest which several of our sister states have experienced." The signers of the resolution also expressed confidence that the legislation adopted would provide the maximum "freedom of choice."

When the resolution was first released, it had 960 signatures, in addition to its 26 sponsors. Among the signers were John W. Dent of Cartersville, president of the Georgia Chamber of Commerce. A letter transmitting the resolution to Vandiver and the legislature was signed by H. E. Benson of Benson's, Inc., in Athens. Benson said additional signatures would be forwarded to the governor and legislators as they were received. Benson also said that the resolution originated with him and a group of his friends in Athens. He explained that about 50 leading Georgia businessmen were contacted at first and 26 agreed to sponsor the resolution. The 960 signatures were collected over a period of ten days.[23]

During the last five days of January, 1961, the Georgia legislature, with the support of a substantial amount of the state's public opinion, officially abandoned massive resistance to school desegregation. On January 27 and 30, the general assembly passed several bills which: repealed six anti-integration laws; granted aid for pupils who chose to attend private, nonsectarian schools; permitted local boards of education to set academic, psychological, and other standards governing pupil transfers (this had formerly been a state function); authorized local elections on whether to close desegregated schools; and passed a constitutional amendment, to be voted on in 1962, that asserted that "freedom from compulsory association at all levels of public education shall be preserved inviolate." This amendment was to

23 Atlanta *Constitution*, January 21, 23, 1961; Atlanta *Journal* January 21–23, 1961.

replace a constitutional requirement for "separate schools . . . for white and colored races." On January 31, 1961, Governor S. Ernest Vandiver signed the "open-schools package" into law, commenting, "These are the four most important bills to be signed in this century in Georgia."[24]

The last twenty-five days of January, 1961, had indeed been among the most momentous in the history of the state of Georgia. The University of Georgia crisis had not only opened the state's institutions of higher education to blacks, but had forced the state to abandon massive resistance to school desegregation at all levels. Since, at the time, only the Atlanta public schools were threatened with disruption due to desegregation, it is certainly no exaggeration to conclude, as others did at the time, that the university crisis saved the Atlanta public schools; for until that crisis erupted, Georgia's political leaders were adamant in their view that desegregation would be eternally resisted, even if public education had to be sacrificed. While these leaders spouted demagogic rhetoric, the business, religious, and educational leaders of the state remained, for the most part, silent. With the exception of black advocates of desegregation, the group of white moderates known as HOPE and a scattering of other white Atlantans and Georgians were the only voices calling for retention of public education, even with desegregation. Notable among this group, however, were the members of the Atlanta Chamber of Commerce.

The first major crack in the wall of massive resistance in Georgia, it must be said, was the report by the Sibley commission. No one really expected that the group, in its survey of the state's ten congressional districts, would find a groundswell of support for integration. On the other hand, the fact that two-fifths of those testifying and presenting resolutions suggested that they would tolerate some desegregation came as a real surprise to almost everyone. This report was a welcome weapon in the arsenal of HOPE, the blacks, and others who advocated compliance with federal laws. Once the state's major university was threatened, politicians were in the forefront of those admitting that changes in the state's centuries-old caste system must be

24 Atlanta *Constitution*, January 28–31, February 1, 1961; Atlanta *Journal*, January 28–31, February 1, 1961.

made. They immediately garnered support from a cross-section of public opinion in the state. One of the most influential groups, the white businessmen, were late, except in Atlanta, in adding their voices to the chorus of "open school" advocates, but when they did they came down solidly and unequivocally on the side of change.

White and black businessmen who were active at the time recall that they were concerned about the adverse economic effects on the state which would result from continued defiance of the law, school closings, and violence of the sort that had rocked Little Rock and New Orleans. The state's illiteracy rate was already one of the highest in the nation, and disruption of public education would certainly not help in the solution of this problem. Atlanta, especially, was becoming a "boomtown" for commerce and industry as more and more northern corporations were establishing regional offices there. Other parts of the state were also energetically pursuing industry. All of these advances could be set back by prolonged turmoil over desegregation. Thus, as reluctantly as any portion of the white population, the business sector endorsed limited desegregation in its own interest and in the interest of the state's welfare.[25]

Atlanta Mayor William B. Hartsfield had said in the early days of the university crisis that the city would watch the rapidly unfolding events with great interest. After January 31, he and most Atlantans could breathe a bit easier. The actions of the governor and the legislators, no matter how painful to them, had paved the way for the desegregation of Atlanta's public schools. Atlanta's political leaders, while not entirely "slaves" to the black bloc vote (as some segregationists charged), but certainly unable to ignore it, now set out to achieve the first peaceful desegregation of public schools in a major Deep South city. In this quest, they were supported by a substantial cross-section of Atlanta public opinion. Professional, religious, and even social groups seemed to be trying to outdo one another in adopting resolutions calling for peaceful desegregation. This time, the business community was also in line with the chorus. As one business leader recalled, they were very concerned about the

25   Interview with Lyndon Wade by Marcellus C. Barksdale, September 12, 1978; interview with J. R. Wilson by Cynthia G. Fleming, September 7, 1978; interview with Robert Clark by Marcellus C. Barksdale, September 6, 1978.

prospects for violence and "wanted to get on with it [desegregation]." The Atlanta newspapers, particularly the Atlanta *Constitution*, which had consistently lent its powerful voice to the movement for "open schools" and peaceful desegregation, were buoyed by these efforts and gave them a prominent place in their pages.[26]

In the face of these widespread efforts for peaceful desegregation, the extremist ravings of die-hard segregationists like restaurateur and mayoral candidate Lester Maddox were all but drowned out. Maddox was vehemently opposed to any desegregation and ridiculed white leaders for encouraging and "planning to invade every white high school in Atlanta, with negro students, in September this year. In the meantime, white race-mixers, working with negro children during the spring and summer, so that when school starts in September, the children will be sweethearts and friends—rather than strangers." "After a few years of this," Maddox predicted, "stories about young white girls being found in negro hotels will not even make the newspapers."[27]

As Atlanta school officials prepared to test more than a hundred black students for the limited desegregation scheduled for the fall, a sit-in blitz hit the city. Early in February, Atlanta's black college students began their second year of demonstrations designed to end lunch counter segregation. The new sit-ins deeply troubled many Atlantans, as they saw them jeopardizing the plans for peaceful school desegregation. Ironically, business leaders who were now in the forefront of the move for peaceful desegregation remained steadfast in their opposition to desegregation of their own lunch counters. Since one school crisis had just been met and there were uncertain days ahead in the fall, some business and political leaders viewed the new sit-ins as most untimely. They could only further inflame passions and make violence in September a likelihood. The Atlanta newspapers adopted this view in their editorials and it was even supported by several black leaders.[28]

26   Wilson interview; Clark interview; interview with Benjamin E. Mays by Cynthia G. Fleming, September 7, 1978; Allen interview. A new organization called Organization Assisting Schools In September (OASIS) joined HOPE as the most vocal prodesegregation group among white moderates.
27   Atlanta *Constitution*, February 25, 1961.
28   *Ibid.*, February 1, 20, 28, 1961.

The view that peaceful school desegregation was the most important issue facing the community and that continued pressure for immediate lunch counter integration would threaten it was eventually accepted by all of the parties involved. On March 7, student and adult black leaders signed an agreement with downtown merchants which ended the sit-ins with a promise of lunch counter desegregation following school desegregation. The six months' delay was soon denounced by younger blacks who threatened to renege on the pact and resume sit-ins. It took a personal plea from Martin Luther King, Jr., to convince them to accept the delay.[29]

On August 30, the nine black students who had survived the rigorous testing and other procedures to qualify for transfers entered schools in each of Atlanta's four quadrants without incident. Desegregation in Atlanta had become a reality, peacefully.

The history of public school desegregation in Atlanta is still an open chapter. Even today, a suit is pending in the federal courts aimed at ending the resegregation of the school system. The proponents of further desegregation argue that the school system is virtually all-black because of white flight to the suburbs and suggest cross-county busing as the only means of achieving real integration. Nevertheless, the accomplishments of 1961, small as they may seem now, were immensely significant, not only for Atlanta, but for the entire nation. Dallas, Houston, and even New Orleans, as well as several smaller places, were now able to say, "We can do it too." And the federal government had, and willingly used, "a showplace for peaceful desegregation."

29 *Ibid.*, March 8, 11, 1961.

WILLIAM BROPHY

ACTIVE ACCEPTANCE—ACTIVE CONTAINMENT

THE DALLAS STORY

Dallas, Texas, has suffered a negative image for much of its recent history. The city has been viewed as the community where people spat upon Lady Bird Johnson and Adlai Stevenson, where Adlai Stevenson was hit with a placard, and above all where President John F. Kennedy was assassinated. Many Americans perceived Dallas as a city of hate. This view has considerable basis in fact. During the 1920s a xenophobic atmosphere enabled Dallas hatemongers to create one of the nation's most powerful and violent chapters of the Ku Klux Klan. Even in the 1940s, 1950s, and 1960s the city was fertile ground for right-wing organizations seeking to raise money for the crusade against liberalism, socialism, and communism. In sharp contrast to this negative image was the success that Dallas achieved in handling the desegregation crisis of the early 1960s.

The desegregation story in Dallas began a few months after the Supreme Court's implementation decision of May 31, 1955, in the case of *Brown* v. *Board of Education*. In September, 1955, the National Association for the Advancement of Colored People filed suit in behalf of twenty-four Negro plaintiffs in the case of

Bell v. *Rippy.*[1] The two principal attorneys for the NAACP, W. J. Durham and C. B. Bunkley, were both citizens of Dallas and veterans of the civil rights struggle. Durham and Bunkley had been the attorneys in the cases of *Smith* v. *Allright* (the white primary case) and *Sweatt* v. *Painter* (the University of Texas School of Law desegregation case).[2]

For the five years and four months following the initiation of the suit in 1955, Durham, Bunkley, and the attorneys for the Dallas Independent School District engaged in a legal battle.[3] During this time, the NAACP did not anticipate a favorable decision at the district court level before either Judge William T. Atwell, who heard the *Bell* cases, or Judge T. Whitfield Davidson, who heard the *Borders* cases. Instead, Durham and Bunkley thought that the Fifth Circuit Court of Appeals in New Orleans would rule in their favor. By February, 1960, it became evident that the NAACP's strategy was working. In that month the fifth circuit court ordered the school district to have a desegregation plan by May of that year.[4]

In compliance with the court order the Dallas Independent School District presented Judge Davidson with a stair-step grade-per-year plan. The plan was submitted in April and rejected by Judge Davidson in May. Davidson favored a "salt and pepper" plan under which all grades in selected schools would be desegregated on a voluntary basis. The influential Dallas *Morning News* praised Davidson's approach because it complied "with the letter of the high court's decree but at the same time [stayed] in line with the Constitution, with individual liberty and with parental control over child welfare." Durham condemned the "salt and pepper" plan as being unconstitutional. According to Durham, Judge Davidson's approach involved "no plan at all in that it permits one's constitutional rights to be dependent upon the will of another." In November of the same year

1   *Bell* v. *Rippy*, 133 F. Supp. 811 (1955).
2   Interview with Judge Lewis A. Bedford, Jr., by John Bodnar, March 28, 1977, p. 7, in the Oral History Collection of North Texas State University, Denton, Texas.
3   See *Bell* v. *Rippy*, 133 F. Supp. 811 (1955); *Bell* v. *Rippy*, 184 F. Supp. 485 (1956); *Borders* v. *Rippy*, 184 F. Supp. 402 (1960); *Borders* v. *Rippy*, 188 F. Supp. 231 (1960); *Borders* v. *Rippy*, 195 F. Supp. 732 (1961).
4   Bedford interview, 19, 20, 23; *Borders* v. *Rippy*, 184 F. Supp. 402 (1960).

the fifth circuit court rejected the Davidson plan and approved the grade-per-year one. At the same time the court invalidated a 1957 Texas referendum law. Under this law no school district could desegregate and receive state funds unless a majority of the voters in a referendum approved of desegregation. In August, 1960, Dallas voters had rejected school desegregation by a vote of 30,324 to 7,416. Finally, in January, 1961, the fifth circuit court gave the Dallas Independent School District ninety days to make an appeal before the Supreme Court. Henry W. Strasburger, the attorney for the school district, advised the school board not to appeal. In Strasburger's opinion such an appeal would be futile. The school board agreed with their attorney and the way was cleared for school desegregation to begin in September, 1961.[5]

On September 6, 1961, eighteen black first graders attended eight formerly all-white schools. These eighteen children were not confronted with angry mobs and the sounds of angry parents, nor were they met by classmates who called them "niggers." There were no significant racial incidents in Dallas on September 6. The absence of scenes such as those which had occurred at Little Rock and New Orleans or those which would occur in other cities was not an accident. Leaders from both the white and black communities had made a commitment eighteen months earlier to ensure that Dallas would not be the scene of racial violence.

In early 1960 a group of black leaders had asked Dr. Luther Holcomb, the director of the Dallas Council of Churches, to talk to Mayor R. L. Thornton. These black leaders wanted the city commission to establish a human relations commission. City officials rejected the proposal because it would be politically untenable. Instead, Mayor Thornton went to the powerful Dallas Citizens Council (DCC) and asked its leaders to work with representatives from the black community. The DCC was a civic organization composed of over two hundred leading white businessmen. The association, which was not related to the White Citizens Council, had been established during the 1930s. Beginning with the DCC's original success of making Dallas the focal

5   Dallas *Morning News*, September 8, 9, 1960; *Southern School News*, September, 1960, p. 16, January, 1961, p. 14, February, 1961, p. 3, May, 1961, p. 4.

point of the 1936 Texas Centennial Celebration, the organization had consistently worked for the betterment of Dallas. DCC members constituted the city's power elite. From its creation the DCC was composed of individuals who had the authority to commit their companies to civic projects without having to contact officials at a home office.[6]

DCC leaders agreed to a plan in which seven prominent whites would meet with seven eminent black spokesmen on a regular basis. This fourteen-person biracial committee spearheaded the desegregation movement in Dallas.[7] The Negro members of the committee were: George Allen, president of the Great Liberty Life Insurance Company; W. J. Durham, the attorney involved in the *Bell* and *Borders* cases; Rev. E. C. Estell, president of the Interdenominational Ministerial Alliance; C. J. Clark, undertaker and spokesman for the various fraternal associations; Rev. B. E. Joshua, president of the Baptist Ministerial Alliance; E. L. V. Reed, a tire dealer; and A. Maceo Smith, a leading black businessman and one of the most prominent Negro leaders in Texas. The seven whites were: James Aston, president of the Republic National Bank; Carr P. Collins, Sr., president of the Fidelity Union Life Insurance Company; Karl Hoblitzelle, chairman of the board of the Republic National Bank; W. W. Overton, board chairman of the Texas Bank and Trust Company; John Mitchell, cotton machinery manufacturer; Julian Scheppes, wholesale liquor dealer and a leading Jewish layman; and C. A. Tatum, president of the Dallas Power and Light Company. Tatum was selected as the chairman of the biracial committee.[8]

The members of the biracial committee were major economic and political figures in the black and white communities and therefore had the respect of most Dallas residents. Equally important, however, was the fact that white Dallasites played no role in the selection of the committee's black members. The Negro members were selected by, and responsible to, the Negro community. Each Saturday the black community received a re-

6   Dallas *Morning News*, September 17, 1961.
7   *Christian Century*, September 26, 1961, in *Facts on Film* (Nashville: Southern Education Reporting Service, n.d.), article K, roll 8, frame 88.
8   Dallas *Morning News*, May 14, 1962; New York *Times*, July 30, 1961; *Southern School News*, October, 1961, p. 9.

port from its committee members. Had the seven blacks been selected by whites or had they been unable to bring reports of progress to their people during the period prior to September, 1961, racial strife rather than relative harmony would probably have prevailed in Dallas.[9] Success was dependent upon the cooperation of the people of Dallas.

A primary objective of the DCC was to avoid the type of racial crisis that had occurred in Little Rock, Arkansas, in 1957. Two of the most important people involved by the DCC in the effort to have a peaceful transition in Dallas were Chief of Police Jesse Curry and Sam R. Bloom of the Bloom Advertising Agency. Curry was asked by the DCC to study the effect of the Little Rock crisis on that city's police department; Bloom was asked to cover all areas not related to police activities. Of great concern to the members of the DCC was the bifurcating effect of the desegregation crisis upon the city of Little Rock.[10]

The children of Dallas, both black and white, were of special concern to the city's leaders. Dr. Percy Luecke, chairman of the Dallas Medical Society's Mental Health Committee in 1961, became involved in the desegregation story because of the medical society's concern with the impact of violence upon the mental health of children. The children were the ones who had to pay the price for adult-created racial situations. Bloom believed that children have a difficult time coping with violence. Responsible citizens such as Bloom and Luecke were concerned with what happens to a child who witnesses the perpetration of violence by one of his parents. Both black and white leaders were also concerned with the impact of racial intolerance on the minds of Negro children.[11]

City leaders were also worried about the effect that extremism would have on the image of Dallas. Dick West, editorial page editor of the Dallas *Morning News*, told approximately two hundred top business officials in Dallas that Little Rock had lost fifteen industries because of the segregation crisis. The vice-president and executive editor of the Dallas *Times Herald*, Felix

9   Interview with Sam Bloom by the author, July 15, 1978.
10   *Ibid.*
11   Interview with Dr. Percy Luecke by the author, June 28, 1978; Bloom interview.

McKnight, spoke to the same group of businessmen about the need to keep Dallas from being regarded as a rebellious city.[12]

To avoid what had happened in Little Rock and New Orleans, leaders in Dallas decided to create a pattern of behavior conducive to peaceful change. A film, *Dallas at the Crossroads*, was used to help establish the desired behavioral pattern among whites. A photographer for the National Broadcasting Company, Morris Levy, produced the film. Levy had witnessed the 1960 violence in Montgomery, Alabama, and told Dr. Luther Holcomb that he would donate his services to Dallas to help the city avoid a similar breakdown of law and order. Walter Cronkite of CBS volunteered his services to narrate the film.[13]

The film began with a depiction of Dallas as a friendly, progressive city. Juxtaposed against the image of a progressive Dallas were scenes of troops in Little Rock and screaming mothers holding their small children in New Orleans. There were also short comments in the film by leading Dallas citizens. Police Chief Jesse Curry, for example, promised to see that the law was obeyed. *Dallas at the Crossroads* concluded with an appeal to patriotism. Hundreds of uniformed Boy Scouts marched with flags to patriotic music.[14]

The film was shown to small groups of people who were members of a church organization, civic club, neighborhood association, or lodge. The small-group approach was used because Bloom and others believed that an individual would be less prone to denounce desegregation before limited numbers of his peers than he would before a larger impersonal audience. In the months prior to September, 1961, the film was shown approximately a thousand times. While produced primarily to be seen by whites, the film was occasionally viewed by blacks. When this occurred the audience was informed that the film was made to make whites aware of their responsibilities. On the day before the implementation of the desegregation order *Dallas at the Crossroads* was televised.[15]

12   *Southern School News*, July, 1961, p. 3.
13   Bloom interview; *Christian Century*, September 26, 1961.
14   *Dallas at the Crossroads*. Copies of this film are in possession of the Bloom Advertising Agency in Dallas.
15   Bloom interview; Dallas *Morning News*, September 2, 1961; New York *Times*, July 30, 1961.

The DCC-supported behavior modification program also involved the distribution of pamphlets, with titles such as *Dallas at the Crossroads* and *Dallas Opportunity*, which were printed and distributed by the hundreds of thousands. Various companies handed out printed material along with paychecks. On the Sunday prior to school desegregation the Dallas Council of Churches sponsored a panel discussion concerning the impending event on the television program "Your Church Presents."[16]

Analyses of the various films, pamphlets, and television productions reveal two significant and related factors. Civic leaders in Dallas decided that the issue should be presented to the people as one of law and order versus civil disorder and violence. Neither the members of the biracial committee nor the DCC wanted Dallasites to see the issue solely in terms of race. Violence was described as "a problem that effects the whole community and not merely a few isolated segments of the school or business public. Violence destroys a community. It not only disrupts business and education, but undermines the health and moral fiber of all citizens. Extremist elements and self-seeking individuals come into control, and the city's children are forced to bear alone a burden which rightfully is an adult responsibility."[17] In short Dallas was not going to accept "any sort of action that scars the life and warps the memories of our six-year-old children of whatever race."[18]

In this carefully orchestrated plan the printed and spoken words of civic leaders were reinforced by city officials. Prior to the date of school desegregation Mayor Earle Cabell called both blacks and Ku Klux Klan types to his office. Cabell made it perfectly clear that there would be "ample policemen on the job and that the first person who made any move that would tend toward disorder, be he white or black, was going to jail and then we'd ask questions later."[19]

The police department monitored the activities of those who were deemed to be extremists and compiled a collection of mug

16 Dallas *Morning News*, August 6, September 2, 1961.
17 *Dallas Opportunity*, quoted in the Dallas *Morning News*, August 6, 1961.
18 Comment made before a group of businessmen by supermarket chain chairman Robert McCullum, quoted in *Southern School News*, July, 1961, p. 3.
19 Interview with Earle Cabell by Ronald E. Marcello, October 2, 1974, in the Oral History Collection of North Texas State University, 170–71.

shots of such individuals. On the actual date of school desegregation the police had a special force of officers who surveyed the schools affected by the process. The Dallas plan worked well enough that the special force had an uneventful day with no significant incidents and no arrests.[20]

The effort to create a favorable climate of opinion among whites was not in itself sufficient to ensure peaceful school desegregation. Orderly transition was also dependent upon the black community remaining calm and patient. To attain the desired behavior pattern among blacks, white Dallas had to indicate clearly to the black community that an atmosphere of good faith existed. Good faith could not be demonstrated by words alone; Negroes had to be shown that specific actions had taken place.[21]

Each Saturday the seven Negro members of the biracial committee met with the representatives of approximately 125 black organizations. At these meetings the individuals on the biracial committee discussed the rate of progress. Representatives from the various groups attending the meeting then informed the larger black community. At these weekly gatherings the members of the biracial committee were also asked to deal with specific grievances. The black members then met with the seven whites on the biracial committee to discuss and possibly resolve the grievance. The following Saturday the Negro leaders would report to those at the weekly meeting on the rate of progress in redressing the complaint.[22]

One of the primary complaints of black Dallasites was the existence of segregated cafeterias, restaurants, and lunch counters in the downtown area. As was the case throughout the South, Negroes in Dallas resented merchants who accepted their money for goods purchased in their stores but who would not allow a black person to eat in the establishment's restaurant. In the quest for lunch counter desegregation black leaders advised their followers to utilize both the boycott and the sit-in.

Among the black organizations advocating the use of boycotts and/or sit-ins were the Dallas Community Committee, the Interdenominational Ministerial Alliance, and the Youth Coun-

20   Dallas *Morning News*, September 2, 1961; *Christian Science Monitor*, September 5, 1961.
21   Bloom interview.
22   *Ibid.*; New York *Times*, July 30, 1961.

cil of the NAACP. A serious effort to integrate eating facilities began in January, 1961, when W. J. Durham, a member of the biracial committee, spoke to a thousand people attending a meeting at Saint John's Baptist Church. At this particular time, Durham was concerned about an apparent impasse over the complete integration of the Texas State Fairgrounds. In his speech Durham urged blacks to sit-in and to boycott several stores, including Titche-Goettinger, Sanger's, H. L. Green, and S. H. Kress & Company. These stores, as well as Neiman-Marcus and A. Harris, became the primary targets of the sit-in and boycott campaigns.[23]

For several months limited protests occurred. Through a tacit agreement the city's major newspapers refused to cover the demonstrations. The intent of this agreement was to deny publicity to those engaging in acts of civil disobedience and thereby minimize the tension level in the city. Even the Dallas *Express*, the leading black-owned newspaper in the city, largely ignored sit-in activities. The city council, however, passed an ordinance which prohibited people from "standing, remaining or congregating on any public street or sidewalk, or at the entrance, alcove or steps of any public or private building so as to obstruct, prevent or interfere with its use."[24]

The desegregation campaign continued throughout the spring and early summer of 1961. Easter was normally a profitable season for clothing merchants, and black leaders hoped to apply pressure on the merchants by reducing the Easter profits at the boycotted stores. The Reverend E. C. Estell, a member of the biracial committee and the president of the Dallas Citizens Committee, called for an Easter boycott against Neiman-Marcus, Sanger's, A. Harris, H. L. Green, S. H. Kress, and Titche-Goettinger because representatives from these stores had been unable to reach a desegregation agreement with the biracial committee.[25]

The boycott effort continued after Easter and its apparent effectiveness increased with the passage of time. On May 27, 1961, the Dallas *Express* contained a full page advertisement in

---

23 Dallas *Express*, January 14, February 4, 1961; Dallas *Morning News*, January 9, 1961.
24 Luecke interview; Oklahoma City *Times*, January 31, 1961, in *Facts on Film*, article J, roll 6, frame 2977.
25 Dallas *Express*, February 18, 1961.

support of the boycott. The advertisement consisted of the names of approximately 1,100 people who had pledged themselves not to purchase goods from the target stores.[26]

After months of the boycott, negotiations between the members of the biracial committee resulted in an agreement with the merchants. On July 26 approximately forty business establishments allowed blacks to eat at the lunch counters. Significantly, the 159 blacks who participated in the activities of July 26 were not confronted by hostile mobs. There were no incidents at any of the business establishments and there were no arrests. Other than the facilities at the aforementioned stores, restaurants and lunch counters were integrated at Sears, Walgreen's, Love Field (the city's old airport), the Continental Bus Depot (the lunchroom of the Greyhound Bus Depot was already desegregated), and the Union Fidelity Life Insurance Building. Immediately after the successful desegregation effort in downtown Dallas, the boycott was ended.[27]

Analysis of the lunch counter desegregation process suggests that success was a result of hard work and excellent communication between the city's black and white communities. During the period prior to July 26, the negotiations were carried out in good faith by both sides. Power elites from both the black and white sectors of the population were deeply involved in the desegregation effort. The DCC, through its members on the biracial committee, was very much involved in the process and represented the interests of the white power structure. Both Estell and Durham were outstanding Negro leaders respected by the black citizens of Dallas.

The atmosphere in Dallas also contributed to the successful effort. By July the behavior conditioning program was near its end. The film, *Dallas at the Crossroads*, and the various pamphlets had been widely circulated and had created the desired effect. Too, the near absence of news media coverage of the demonstrations contributed to a climate that, by southern standards of the period, was relatively free of hostility.

As part of the overall racial picture in Dallas, the desegregation of the restaurants was significant. Desegregation was perceived by those working for peaceful transition as an adult

26   *Ibid.*, May 27, 1961.
27   New York *Times*, July 28, 30, 1961; Dallas *Express*, August 5, 1961.

problem. Once the crisis was defined as being adult in nature, the biracial committee decided that the city's grown-ups and not the children should bear the burden of the initial integration experience. If, as was the case in Dallas, the adult population accepted its responsibility, an example for the children would be set.[28] The restaurant desegregation process was also important because it was but one of several events which demonstrated good faith on the part of the white leadership to the black community.

Prior to September, 1961, efforts were also under way in Dallas to change the job situation for blacks. At the beginning of 1961, Dallas Negroes performed 139 different jobs listed under the categories of janitor or porter. As a result of a reclassification system, blacks began to receive job titles which more accurately described their work functions. Thus, an individual who had been classified as a porter but who had been doing the work of a receiving clerk was called a receiving clerk.[29]

Black Dallasites also expressed concern about other types of job discrimination. In May, 1961, the Phylon Salesmanship Club, a Negro organization, asked retailers in Negro areas not to purchase Pearl Beer because the Pearl Brewing Company did not employ Negro route salesmen. One week after the complaint was lodged a Negro, William G. Reed, who had been with the company for eight years, was promoted to route salesman. At approximately the same time the NAACP filed a complaint alleging that Negro workers in Dallas were being denied promotions on the basis of race at a Western Electric Company plant in the city. The NAACP further contended that Local 6295 of the Communications Workers of America was in collusion with the company. Within a year the Western Electric Company had eliminated its "housekeeping department" and had transferred blacks to the formerly all-white production department where promotions became possible. The action by the Western Electric Company brought a citation from the President's Committee on Equal Job Opportunity.[30]

Comparable job-related changes were taking place else-

28   New York *Times*, July 30, 1961.
29   Dallas *Morning News*, August 6, 1961.
30   Dallas *Express*, May 20, 27, 1961; Dallas *Morning News*, May 27, 1961, April 24, 1962.

where in Dallas. In late January, 1961, the Dallas Transit Company was asked to hire black bus drivers. By February 25 of the same year the transit company announced that henceforth its hiring policies would be based on the ability of the applicant and not upon his race or religion. Two months later city officials stated that they were looking to the day when Negroes would be hired as firemen. Blacks had been on the police force for more than fourteen years.[31]

Equal employment opportunity was an objective of civil rights advocates but both black and white leaders believed that substantive changes in the job market were contingent upon improved race relations in other areas. Sam Bloom and Lewis A. Bedford, Jr., a Negro attorney in Dallas, believed that economic equality could not be attained until whites accepted blacks on an equal basis in places of public accommodation and in the schools. Dallas blacks in the early 1960s could, therefore, expect only modest gains in the job market. Coequality in the economic sector would have to wait until some date after whites accepted desegregated schools and integrated public accommodations.[32]

The gradually changing policies of the hotel owners in Dallas also contributed to the city's "good faith" approach to the desegregation crisis. In December, 1960, and January, 1961, Dallas was the host city for a Presbyterian church convention. Although black delegates could not stay overnight in the same hotels as their white counterparts, the Adolphus Hotel did provide the group with private eating and meeting facilities. By August, 1961, a representative of the Dallas hotel owners, Tom Pendergraft, stated that successful school desegregation would be followed by the gradual desegregation of the hotels. The hotel owners, according to Pendergraft, would cooperate with the DCC. The initial action on the part of the hotels involved the acceptance of Negro government officials. Within six months of the school desegregation date the hotels in Dallas were accepting guests without regard to race.[33]

31 Dallas *Express*, February 25, 1961; Dallas *Morning News*, February 1, April 10, 1961.
32 Bedford interview; Bloom interview.
33 Dallas *Morning News*, January 1, August 16, 1961; Houston *Post*, February 13, 1962.

Local government agencies also adopted changes which improved race relations. In July, 1961, two Negroes, Dr. Frank Jordan and H. B. Revis, were appointed to boards by the city council. Dr. Jordan was made a member of the Advisory Public Health Board and Revis was selected to serve on the City-County Civil Defense and Disaster Commission. Of greater significance was the desegregation of public recreational and cultural facilities. Without litigation various city parks, the facilities at White Rock Lake, the Dallas Garden Center, the museums of fine arts, science, and natural history, the city's public golf courses, the memorial auditorium, and the zoo were desegregated by the end of 1961. Public swimming pools remained segregated until 1963, but there were swimming pools in black neighborhoods.[34]

The desegregation story in Dallas was a successful one. Dallas avoided the hatred, violence, and mental anguish which characterized the desegregation effort in other cities. What happened in Dallas was not a result of the city being blessed with a uniquely tolerant population. Indeed, the August, 1960, vote in opposition to school desegregation suggests that white Dallasites held racial views comparable to other white southerners. White Dallasites, however, probably did not feel threatened by the emerging blacks as did whites elsewhere in the South. In 1960 only 14.5 percent of the 951,527 people living in Dallas County were black. Of primary significance was the presence in Dallas of black and white leaders who wanted to prevent violence and preserve the community's image. The biracial committee was able to convince whites that the old order had to be changed and blacks that it had to be changed gradually.

The Dallas Citizens Council was instrumental in bringing peaceful transition to the city. The businessmen belonging to the DCC controlled the economic life of Dallas. Had the DCC shirked its responsibility, Dallas would probably have experienced the same kinds of civil rights disturbances encountered elsewhere.

Perhaps equally important to the role of the DCC were the decisions made by various groups in Dallas. The press in Dallas tacitly agreed not to cover major news stories relating to civil rights because it believed that such reporting would help create racial strife in the city. Both black and white leaders agreed that

34 Dallas *Express*, July 15, 1961; Birmingham *News*, January 9, 1962; Dallas *Morning News*, June 16, 1963.

desegregation was a local problem and should be dealt with at the local level by citizens of the city. No lawsuits were filed to desegregate municipal golf courses, museums, and parks. When Attorney General Robert F. Kennedy offered to send federal employees to help the city, he was politely rejected. The Congress of Racial Equality (CORE) did not conduct freedom rides in Dallas. CORE people came to Dallas but decided that their services were not needed in the city.[35] Black leaders in Dallas, such as the Reverend James Rhett, president of the local NAACP in 1962, urged Negroes to remain peaceful and to accept what he considered to be token integration.

There were, to be sure, differences of opinion in Dallas. Clarence Laws, the regional director of the NAACP, was openly opposed to the type of integration that took place in the Dallas schools. He and other members of the local NAACP engaged in a campaign to persuade Negro parents to enroll their children in formerly lily-white schools. The projected goal of the NAACP was to enroll two hundred black children on the first day of desegregation; the eventual total of eighteen fell far short of the objective. Complaints were also heard about the inferior quality of housing for poor people. Too, the hiring of black bus drivers, the changing of job titles for Negroes, and improved promotion policies in selected industrial plants were beneficial, but positive change in the job market was still needed.[36]

Although racial problems continued to exist in Dallas after the 1961 desegregation experience, the effort for peaceful change was successful. The people of Dallas demonstrated that a community of individuals working together can resolve fundamental problems. The key to the Dallas approach of "active acceptance-active containment" lay with the leadership. Prominent Dallasites, both black and white, controlled the situation. Indeed, the leadership orchestrated the movement toward desegregation. Within the limits of the possible, the residents of Dallas were not forced to react to unforeseen events. As planned by the biracial committee, whites accepted limited change and blacks accepted change that was limited.

35 New York *Times*, July 30, 1961; *Southern School News*, October, 1961, p. 9.
36 NAACP Press Release, August 14, 18, 1961, in *Facts on Film*, July, 1961– June, 1962, Supplement Roll 12; Dallas *Morning News*, July 28, 1961.

JAMES C. COBB

YESTERDAY'S LIBERALISM

BUSINESS BOOSTERS AND CIVIL RIGHTS
IN AUGUSTA, GEORGIA

Although the post-Reconstruction South often seemed to choose the past over the future, the region's remarkable capacity for simultaneous displays of progress and primitivism suggested that whenever possible southerners simply avoided such a choice. In the years before racial practices in Dixie became offensive to mass society values, Henry Grady and the early twentieth-century boosters who followed his lead experienced little difficulty in crusading for industrial development while extolling the merits of white supremacy.[1] After World War II, however, mounting civil rights pressures complicated efforts to pursue economic growth. As the postwar apostles of industrial expansion came under increasingly critical national scrutiny, they seemed to confront at last the oft-postponed decision be-

1 C. Vann Woodward, *The Burden of Southern History* (Baton Rouge: Louisiana State University Press, 1960); John Hope Franklin, "The Great Confrontation: The South and the Problem of Change," *Journal of Southern History*, XXXVIII (February, 1972), 3–20; Paul M. Gaston, *The New South Creed: A Study in Southern Mythmaking* (New York: Alfred A. Knopf, 1970); Blaine A. Brownell, *The Urban Ethos in the South, 1920–1930* (Baton Rouge: Louisiana State University Press, 1975); Charles P. Garafalo, "The Sons of Henry Grady: Atlanta Boosters in the 1920s," *Journal of Southern History*, XLII (May, 1976), 187–204.

tween emotional attachments to yesterday and grand ambitions for tomorrow.

For community leaders in Augusta, Georgia, this choice seemed especially traumatic. Founded by James Oglethorpe in 1735, antebellum Augusta was both a bustling riverport and a resort center famous for its beauty and genteel hospitality. In the twentieth century, Augusta's reverence for tradition charmed visitors to the annual Masters Golf Tournament and caught the eye of Dwight Eisenhower, who selected it as the site of his presidential retreat.[2]

Determined to keep southern racial customs intact in their city, Augusta's white officials and prominent white citizens responded to the 1954 *Brown* v. *Board of Education* decision with angry denunciations of would-be race-mixers. Local lawyer and publisher Roy Harris was a mainstay of the Citizens Council movement whose antics earned him the title "Mr. Segregationist." Reflecting the views of many of Augusta's citizens, Harris' newspaper damned northern liberals, Supreme Court tyrants, "communistic" civil rights agitators and politicians who sought black votes.[3]

Augusta appeared to be a citadel of defiance in 1954, a place where integrationists could expect last-ditch resistance. Yet less than a decade later, in 1962, peaceful and to some extent voluntary desegregation allowed blacks to eat at the city's lunch counters and be entertained at its theaters. This apparent breakthrough was largely attributable to the influence of growthminded civic and business leaders who feared that continued refusal to desegregate would undermine their efforts to lure new industries to the area.[4] Although economic concerns may have

2   Federal Writers Project in Georgia, Works Progress Administration, *Augusta* (Augusta: Works Progress Administration, 1938). For an affirmation of the persistence of tradition in Augusta, see E. J. Kahn, Jr., "Profiles: Georgia, from Rabun Gap to Tybee Light" (Part II), *New Yorker*, February 13, 1978, pp. 46–48.
3   Editorial, Augusta *Chronicle*, May 1, 1954. See editorial in Augusta *Courier*, May 31, 1954, for Harris' thoughts on "rape by judicial fiat."
4   For optimistic views of the impact of industrialization on southern race relations see Joseph J. Spengler, "Demographic and Economic Change in the South, 1940–1960," in Allen P. Sindler (ed.), *Change in the Contemporary South* (Durham, N.C.: Duke University Press, 1963), 54; J. Milton Yinger and George E. Simpson, "Can Segregation Survive in an Industrial Society?" *Antioch Review*, XVIII (Spring, 1958), 15–24.

triumphed temporarily over the caste system in Augusta, the pace of black progress during the rest of the decade was painfully slow. After yielding so gracefully in 1962 city officials used tokenism and ballyhoo to create an illusion of cooperation and harmony and crusaded for expanded prosperity without further compromising their racial philosophies or their economic and political advantages.

The booster spirit which was to have such great impact on early desegregation efforts in Augusta emerged in 1946 when a reform movement toppled the Cracker party, a political machine which governed with benevolent but wasteful and provincial despotism. The Crackers gave way to the Independent party, a group of businessmen and professionals who promised an efficient and modernized government that would work to attract the industries which had shunned the city under their predecessors.[5]

In spite of their forward-looking platform, the Independents took as the symbol of their crusade one Col. W. Seaborn Effingham, a southern aristocrat of the old school. As the hero of *Colonel Effingham's Raid*, a film based on a novel written by Independent leader Berry Fleming, Effingham urged citizens to rise up against machine rule in the fictional city of Fredericksburg. Like the ghostly planter used by cartoonists to represent the New South movement, the colonel helped assure the public that a new commitment to progress need not supersede an old obligation to tradition.[6] More specifically, his figurative presence at the head of the reform crusade also indicated that the Independents had no intention of discarding the doctrine of white supremacy. This was a significant contribution because 1946 was the first year since Reconstruction in which blacks were allowed to vote in southern Democratic primaries. True to the sacred principles which Effingham invoked incessantly, the reformers promised fairness to blacks and nothing more. Physical and economic growth would come, but everything else would remain the same.

5   For a full treatment of the overthrow of the Crackers see James C. Cobb, "Politics in a New South City: Augusta, Georgia, 1946–1971" (Ph.D. dissertation, University of Georgia, 1975), 23–48.
6   Berry Fleming, *Colonel Effingham's Raid* (New York: Duell, Sloan and Pearce, 1943). Fleming was kind enough to arrange a special showing of the movie for the author.

The Independents quickly fulfilled their pledge to modern-ize Augusta's government. Under the Crackers, municipal pol-icy-making had conformed to the "caretaker" model, offering a minimal level of general services and providing special atten-tion to the interests and problems of individual wards as deter-mined by their city council representatives.[7] The Independents scuttled the Cracker approach for one which emphasized "good government," economic growth, and extension of public ameni-ties. In 1951, Independent Hugh Hamilton was elected mayor on a platform promising businesslike leadership and a number of improvements designed to please Augusta's expanding middle class. Under his expert guidance Augusta became one of the first southern cities to receive federal urban renewal funds. Hamilton's first administration was also a period of significant economic growth. In 1951 construction began on the mammoth Savannah River Nuclear Plant at nearby Barnwell, South Caro-lina, and by 1952 retail sales and building expenditures had doubled their 1949 totals.[8]

The affluence such growth could bring helped convert some of the skeptics who had resisted the Independent sales pitch for industrial expansion. The predictable economic slump that came when the huge plant was completed also provided an ex-cellent opportunity to recall the stagnation of the Cracker years.[9] Having tested the fruits of prosperity, Augusta's busi-ness and professional leaders supported the governmental phi-losophy most likely to restore it.

The election of Millard Beckum as mayor of Augusta in 1957 reflected the impact of a strengthened commitment to eco-nomic growth on the city's political climate. Beckum had begun his career as a member of the Cracker machine, but his experi-ence as a Chamber of Commerce executive had prepared him to lead the crusade for renewed growth and he received strong, broad-based support from the city's voters.[10]

---

7   For a description of this model, see Oliver P. Williams and Charles R. Adrian, *Four Cities: A Study in Comparative Policy Making* (Philadelphia: University of Pennsylvania Press, 1963), 23–29.
8   Augusta Chamber of Commerce, *For You Sir, a Brief on Industrial Augusta* (Augusta: n.p., 1953).
9   "The Boom That Went Awry," *Business Week*, August 4, 1956, p. 138.
10   Augusta *Chronicle*, October 6, 1957. Beckum carried every one of the city's eight wards, receiving at least 60 percent of the vote in all but two.

Beckum made industrial expansion the byword of his administration. Early in 1959 he led a number of businessmen in a three-day campaign to raise eighty thousand dollars toward the purchase of a site for a plant that Continental Can Corporation decided to locate near Augusta. Elated, the city's boosters intensified their determined, single-minded search for new industry. They failed to get the county commission's approval for the use of convict labor to prepare industrial sites, but the city council cooperated by voting to enlarge the airport to accommodate jet traffic. The daily papers, the *Chronicle* and *Herald*, nervously observed potential investors who toured the city, hoping to see "smokestacks follow in their wake."[11]

When it came to industrial promotion Augusta's journalists were more like cheerleaders than objective reporters. The papers repeatedly cited the need for economic growth and warned of the dangers of unionization. Urging others to do likewise, they contributed heavily to the funding of the Committee of 100, the area's major industrial development organization. The executive editor of the jointly owned papers cited several cases in which the papers had suppressed information about delicate negotiations with prospective industries. For example, when Continental Can decided to locate in Augusta, the newspapers kept quiet about the governor's decision to advance Richmond County its state highway funds for the next three years in order to facilitate construction of an access road for the new plant. The papers also spearheaded a drive to raise $250,000 to purchase extra land for future expansion by Continental Can. Local firms seemed most appreciative of media support; one executive felt he had such a good relationship with the press that editors and reporters would notify him if they encountered any "adverse publicity" concerning his company.[12]

The newspapers, which had supported reformers in 1946 and had consistently expressed the "what's good for business" point of view, warned that luring new industries demanded greater attention to appearances. Editorials urged that squatters be chased out of their shacks on Augusta's levees near the Savannah River and moaned that the city's illegal garbage

11 Augusta *Chronicle*, March 12, 1958, January 20, 22, 1959, March 22, December 8, 1960.
12 Louis C. Harris, "Don't Overlook the Newspaper's Role," *Industrial Development*, CXXXVI (March–April, 1967), 21–23.

dumps were enough to make Erskine Caldwell say, "I told you so!"[13] Joining in the chorus, business leaders and elected officials seldom missed an opportunity to warn of the need to maintain a progressive image. This fervent concern with appearances made the city vulnerable to black protests against segregation and discrimination.

Although some blacks spoke out against racial injustices in Augusta in the early postwar period, whites effectively ignored their complaints until the late fifties and early sixties when students from all-black Paine College swelled the ranks of protestors. In 1960, Paine students went to court seeking an end to segregated seating on city buses and later staged a lunch counter sit-in which resulted in some scuffling with whites before the students were arrested.[14]

The civil rights demonstrations of the late 1950s and early 1960s posed a significant threat to the Independents' commitment to defend tradition as vigorously as they pursued progress. Roy Harris was not the only influential Augustan who felt that the South's racial customs were the most precious elements of its regional heritage. In fact, some of the veterans of the 1946 defeat of the Crackers emerged as architects of Augusta's defenses against integration. In 1958 Berry Fleming suggested that when (and if) segregation became legally indefensible, students in Augusta schools should be segregated by sex in order to provide a better "out" for whites and a less tempting "in" for blacks. When school segregation finally came under fire, former Independent leader Scott Nixon urged the school board to defend its position by explaining that its charter required a dual school system.[15]

As black protests gathered steam and began to attract more attention, Mayor Millard Beckum decided to avoid the kind of resistance advocated by Nixon. Though hardly sensitive to black problems, Beckum was an astute politician who realized that an uncompromising attitude would create the kind of publicity likely to "bring in Martin Luther King." With federal interven-

---

13   Editorial, Augusta *Chronicle*, October 21, 1960.
14   *Ibid.*, April 5, December 14, 1960.
15   Augusta *Chronicle*, December 28, 1958; Minutes, Board of Education of Richmond County, April 11, 1963, in Richmond County Board of Education Office, Augusta.

tion changes would come inevitably, and he saw no need to damage the city's image in a futile struggle. Consequently, after black activists served notice that they would not be dissuaded, the mayor met with them and reached an understanding about the methods to be used in initiating desegregation in Augusta.[16]

On March 29, 1962, approximately 150 black youths, most of them high school students, peacefully integrated the city's lunch counters. There was no show of force by police, but they were standing by in the event of trouble. After meeting with Beckum the protestors returned to the Tabernacle Baptist Church of NAACP leader Rev. C. S. Hamilton. A few days later a similar group successfully defied Jim Crow seating practices in downtown theaters.[17] One student of the civil rights movement in Georgia attributed the success of these sit-ins to threats that there would be massive demonstrations during the annual Masters Golf Tournament which attracted thousands of spectators who spent thousands of dollars in Augusta. Before they agreed to token desegregation, city officials apparently concluded that the likelihood of disruptive protests would hurt Masters attendance.[18]

Once the wall of solidarity cracked, the *Chronicle*, which had been a consistent critic of civil rights demonstrations, suggested "The Time Has Come!" The editor noted the agonies of intransigent New Orleans and cited the damage done to that city's image in the eyes of potential investors. To him voluntary desegregation seemed to be the best means of insuring a prosperous future for Augusta.[19]

The concern of business and civic leaders with Augusta's reputation had helped to undermine the practice of segregation, an achievement of some significance in a city so enamored of its past. Yet Augusta's leaders, rather than admitting that racial discrimination was wrong, had merely conceded that further resistance would be futile and economically unwise. The *Chronicle* did not reinforce its call for desegregation with similar editorials but returned instead to its past policy of attempting to

16   Interview with Millard Beckum by the author, August 19, 1974.
17   Augusta *Chronicle*, March 30, 1962; Beckum interview.
18   Paul D. Bolster, "The Civil Rights Movement in Twentieth Century Georgia" (Ph.D. dissertation, University of Georgia, 1972), 194–95.
19   Editorial, Augusta *Chronicle*, July 14, 1963.

discredit the motives of civil rights advocates. When a small group of blacks visited city hall and quietly asked for integration of all municipal facilities, the mayor and council quickly pointed out that no legal sanction existed for segregation; it was largely a matter of tradition. A return visit elicited a plea by a leading councilman for respect for the city's customs which he felt were "not ill advised."[20] Despite the changes which had occurred, in the absence of continuing agitation by blacks, Augusta's white leaders refused to make a clean break with past discriminatory policies.

The inability of blacks to speed school desegregation suggested that without the threat of embarrassing protests they were unable to gain concessions that whites considered significant. Superintendent of Schools Roy Rollins continually voiced his opposition to integration, which when it came as a result of legal action in 1964, involved only eleven students. By 1969 only eight of thirty-seven schools for which such data were available had more than a 10 percent racial mixture and eleven had none at all. Desegregation proceeded slowly and not very well. HEW received a number of complaints about Rollins, who insisted that school choice forms mailed to parents bear the inscription "required and dictated by the federal government."[21]

In spite of their anger at Rollins, blacks failed to mount a significant protest effort against him, choosing instead to wage a tedious legal battle against segregation. This decision resulted from a combination of several factors. In an effort to forestall black protests, in the 1950s the board of education had begun to build new and modern black schools. The result was that by 1970 the National Urban League could find remarkably few physical discrepancies between black and white educational facilities in the city. The presence of committed and capable black

20   Augusta, Georgia, Minutes of the City Council, April 2, 5, May 6, 1963, in City Hall, Augusta.
21   Augusta *Chronicle*, August 27, 28, 1964. The following documents are all located in the office of the Department of Health, Education and Welfare, Civil Rights Division, Atlanta, Georgia: "Anticipated Enrollments and Staff of Each School Within the System: Richmond County, 1969" (these estimates were submitted at the beginning of the school year); "Preliminary Investigation of Richmond County, Georgia" (Augusta); Letters of complaint (confidential), August 27, 29, 1965; Sworn statements (confidential), April 25, 1968, January 26, 1967; Ruby Martin, Office for Civil Rights, to Roy E. Rollins, September 28, 1967.

lawyer John Ruffin undoubtedly gave blacks confidence that they could secure legal redress. Finally, several principals to whom the black community looked for leadership were subject to obvious pressure from the school board.[22]

Whatever their reasons, the decision by blacks to fight school segregation in the courtroom instead of the streets proved to be a serious tactical error. Because the primary impetus for integration actually came from the courts, Superintendent Rollins, who remained convinced that the majority of whites agreed with him, never moved to speed desegregation without first explaining that a judicial decree had forced him to act. Fear of further protests might have led Augusta's influential economic leaders to exact more cooperation from school officials, but once the lawsuits began to force token increases in integration and the *Chronicle* could point to these as "progress," the cause of appearances had been served and the city's boosters were satisfied.

As was the case with legal action, Augusta blacks discovered that political participation produced only limited advancement toward racial equality. This was true in part because an important element of Augusta's new image was a commitment to efficient, thrifty, and depoliticized municipal government. The emergence of a good government-economic growth consensus destroyed partisan political activity in city elections, and by the beginning of the 1960s organizations either made joint endorsements with the groups they had formerly opposed or in many cases simply expressed no preferences at all. In the city elections for 1961 the Independents and the Richmond County Democratic Club, a former haven for ex-Crackers, had common endorsees in six of the eight races.[23]

In 1963, both George A. Sancken and W.T. Ashmore promised progressive government and economic growth if elected mayor. Sancken, who won by a narrow margin, received the *Chronicle's* endorsement because of his greater "business experience," but the editor also cited Ashmore as an attractive can-

22   National Urban League, "The National Urban League Serves a Concerned City: A Community Audit of Augusta, Georgia," 1970, pp. 80–81, mimeographed copy in University of Georgia Library, Athens; "Preliminary Investigation of Richmond County, Georgia."
23   Augusta *Chronicle*, September 19, 1961.

didate. As members of the city council both men represented affluent middle-class wards and from a policy perspective there seemed to be little difference between them.[24]

Once in office Sancken continued most of Millard Beckum's policies. Greatly concerned about Augusta's image, he dreamed of a new convention center, supported a $160,000 renovation of the municipal auditorium, and fretted over the city's orchid collection. On the other hand, Sancken displayed less interest in combating the poverty which dominated the lives of many black Augustans. The mayor criticized federally funded low-cost housing programs, prompting a local NAACP leader to charge that city officials were insensitive to the poor.[25] In spite of such allegations Sancken won reelection in 1966 with only token opposition, and in 1969 Millard Beckum easily gained another term as mayor.

Augusta's new politics was not only bland, it was unresponsive to individuals or interest groups forced to operate outside the good government-economic growth consensus. Whereas in the years of sharply contested campaigns elected leaders had to learn to manage conflicts of interest, the advent of nonpartisanship encouraged them to avoid such problems. The reformers who had unseated the Crackers in 1946 replaced the machine's brand of special interest politics with an aboveboard, debit-credit approach to government that promised "fairness" but not the special attention or extra support which blacks wanted.[26]

Businessmen steeped in fiscal conservatism became the Chronicle's preferred candidates for office and serious aspirants had to espouse the gospel of efficiency if they expected newspaper support. The notion that a good government was a thrifty government offered little hope for impoverished blacks; for example, in 1960 the city council's appropriation of twenty-five thousand dollars for public welfare was only half the amount requested and by 1967 this figure had been cut by 14 percent.[27]

24   Editorial, Ibid., October 2, 1963.
25   Augusta Chronicle, August 20, 1963, June 21, 1968, August 12, 1969.
26   See Seymour Spilerman, "The Causes of Racial Disturbances: Tests of an Explanation," American Sociological Review, XXXVI (June, 1971), 437. Spilerman found that racial disturbances were more prevalent in southern cities which had nonpartisan elections and mayor-council governments.
27   Augusta Chronicle, March 23, 1960; U.S. Bureau of the Census, County

Black needs, created and shaped by generations of deprivation, could not be served by a city government dedicated to traditional efficiency at the expense of sorely needed services.

When blacks represented a relatively small percentage of the city's eligible voters, white politicians with ties to the old Cracker machine had at least offered minor concessions or small monetary payments in exchange for their support. Ironically, by the 1960s when black registrants comprised nearly 50 percent of the electorate, no white office seeker with a chance of winning made such an overture.[28] Racism encouraged whites to shun appeals for black support, but serious candidates also knew that any "deals" with blacks would conflict with the desire for businesslike conduct of public affairs which dominated the city's politics. In the long run the good government-economic growth consensus helped to prevent black voters from becoming the balance of political power in Augusta.

When blacks first began to seek public office, whites resorted to race-baiting, vote buying, changing to at-large elections, and redrawing ward boundaries in vain efforts to discourage them.[29] Yet, after three blacks held city council posts, boosters pointed to them as symbols of Augusta's "progressive" racial climate. Actually, in spite of their efforts to represent their constituents, black elected officials hardly made a dent in the white recalcitrance that denied them the influence they should have had in the decision-making process. Black councilmen worked to equalize city hiring practices and integrate governmental commissions, but by 1970 90 percent of black city employees still held only menial positions. On one occasion an apparently well qualified candidate for the planning commis-

---

and *City Data Book, 1967: A Statistical Abstract Supplement* (Washington, D.C.: U.S. Government Printing Office, 1968).

28   In 1963, W. T. Ashmore, one of the leading contenders in the mayoral race, did make an effort to gain black votes by making vague promises of economic equality, but blacks still remembered Ashmore's plea for segregation a few months earlier; and they gave enough support to a minor candidate to deny Ashmore the election. The winner, George Sancken, Jr., scorned any appeal for black support.

29   Vote buying was usually accomplished by paying "voter league" members to work at the polls. Such a practice occasionally resulted in black votes being delivered to staunch segregationists like Mike Padgett, a Marvin Griffin supporter. Augusta *Chronicle*, June 8, 19, 21, 1964. Rumors of a black's candidacy for city council and a growing black registration prompted initial consideration

sion lost out to the mayor's white nominee who would be absent during several months of his term because he was taking an "extended tour of Europe."[30]

Grady Abrams, the most outspoken black councilman, grew so tired of seeing rubbish pile up in his ward while he listened to talk of beautifying the city's showplaces that he reminded his colleagues: "The area I represent isn't beautiful at all." C. S. Hamilton, a former civil rights activist, found white fellow council members committed to a "do as little as we can get by with" response to black problems.[31] In spite of the persistence of black councilmen, they found no white allies who would support policy measures beneficial to black interests. Black political representatives became increasingly frustrated as they encountered growing disaffection and disunity among their constituents. By the end of the 1960s they faced criticisms from those who remembered promises like "I'll bring city hall to you," and a growing spirit of militance reflected disappointment with established black leadership as well as anger at whites.[32]

More than racial prejudice was involved in white councilmen's failure to respond to black pleas for help. Pursuit of economic growth required that energy and resources be expended to promote and dress up the city. Embarrassing racial and socioeconomic problems with expensive solutions had to be ignored while white leaders confined themselves to superficial concerns. For example, hoping to lure more conventions to Augusta, they tried to convince voters that the city's future hinged on approval of a proposal to allow the sale of mixed drinks and implied that Atlanta businessmen, fearful of competition, hoped the plan would be rejected.[33] The *Chronicle* thought it reasonable to as-

---

of the at-large system. Augusta *Chronicle*, January 9, 16, 1949. Gerrymandering prevented school board member W. C. Ervin, the first black elected official in Augusta, from seeking reelection. Augusta *Chronicle*, August 10, 1956.

30   Interview with B. L. Dent (black councilman) by the author, August 19, 1974; Minutes of the City Council, April 8, 1965, December 18, 1967, February 5, 1968, September 16, 1969.

31   Augusta *Chronicle*, August 28, 1967, September 19, 1969; Minutes of the City Council, October 6, 1969.

32   This was Grady Abrams' campaign slogan. Augusta *Chronicle*, October 3, 1968. Polarization within the black community is discussed in Joseph Yates Garrison, "The Augusta Black Community Since World War II" (M.A. thesis, University of Miami, 1971).

33   Augusta *Chronicle*, November 2, 3, 1965.

sume that "business" liked "culture," so construction of a "cultural center" was one of its favorite daydreams.[34]

Stymied by whites who refused to court their support or recognize their grievances, blacks suffered under conditions which were not part of boosters' portraits of Augusta. In the city's ghetto the mean income for wage earners was only 68 percent of the mean elsewhere and, in spite of the fact that 36 percent of ghetto residences were deteriorating, officials did not enforce minimum housing standards, arguing that to do so would simply leave the poor with no housing at all.[35] The percentage of land used for industry was more than five times higher for the ghetto than for Augusta as a whole while the percentage devoted to parks and playgrounds amounted to only one-third of the same figure for the entire city.[36] In a survey released in 1970 Augusta's low-income blacks cited the lack of recreational and meeting facilities in their neighborhoods as one of the major sources of their dissatisfaction.[37]

Instead of acknowledging that blacks suffered under these conditions, officials called attention to Augusta's urban renewal programs, which actually seemed to be geared toward producing attractive commercial sites instead of improving the living environment of the city's poor. In spite of protests and threats of legal action by blacks these projects allowed little input from those affected by them.[38] As has been the case with other urban renewal efforts, Augusta's produced a large amount of vacant land in a highly visible section of the city.[39]

34   Editorial, *Ibid.*, August 20, 1969.
35   U.S. Bureau of the Census, *Census of Population and Housing, 1970: Augusta, Georgia* (Washington, D.C.: U.S. Government Printing Office, 1971); City of Augusta, Georgia, "Report of the Department of Building Inspection," 1969, 1970, in City Hall, Augusta.
36   These figures were computed from statistics presented in a land use study made public in 1962 by the Augusta-Richmond County Planning Commission.
37   Augusta *Chronicle*, February 1, 1970.
38   Amos O. Holmes, Georgia Field Secretary, "A Supplement to Special Report on Augusta Urban Renewal Controversy," Container 521, in NAACP Papers, Library of Congress.
39   Augusta *Chronicle*, March 25, 1959, February 9, 1960. An explanation of slum residents' attitudes toward their surroundings appears in Marc Fried and Peggy Gliecher, "Some Sources of Residential Satisfaction in an Urban Slum," in Jewell Bellush and Murray Hausknecht (eds.), *Urban Renewal: People, Politics and Planning* (Garden City, N.Y.: Anchor, 1967), 120–35. See also Herbert J. Gans, "The Failure of Urban Renewal: A Critique and Some Proposals," *Commentary*, XXXIX (April, 1965), 28–37.

Meanwhile, in a less conspicuous area the first project's "rehabilitation" zone absorbed many of those being relocated. This neighborhood's increasing population and housing density suggested that instead of transforming a slum, urban renewal had merely transferred it.[40] As for commercial development, the McDonald's restaurant languishing in the middle of a huge cleared space symbolized the disappointing results.

White leaders devoted so much of their energies to the pursuit of new industry because they could see no other means of combating the city's rapid economic decay. As middle-class whites fled to the suburbs, Augusta's population fell from more than seventy thousand in 1960 to less than sixty thousand by 1970, while the population of Richmond County increased by twenty-seven thousand in the same period.[41] This exodus helped to explain why Augusta had the lowest median family income for whites of any city in Georgia and one of the lowest overall median family incomes in the urban South.[42]

While Augusta suffered, the influx of whites from the city and an increase in industrial and commercial development strengthened Richmond County's economy and widened the suburban–central city disparity; for example, in 1960 Augusta's median family income was 84.5 percent of Richmond County's, but by 1970 this figure had fallen to 77.5. Manufacturing and retail sales in the city also failed to keep pace and the growing differences in financial resources available to the respective governments reflected the heightened contrast in economic conditions.[43]

---

40   Between 1960 and 1970 the rehabilitation area's population increased by 30 percent while the population of the census tract in which it was located declined by 17 percent. *Census of Population and Housing, 1970: Augusta, Georgia*; U.S. Bureau of the Census, *Census of Population and Housing, 1960: Augusta, Georgia* (Washington, D.C.: U.S. Government Printing Office, 1963).

41   *Census of Population and Housing, 1960: Augusta, Georgia*; *Census of Population and Housing, 1970: Augusta, Georgia*.

42   U.S. Bureau of the Census, *County and City Data Book, 1972: A Statistical Abstract Supplement* (Washington, D.C.: U.S. Government Printing Office, 1973).

43   *County and City Data Book, 1972*; U.S. Bureau of the Census, *County and City Data Book, 1962: A Statistical Abstract Supplement* (Washington, D.C.: U.S. Government Printing Office, 1962). The city's manufacturing payroll, which was 78 percent of the county's in 1960, had declined to 59 percent by 1970. Augusta's total operating revenue, 42 percent of the county's in 1960, shrank to only 20 percent by 1970.

After the mid-1950s attempts to allow Augusta to share in suburban affluence through annexation failed because the only outlying areas interested in joining the city were unwanted black subdivisions which would bring more problems and demands without an equivalent boost to the city's tax revenue.[44] Proannexationists surmised, probably correctly, that the exodus of middle-class whites further damaged Augusta's prospects for growth. Yet, without the benefits of economic expansion, living conditions in the city would not be made attractive enough to dissuade those thinking of moving to the suburbs. Consequently, Augusta's white leaders persisted in their belief that the only hope of saving their town lay in utilizing the existing resources to sell it as something it was not.

While perhaps unaware of the problems faced by white officials, Augusta's blacks found their socioeconomic and political deprivation an inescapable reality. On May 11, 1970, slightly more than eight years after the initial triumph over total segregation, anger over problems long hidden or ignored erupted in a bloody and destructive riot during which police killed six blacks, all shot in the back.[45] The violence offered clear testimony that Augustans were not too busy to hate; the facade of artificial progress had concealed a festering core of bitterness and frustration. Yet even after the riot white officials refused to face reality. On the day after the violence Mayor Beckum told a tense city: "Everything is calm and we are desperately trying to make them more calm!" To reporters he spoke of the city's "good image," insisting, "We've always had harmonious relations between the races." By the end of 1970 blind boosterism again reigned supreme as the *Chronicle* spoke proudly of a beefed-up police force which it claimed was for the protection of "all the people" and pointed to new "progress" in school integration which had actually come as the result of court decisions.[46]

At different times business and civic leaders were actually

44   Charles Gary Swint, "The Augusta Annexation Attempt of 1966," *Richmond County History*, VIII (Summer, 1971), 27–32; Beckum interview; Dent interview. Augusta was the only major city in Georgia which failed to annex in the 1960s.

45   The best study of the riot is the Southern Regional Council's *Augusta, Georgia, and Jackson State University: Southern Episodes in a National Tragedy* (Atlanta: Southern Regional Council, 1970).

46   *Newsweek*, May 25, 1970, p. 71; Augusta *Chronicle*, December 27, 28, 1970.

on both sides of the struggle to overturn white supremacy in Augusta. By encouraging a strategic retreat from the reactionary folly advocated by Roy Harris and some of the old Independent spokesmen, image-conscious proponents of economic growth played an important role in shaping their city's initial positive response to the civil rights challenges of the 1960s. Ironically, however, the same concern for Augusta's reputation that prompted their early cooperation ultimately encouraged them to de-emphasize black problems and direct attention and support to cosmetic improvements designed to make the community more attractive to industry. By embracing this strategy, political and economic representatives managed to use a few token changes and their own optimistic pronouncements to camouflage their city's weaknesses.[47] Accordingly, after desegregation of public facilities in 1962 boosters assured relocating industrialists that Augusta was a paragon of racial harmony. Meanwhile, the ascendance of the economic growth-good government consensus helped to thwart black efforts to utilize the political process to secure responses to their problems. Nonpartisan, depoliticized decision making and at-large council elections may have impressed potential investors, but they also frustrated efforts to call attention to the plight of the city's blacks.[48]

Augusta's influential businessmen and industrial promoters might have been willing to accept and even advocate more concessions to blacks had incoming industrialists applied pressure, but this coercion apparently never came.[49] In fact, southern industry-seekers probably overestimated the importance that business executives actually attached to a city's race rela-

47   The efforts of Augusta boosters strongly parallel those of New South advocates. See Gaston, *New South Creed*. Gaston's chapter entitled "The Emperor's New Clothes," pp. 189–214, is especially pertinent.

48   Nonpartisanship and at-large elections were compatible with the efforts of influential urban businessmen to utilize the resources of their municipal governments to promote economic growth. See Williams and Adrian, *Four Cities*, 284–85. On the other hand, these two conditions appeared related to urban racial conflicts, especially in the South. See James Q. Wilson, *Negro Politics* (Glencoe, Ill.: Free Press, 1960), 25–33.

49   A survey conducted in 1966 revealed that half of the city's fifteen most influential leaders came from the business and industrial community. Harold L. Nix and Charles J. Dudley, "Community Social Analysis of Augusta-Richmond County," mimeographed report dated February, 1960, in Institute of Community and Area Development, University of Georgia, Athens.

tions reputation. Many of the industries which came to the South in the 1950s and early 1960s accepted the caste system and even took advantage of it. For example, companies with labor needs entailing particularly arduous or distasteful tasks at low pay often sought a predominantly black work force. As a result, some cities advertised their labor surpluses with figures broken down by race. Because many of the firms which came to the region did so seeking cheap, nonunion labor and lower taxes, they were less interested in a community's social progress than companies whose operations were more sophisticated and required skilled and higher-paid employees.

A Tennessee survey of industrial location factors, one of the few to pose the question directly, revealed that only 4 of 308 corporate planners felt an area's success in making racial adjustments had any bearing on its attractiveness as an industrial site. Instead of requesting southern cities to alter their customs drastically, some companies expected little. As late as the 1960s one industrialist was delighted to learn that if his firm built a new plant in Augusta, racially segregated toilets would be unnecessary.[50] Overall, businessmen seemed more interested in the absence of labor turmoil than a city's progress toward racial equality.[51] In view of these attitudes Augusta's boosters must have seen their unremitting positivism as the best approach to pursuing economic growth while maintaining racial stability within their community.

In contrast to Atlanta, concern for economic growth did not open the door to continuously expanding social, political, and economic opportunities for blacks in Augusta. Several factors favored Atlanta blacks in this regard. First, the Georgia capital's commitment to moderation had been painstakingly forged by long-time Mayor William B. Hartsfield whereas Augusta's desegregation of public facilities in 1962 was a last-second attempt to stave off embarrassing protests during Masters week.

50 Ronald E. Carrier and William R. Schriver, *Plant Location Analysis: An Investigation of Plant Locations in Tennessee* (Memphis: Bureau of Business and Economic Research, Memphis State University, 1969); Beckum interview.

51 I have collected numerous industrial location surveys whose data support this conclusion. For example, see A. C. Flora, "Industrial Location in South Carolina," *Business and Economic Review*, X (January, 1964), 1–4; Robert P. Boblett, "Factors in Industrial Location," *Appraisal Journal*, XXXV (October, 1967), 518–26.

Second, Atlanta's large, well organized black community looked back on a stronger, more venerable tradition of activism than did Augusta's. Finally, the Atlanta area's phenomenal growth and carefully cultivated image as a sophisticated commercial center encouraged influential white businessmen and politicians to keep their city's reputation untarnished. Augusta's growth was not dramatic enough to thrust it into the national spotlight.[52]

In the postwar decades Augusta's white leaders managed to stand by the Independents' 1946 promise to preserve white supremacy, forsaking this pledge only briefly in the interest of the city's economic future. Even so, the city's businessmen certainly did more to promote the cause of equality than other respected whites like the ministers who denounced a small group of fellow clergymen for supporting desegregation. This attack was so intense that the prointegration pastors backed down and the potentially positive influence of the church was lost.[53] High-ranking officers at Fort Gordon, a large army installation near Augusta, refused to become involved in the city's racial troubles, thereby forfeiting a chance to wield the base's sizable payroll in behalf of integration.[54]

Through its role in the initial desegregation of public facilities Augusta's business community probably contributed as much to the advancement of blacks as any other group of whites in the city. Although the advocates of economic growth did only what they felt necessary to protect Augusta's image, they might have done more had blacks organized more large-scale protests that called attention to the city's unsolved problems, and more important, threatened its reputation for moderation and order. Also businessmen might have played a greater role in combating discrimination had the pro–civil rights sentiments emanating from Washington penetrated more deeply into the minds

52   For a description of Atlanta's progressive image see Helen Fuller, "Atlanta is Different," *New Republic*, February 2, 1959, pp. 8–11. For an assessment of the traditionally strong black leadership class in Atlanta see Floyd Hunter, *Community Power Structure: A Study of Decision Makers* (Chapel Hill: University of North Carolina Press, 1953), 130–32.

53   Augusta *Chronicle*, April 30, May 1, 6, 1961.

54   Neither Millard Beckum nor Roy Rollins recalled any pressure from Fort Gordon officials. Beckum interview; interview with Roy E. Rollins by the author, August 20, 1974.

and consciences of the industrial executives who established new plants in the South.

For all their progressive pretensions Augusta's boosters never fully transcended their region's racial heritage. As a result they employed minimal concessions and misleading rhetoric to obscure the ugly realities of prejudice and repression in their city. Still, their self-serving tokenism could not have remained viable in a nation willing to make its professed belief in racial equality a meaningful and permanent commitment.

ROBERT CORLEY

IN SEARCH OF RACIAL HARMONY

BIRMINGHAM BUSINESS LEADERS AND
DESEGREGATION, 1950–1963

From Birmingham's very inception in 1871, the history of this
Alabama city has been entwined with the fortunes and decisions
of its businessmen. Birmingham's founders were bankers, land
speculators, and railroad executives who were drawn to this in-
conspicuous valley in Jefferson County by their knowledge of
the untold mineral wealth which laced its foothills, and by the
impending intersection of two major rail routes—the Alabama
and Chattanooga, and the South and North Alabama. Organizing the Elyton Land Company, this varied coalition of businessmen mapped out a symmetrical pattern of streets and avenues
along the rail lines, and during the next two decades, proceeded
to turn a cornfield into a thriving industrial metropolis.[1]

After 1880, and especially after the advent of the Tennessee
Coal, Iron and Railroad Company (TCI) in 1886, Birmingham's
economy was based on the production of iron, steel, and coal.
Attracted to the growing number of industrial and mining jobs

---

1 For the best short summary of Birmingham's founding and early years, see
Carl V. Harris, *Political Power in Birmingham, 1871–1921* (Knoxville: University of Tennessee Press, 1977), 12–38.

around the city were native white and black southerners and a significant number of immigrants, led by the Germans and followed by the Irish and Italians. Blacks, however, quickly established themselves as the largest minority group in the Birmingham area, growing from about 10 percent of the population in 1870 to about 40 percent in 1900, a proportion which remained fairly constant throughout the first half of this century, in spite of substantial white migration into the city and black migration to the North. Indeed by 1920, among cities of one hundred thousand or more persons, Birmingham ranked highest in the nation in its percentage of Negro population. Thus, Birmingham after 1900 was characterized primarily by its heavy industry, its blue-collar workers, and its large black population, all of which presented city leaders with unique problems.[2]

However, as both Carl V. Harris and Blaine A. Brownell clearly demonstrate, Birmingham's leaders were able to establish their dominance without great difficulty. Both these historians agree that political power and influence in Birmingham after 1910 was concentrated in the hands of the top 20 percent of the population, a group which Brownell characterizes as the "commercial-civic elite." In Harris' concurrent view, political power in Birmingham "was roughly proportional to economic power"; therefore, on every political issue which the business elite considered important, the elite more often than not emerged the victor. The most prominent members of this elite group were the iron and steel companies, led by TCI, which had been acquired by United States Steel in 1907, but also including at least half a dozen other industrial firms. Other businesses contributing significantly to the elite were the utility companies, the larger real estate firms, the downtown merchants, and the leading banks.

While this leadership group was by no means monolithic, frequently disagreeing on specific issues where individual in-

2 *Ibid.*, 17–24; Carl V. Harris, "Reforms in Government Control of Negroes in Birmingham, Alabama, 1890–1920," *Journal of Southern History*, XXXVIII (November, 1972), 570; Paul B. Worthman, "Working Class Mobility in Birmingham, Alabama, 1880–1914," in Tamara K. Hareven (ed.), *Anonymous Americans* (Englewood Cliffs, N.J.: Prentice-Hall, 1971), 175; Paul B. Worthman, "Black Workers and Labor Unions in Birmingham, Alabama, 1897–1904," *Labor History*, X (Summer, 1969), 379.

terests conflicted, it was generally committed to the doctrine of "business progressivism." Simply stated, this doctrine promoted economic growth as the primary cure for all social ills, since all citizens theoretically would derive some eventual benefits from an expanding local economy. On questions relating to the problems of Birmingham's blacks, business progressives usually maintained a laissez faire attitude, accepting the dominant assumptions about racial segregation and depending on private welfare agencies to care for the disadvantaged.[3] Once it consolidated its position of influence during this century's first two decades, Birmingham's "commercial-civic elite" was able to sustain its hegemony in local affairs without serious challenge until the civil rights issue emerged in full force during the mid-1950s.

The black discontent which was manifested in the civil rights movement actually had its roots during the crisis years of World War II. As several historians have observed, the war that was then being waged to protect democracy and freedom heightened black awareness of the inequities and injustices which pervaded the nation, and especially the South. Moreover, by according blacks new opportunities both in the armed forces and on the home front, the war disrupted traditional racial patterns and removed many obstacles to economic advancement. As a consequence, World War II instilled within southern Negroes both a new race consciousness and a determination to strive for a higher position in society.[4]

These new Negro aspirations produced divergent views among Birmingham's business leaders. In a 1947 speech, for

3   Harris, *Political Power in Birmingham*, 270–71; Blaine A. Brownell, *The Urban Ethos in the South, 1920–1930* (Baton Rouge: Louisiana State University Press, 1975), 47; Blaine A. Brownell, "Birmingham, Alabama: New South City in the 1920's," *Journal of Southern History*, XXXVIII (February, 1972), 24–25, 42–45. Unless otherwise noted, terms like *business leader* or *community leader* will refer to white businessmen only. Birmingham has always had a small black business community, but its influence before 1963 was minimal, especially when compared to black businessmen in other southern cities such as Atlanta or Durham.

4   Richard M. Dalfiume, "The 'Forgotten Years' of the Negro Revolution," *Journal of American History*, LV (June, 1968), 90–106; Richard Polenberg, *War and Society: The United States, 1941–1945* (New York: J. B. Lippincott, 1972), 99–130; and George Brown Tindall, *The Emergence of the New South, 1913–1945* (Baton Rouge: Louisiana State University Press, 1967), 711–21.

instance, First National Bank president John C. Persons expressed a common opinion of conservative city leaders when he declared that segregation was "wise and essential for the peace, protection, comfort and convenience of the Negro." From Persons' perspective, moreover, there was little reason for blacks to be discontented. The southern Negro, he believed, had made great progress under segregation, having "moved from slavery to respected citizenship." And now, concluded Persons, "he is being educated in our public schools, he enjoys the protection of our laws and the benefits of our social services, and by and large he is happy in the South."[5]

At the same time, however, there were other white leaders in Birmingham who, while they accepted segregation, did not share the conservatives' sanguine views on race relations. These moderate leaders felt that many of the problems encountered by Birmingham's Negroes in such areas as housing, health care, recreation, and police protection needed attention, and they also believed that the white and black communities could work together to formulate definitive solutions. Furthermore, there was always the possibility that "irresponsible" elements might gain control in the black community unless whites took positive action to shift legitimate black dissatisfaction into constructive channels. This moderate faction of the white elite, accordingly, determined to organize a functioning interracial group, composed of "responsible" white and black community leaders who would seek solutions to Negro problems within the framework of established racial customs.

Initially, the moderates attempted to organize a local chapter of the National Urban League. Between 1946 and 1950, a concerted campaign to raise money for the proposed chapter was conducted by Nelson Jackson, the southern field director for NUL, together with a local biracial board of directors headed by Dr. Henry Edmonds, the former minister of a socially prominent church. Although the Urban League effort encountered some opposition from conservative whites and a few moderates, it was very nearly successful, as several business leaders raised four thousand dollars in seed funding. However, the reemer-

5   John C. Persons, "The South," 6–8, undated copy in 1948 files, Robert Jemison, Jr., Papers, Birmingham Public Library (BPL) Archives.

gence of the volatile race issue in Alabama politics following the 1948 Dixiecrat revolt contributed to the growing concern that the Urban League might be a disruptive outside influence. Consequently, the early support for an Urban League chapter within the business community rapidly evaporated. Finally in late February, 1950, a discouraged Nelson Jackson was forced to admit defeat and to discontinue any further efforts on behalf of the NUL in Birmingham.[6]

With an Urban League chapter no longer a possibility, its moderate white supporters were compelled to seek other avenues for improving Birmingham's race relations. By 1950, dynamite bombs had already destroyed three Negro homes involved in a residential zoning dispute, and the Ku Klux Klan had been openly terrorizing both black and white citizens. Meantime, city officials had neither solved these bombings nor seemed able, or willing, to suppress the Klan. With racial tensions at such a critical point, most business and community leaders recognized the need to deal in some organized manner with Birmingham's race problems or face the consequences of racial turmoil. As a result, the moderates, who included industrial, financial, and opinion leaders, convinced those who had been skeptical about an Urban League chapter to join them in organizing a local Interracial Committee which would be funded in part by the four thousand dollars already in hand. According to the moderates' plan, the Interracial Committee would become a division of the Jefferson County Coordinating Council of Social Forces, an independent agency designated by the Community Chest to oversee and rationalize its numerous social welfare programs. On July 20, 1950, Woodward Iron Company president Bradford Colcord, on behalf of a prominent and concerned biracial group, petitioned the Coordinating Council board to create an Interracial Committee of twenty-five black and twenty-five white members, and to hire a Negro executive director who would devote full time to the problems of black housing, health,

6   Edward S. LaMonte, "Politics and Welfare in Birmingham, Alabama: 1900–1975" (Ph.D. dissertation, University of Chicago, 1976), 261–69. The effort to form an Urban League chapter is also vividly told in a series of memos from Nelson Jackson to Urban League executive director Lester B. Granger. These memos, written between 1948 and 1950, are available in the National Urban League Papers, Library of Congress.

education, and police protection. The board unanimously agreed to the proposal, and in September, the full council membership, which was heavily weighted with prominent businessmen, added its endorsement.[7]

The support of Birmingham's business leaders was also clearly evident when the Interracial Committee held its first meeting on April 24, 1951. Of the twenty-five white members, fourteen were leading business executives, such as Arthur Wiebel, president of TCI, Claude Lawson, president of Sloss-Sheffield Steel and Iron Company, and Joe H. Woodward II, a top official of Woodward Iron Company. In marked contrast, there were only three black businessmen on the committee; one was the manager of an insurance office, another was co-owner of a realty company, and the third owned a funeral home.[8] Although these blacks certainly had significant influence in their own community, the whites obviously had greater access to the centers of power in Birmingham and thus could more easily control the priorities and activities of the Interracial Committee.

At this first meeting, the committee approved a statement of objectives which mandated it to "promote public understanding and cooperative relationships" between blacks and whites, to "provide an opportunity for the full and free discussion . . . of the desired ends of interracial collaboration," and most important, to deal with the "interracial aspects of problems involving health and sanitation, industry and labor, education, child and family welfare, housing, police and fire protection, transportation, and cultural and recreational opportunities." Quickly realizing the futility of dealing with such a broad range of problems all at once, the committee voted three months later to narrow its areas of concern to six, appointing subcommittees on hospitals, day care, housing, recreation, transportation, and Negro police.[9]

7   LaMonte, "Politics and Welfare in Birmingham," 271–72; Jackson to Granger, February 28, 1950, in Urban League Papers; Coordinating Council Board Minutes, July 20, 1950, and Coordinating Council Minutes, September 26, 1950, in Jefferson County Coordinating Council of Social Forces Papers, BPL Archives (hereafter cited as Coordinating Council Papers).
8   Interracial Committee Membership List, attached to Interracial Committee Minutes, April 24, 1951, in Coordinating Council Papers.
9   Interracial Committee Minutes, April 24, June 15, 1951, in Coordinating Council Papers.

During the first few years of their activity, some subcommittees proceeded cautiously and gave priority to maintaining Birmingham's tenuous racial harmony, often at the risk of reinforcing the established racial order. For instance, the hospital subcommittee evidenced great reluctance in helping qualified Negro doctors eliminate racial barriers in Birmingham hospitals. In order to affiliate with a hospital, a doctor first had to become a member of the Jefferson County Medical Society. In the spring of 1953, the medical society deleted the word *white* from its membership requirements, apparently signaling its readiness to accept a qualified Negro doctor. The hospital subcommittee noted the society's action as a "progressive" step, but those white members who were also doctors were reluctant to push the matter further. Citing their fear of a "blackball," they counseled potential black applicants to wait "until the situation seems more favorable." While the subcommittee discussed this matter often over the next two years, it did not propose a resolution urging the medical society to admit blacks, nor did it put forth its own candidate, even though one of its own members was a Negro doctor practicing in a Negro hospital.[10] By maintaining silence on this question, the hospital subcommittee avoided controversy, but at the same time, it all but assured that the medical society, and thus hospital staffs, would remain exclusively white.

However, other subcommittees were less cautious. At the same time the hospital subcommittee was delaying action on Negro doctors, the subcommittee on Negro police was actively seeking a solution to the problem of inadequate police protection for Negro areas. Since Birmingham was the only major southern city without any Negro police officers, the subcommittee planned to petition the city commission to hire a minimum of six to patrol only Negro areas. Before submitting a formal proposal, however, the group decided to survey other southern cities employing black policemen and then to publicize its findings "in an effort to create a favorable atmosphere." The survey's positive findings were reported in a pamphlet that the subcommittee distributed to a select group of leading citizens in the spring of 1953. The pamphlet was a model of cogency and reasonableness

10   Interracial Committee Minutes, June 23, December 9, 1953, June 1, 1954, May 17, 1955, in Coordinating Council Papers.

as it detailed Birmingham's regional isolation with regard to Negro police. In addition, it provided the opinions of leading black and white citizens of Birmingham, who were nearly unanimous in favor of Negro police; the lone dissenter felt it was the wrong time to consider the matter.[11]

Unfortunately, despite the pamphlet's persuasive arguments, it failed to generate the anticipated public response. In June, 1953, the executive secretary reported to the full Interracial Committee that there had been few individual responses to the pamphlet and that "almost no groups" had expressed any opinion. Because the subcommittee had expended so much effort on its publicity campaign, its failure to achieve the desired public support for hiring Negro police left the group uncertain about the next step. Finally, in July, 1954, the subcommittee adopted a different strategy, agreeing to proceed "without publicity" and to consult privately on the question with the city commission and the personnel board, both of which would have to approve any black applicants.[12]

Thus, as the Interracial Committee entered its fourth year of active existence, the accomplishments of its subcommittees constituted a mixed record. Some, such as the hospital subcommittee, had shunned opportunities to make breakthroughs in Birmingham's race relations; others, such as the police subcommittee, had taken positive steps to achieve their objectives and thus improve the quality of black life in the city. More important, Birmingham had a functioning interracial organization in which both blacks and whites could grapple with the city's racial problems and perhaps reach mutual solutions. However, in that spring of 1954, the U.S. Supreme Court ruled in the case of *Brown v. The Board of Education of Topeka* that public school desegregation was unconstitutional, and this decision eventually determined not only the potential effectiveness of the Interracial Committee, but its very existence as well.

The initial reaction of both black and white leaders in Bir-

11   Subcommittee on Negro Police Minutes, January 17, 1952, Subcommittee on Negro Police to Executive Committee, February 18, 1952, and "Report on a Study of Negro Police Made by the Jefferson County Coordinating Council of Social Forces," Spring, 1953, all in Coordinating Council Papers.
12   Interracial Committee Report to Coordinating Council, June 23, 1953, Interracial Committee Minutes, June 18, 1953, and Subcommittee on Negro Police Minutes, July 28, 1954, all in Coordinating Council Papers.

mingham was tentative and cautious, and consequently, there were few overt appearances of racial controversy during 1954 and 1955. This period of relative calm permitted the Interracial Committee to score some significant victories for improved race relations. The transportation subcommittee, for instance, had been pressing owners of downtown office buildings to desegregate their elevators, and in December, 1955, the subcommittee chairman reported that "with only one or two exceptions," all elevators were open to both races. In addition, the Interracial Committee organized a biracial "Educational Institute on Race Relations," which was held at Birmingham-Southern College on March 31 and April 1, 1955. Significantly, the committee convinced city officials to permit nonsegregated seating at the meetings because admission would be restricted, and the institute would be held on college, not public, property. Thus, when the approximately eight hundred black and white delegates gathered on the Birmingham campus for this institute, they constituted the first sanctioned desegregated audience of this size in the city's history.[13]

Early in 1956, however, the racial climate in Alabama and Birmingham heated up considerably. Militant prosegregation groups, such as the White Citizens Councils, began to organize in a growing reaction to new black initiatives against Jim Crow, represented most notably by Martin Luther King's bus boycott in Montgomery and Autherine Lucy's abortive effort to desegregate the University of Alabama. As Birmingham's most prominent example of biracial cooperation, the Interracial Committee soon became the focus of attack for segregationists, who charged that the committee's goals were "identical with, or closely parallel to NAACP objectives."[14]

13   The best study of Birmingham's racial climate during 1954 is George R. Stewart, "Birmingham's Reaction to the 1954 Desegregation Decision" (M.A. thesis, Samford University, 1967). See also memo from L. N. Shannon to Subcommittee on Transportation, December 20, 1955, in Coordinating Council Papers; *Southern School News*, May 4, 1955; Program for "An Educational Institute on Race Relations," in Roberta Morgan Papers, BPL Archives.
14   Benjamin Muse, *Ten Years of Prelude* (New York: Viking Press, 1964), 52–54; Paul Anthony, "A Survey of the Resistance Groups of Alabama, July 1956" (Field Study in Southern Regional Council [SRC] Papers, Atlanta); American States' Rights Association, "Memorandum to Members," March, 1956, in Vertical File, Tutwiler Collection of Southern History and Literature, BPL.

Such assaults and the generally worsening racial climate soon took their toll on the members of the committee, straining fragile lines of communication between the races and threatening the group's existence. Attendance at meetings dropped off, internal disputes over policy flared up, and after a two-month search, the nominating committee was still unable to secure a chairman for 1956. Furthermore, as a direct consequence of the segregationist attacks on the committee, numerous contributions and pledges to the Community Chest were canceled in 1956, and some of the committee's strongest white supporters began to question its continued usefulness in a climate so filled with racial tension.[15]

On April 2, 1956, the Community Chest and Red Cross executive committees met jointly to consider their support of the Interracial Committee. Present at this impressive meeting of white community and business leaders were some of the Interracial Committee's earliest supporters, along with some conservative backers of the White Citizens Councils. After some discussion, this group voted to dissolve the Interracial Committee because it constituted a "campaign hazard" for the Community Chest and the Red Cross, and because the "present climate of thinking" had changed, especially among "the Negro members concerned." On April 6, the Community Chest Board of Directors endorsed the executive committee's action, and a week later, the Coordinating Council board made it unanimous, thus officially terminating the work of the Interracial Committee.[16]

The demise of the Interracial Committee was a crippling blow for the racial moderates in Birmingham's business elite. Since 1951, the committee had been the city's primary forum for the discussion of black problems, and the participation of many of Birmingham's most prominent white leaders had afforded the group both respectability and visibility. Moreover, the commit-

15 Interracial Committee, Nominating Committee Minutes, December 19, 1955, and Executive Committee Minutes, February 2, 1956, in Coordinating Council Papers; LaMonte, "Politics and Welfare in Birmingham," 275–76; and Birmingham *Post-Herald*, April 2, 1956.

16 Joint Community Chest-Red Cross Executive Committees Minutes, April 2, 1956, Community Chest, Board of Directors Minutes, April 6, 1956, and Coordinating Council, Resolution, April 13, 1956, all in Coordinating Council Papers. Some business leaders mounted a brief effort to persuade the city commission to appoint a successor biracial group, but their pleas were rejected.

tee had served as an invaluable symbol of biracial cooperation and trust. Once the tenuous lines of interracial communication had been severed, however, both black and white community leaders abdicated their responsibility for maintaining racial harmony and withdrew into their respective communities, each blaming the other for their failure to communicate or preserve order.

The silence of moderate voices after 1956 permitted Birmingham to become the scene of some of the most violent episodes in the desegregation conflict, as white supremacist ideologues and civil rights activists clashed head on without restraint. While the Negro rights advocates preached nonviolence and practiced it, white extremists were not similarly constrained. Between 1957 and 1963, there were at least eighteen race-related bombings in Birmingham, and in the lone case which was solved, the all-white jury recommended probation. Two of these bombings involved the home and church of the Reverend Fred L. Shuttlesworth, a local rights leader who was also attacked and severely beaten in 1957 when he attempted to enroll his daughter in a white high school. The Ku Klux Klan and other extremist groups were unfettered by any official sanction during the late 1950s, and although community leaders spoke out consistently against Klan tactics, the group's acts of violence and intimidation just as consistently went unpunished. Thus by 1960, Birmingham had earned a deserved reputation as the "toughest city in the South" where, in the words of New York *Times* reporter Harrison Salisbury, "every channel of communication, every medium of mutual interest, every reasoned approach, every inch of middle ground has been fragmented."[17]

With the moderate faction of the business community thus isolated, the conservatives momentarily gained the ascendancy and became Birmingham's most visible spokesmen. A number of them even became financial backers and members of states-rights and prosegregation groups, such as the White Citizens Councils and the Committee for Constitutional Government. Despite the certainty of their convictions, these conservative lead-

17   Michael Cooper Nichols, "'Cities Are What Men Make Them': Birmingham, Alabama Faces the Civil Rights Movement, 1963" (Senior honors thesis, Brown University, 1974), 84–108; Joseph Ellwanger, President, Birmingham Council on Human Relations, to Editor, Birmingham *News*, September 1, 1963; *Time*, December 15, 1958, p. 16; and New York *Times*, April 12, 1960.

ers exhibited an acute sensitivity to any criticism of Birmingham's worsening racial climate or of their own role in the defense of segregation. In an effort to counteract this criticism and erase the city's "erroneous" image, a number of business leaders in 1959 organized a "Metropolitan Audit" to examine Birmingham's assets and then report them to the nation. This audit was conducted under the auspices of the Southern Institute of Management, but the data itself was gathered by local leaders. To the dismay of the audit's prominent backers, the survey report, published in 1960, concluded that Birmingham's leaders were "marked by a tendency to be negative and defensive," especially when dealing with racial problems. Further contributing to this hypersensitivity, the report added, was a vague "feeling of insecurity" about the city's economic future. The audit's finding shocked many in the business community and forced these leaders for the first time since 1956 to give renewed consideration to the city's long-standing racial troubles.[18]

Then, in the spring of 1961, an event occurred which finally prompted business leaders to take the central role again in guiding Birmingham toward racial harmony. On May 14, 1961, "Freedom Riders," sent out by the Congress of Racial Equality to desegregate interstate buses and terminals across the South, arrived in Birmingham as scheduled. At the Trailways station to meet them were a large number of Klansmen, a few newsmen, and no policemen. In the melee which ensued, nine people were severely injured, only two of whom had any connection with the Freedom Riders. The police did not arrive until fifteen or twenty minutes after the attack ended, and by that time, the guilty Klansmen had disappeared.[19]

The beatings and the absence of the police produced an outburst of indignation from Birmingham's leaders. On the following day, the *News* summed up the feelings of most citizens with the headline to their front-page editorial which read, "People are

18   Numan V. Bartley, *The Rise of Massive Resistance: Race and Politics in the South During the 1950's* (Baton Rouge: Louisiana State University Press, 1969), 87–89; Committee for Constitutional Government to Robert Jemison, February 24, 1957, and Executive Committee, Birmingham Metropolitan Audit, to Jemison, January 12, 1959, both in Jemison Papers; Southern Institute of Management, Inc., "The Birmingham Metropolitan Audit, Preliminary Report, 1960," Report Number 1, pp. 13–14, Report Number 2, pp. 1, 6–7, 13–14, 24–25, Report Number 3, pp. 22–25.
19   Birmingham *News*, May 15, 1961; New York *Times*, May 16, 1961.

asking: 'Where were the police?'" Although the editorial was typically critical of the Freedom Riders and their methods, the *News* placed the entire blame for the violence squarely on Bull Connor, the city's flamboyant segregationist public safety commissioner. In the past, the *News*, which was a prominent voice for the business elite, had been circumspect in its criticism of Connor, despite some of his questionable tactics against dissenters and civil rights activists. But in this instance, the *News* was blunt in its denunciation, charging that Connor knew about the potential for violence at the bus depot, yet did nothing. The editorial then concluded with a call to action: "Today many are asking 'Where were the police? *The News* asks that too, but *The News* also asks: When will the people demand that fear and hatred be driven from the streets?"[20]

Birmingham business leaders were quick to recognize the harm which such disorders could do to the city's fragile economy if they should continue. Sidney W. Smyer, an erstwhile supporter of the Citizens Councils and the president of the Chamber of Commerce in 1961, admitted that "these racial incidents have given us a black eye we'll be a long time trying to forget." In an effort to forge a new approach to race relations and to prevent further violence, three civic and business groups— the Chamber of Commerce, the Committee of 100, and the Birmingham Downtown Improvement Association (BDIA)—resolved in late May to form a joint biracial committee to study the "means of creating better relations with all groups, regardless of their race or religion."[21] With this action, and with the open admission that Birmingham's economic future was at stake, the business elite were clearly hoping to reopen lines of interracial communication and lead the city back to racial peace. As events would prove, however, they faced an arduous task.

Part of the difficulty stemmed from the controversial nature of what these businessmen were attempting. In the heated racial atmosphere of the early 1960s, even the hint of a compromise

20   Birmingham *News*, May 15, 1961. Duard LeGrand, then city editor at the *Post-Herald*, later stated that Connor and the police had to have known about the time and place of the Freedom Riders' arrival, because the only way LeGrand himself knew was by calling the police department. Interview with Duard LeGrand by the author, March 29, 1977.
21   *Wall Street Journal*, May 26, 1961; Washington *Post*, June 14, 1961; Birmingham *News*, May 19, May 23, 1961; Birmingham Downtown Improvement Association Board Minutes, May 23, 1961, in Jemison Papers.

with black demands was regarded as a profound betrayal of principle by most segregationists. Consequently, then, a great deal of the work towards racial harmony had to be done in secret, which made it all the harder to build broad community support for the leaders' objectives. Nevertheless, by the fall of 1961, a small and confidential group of businessmen was attempting to organize support for limited school desegregation plans similar to those which had succeeded in Dallas and Atlanta.[22]

Business and other community leaders were also willing to make accommodations on the desegregation of parks and other public recreational facilities, and in fact, were quite open about it. When Federal Judge H. H. Grooms ruled on October 24, 1961, that these facilities must be desegregated, the response from Connor and the other commissioners was that the parks would be closed instead. The opposition of community leaders to such a drastic step was immediate and resolute. Some business leaders who had previously been silent now spoke out boldly in favor of keeping the parks open, even if it meant desegregation. Under the threat of additional economic losses, the *Wall Street Journal* observed, Birmingham's leadership had exhibited a "significant realignment of forces." The BDIA board of directors, for example, met in executive session a week after the ruling and decided that "ways and means must be found to keep public facilities operating without drastic measures." On December 12, they unanimously passed a well publicized resolution to the city commission, urging its members to "take no action which would close down or eliminate the facilities for better living that have made our community healthy and progressive." In addition, the Chamber of Commerce and both daily newspapers actively supported open parks, even in the face of late-night threatening phone calls. Finally, the business leaders circulated a petition for open recreational facilities and obtained 1,260 signatures. When the petition was presented to the city commissioners in early January, 1962, they angrily rejected it. On January 15, the parks were closed.[23]

22   Norman Jimerson, Executive Director, Alabama Council on Human Relations, to Paul Rilling, September 18, November 9, 1961, Jimerson to Leslie W. Dunbar, October 26, 1961, all in SRC Papers.
23   *Southern School News*, November, 1961; *Wall Street Journal*, March 12, 1962; Jimerson to Dunbar, October 26, 1961, Jimerson to Rilling, December 27, 1961, both in SRC Papers; BDIA Board of Directors Minutes, October 31, December 12, 1961, in Jemison Papers; Birmingham *Post-Herald*, January 11, 1962.

This dispute over open parks drove a deep wedge between the city commission and Birmingham's business elite. Since February, 1961, at the behest of Chamber president Smyer, a Birmingham Bar Association committee had been studying the procedures for changing the city's form of government. Following the Freedom Riders incident and the park closings, support for the governmental change grew rapidly among businessmen, who viewed it as a convenient way to remove the intransigent commissioners before the next election and replace them with more conciliatory government leaders. However, since most of these businessmen lived in the suburbs around the city, they chose to stay in the background, providing substantial financial support but declining to lend their prestige to the effort. As a consequence, the drive to change the form of government was spearheaded publicly by a new leadership group, the Young Men's Business Club, which backed two of its members, attorneys David Vann and Erskine Smith, in organizing a grassroots movement called "Birmingham Citizens for Progress."[24]

The "Citizens for Progress" prepared petitions to be signed at polling places on the day of a special election in late August, 1962. These petitions requested an election, as provided by state law, which would permit Birmingham's voters to choose the form of government they wanted. The idea was favorably received, as over 11,000 voters signed the forms, well in excess of the 7,500 needed. On November 6, 1962, as city voters cast their ballots in the regular election, they also decided the fate of their local government. When the votes were counted, the mayor-council form had beaten the commission form by nearly 3,000 votes, and another election to choose the members of this new government was immediately set for March, 1963.[25]

In the meantime, as business leaders were striving to change the city government, they were also working quietly with black leaders in an effort to head off a growing Negro protest movement. There had been intermittent contacts between whites and blacks since the summer of 1961, and these had in-

24 LaMonte, "Politics and Welfare in Birmingham," 284–88; Mary Phyllis Harrison, "A Change in the Government of the City of Birmingham, 1962–63" (M.A. thesis, University of Montevallo, 1974), 23–29.
25 LaMonte, "Politics and Welfare in Birmingham," 296–97; Harrison, "Change in Government," 31–32, 39–40.

creased in number during the crisis over the parks. Then in early 1962, students at Miles College, a local black institution, threatened to organize a boycott of downtown stores unless merchants hired black clerks and desegregated their lunch counters, drinking fountains, and rest rooms. White merchants and other business leaders met with Miles president Lucius Pitts and the students on several occasions between December, 1961, and March, 1962, but their compromise proposals were consistently rejected by the students as inadequate. Thus, in mid-March the boycott began. Initially, this "selective buying" campaign was extremely effective, cutting off 90 to 95 percent of the merchants' black trade and generating great concern among business leaders. Despite their concern, the merchants still refused to grant any concessions, and during the summer the boycott faltered and finally failed. Nevertheless, the lesson had not been lost on the store owners. They saw how badly their business could be hurt by the loss of black buyers, and they knew the downtown economy could not sustain many more such boycotts.[26]

Furthermore, the threat of massive street demonstrations loomed large. In September, 1962, Martin Luther King's Southern Christian Leadership Conference planned to hold its annual meeting in Birmingham and seriously considered mounting demonstrations at the same time. Responding to this threat and fearing violence, a small group of businessmen, led by Sidney Smyer, made contact with local civil rights leaders and King lieutenant Rev. Fred Shuttlesworth. These white leaders belonged to the prestigious "Senior Citizens Committee," which had been organized by the Chamber in late August, 1962, and represented businesses and industries employing 80 percent of Birmingham area workers.[27]

26   George R. Osborne, "Boycott in Birmingham," *Nation*, May 5, 1962, pp. 397–401; Nichols, "'Cities Are What Men Make Them,'" 159–62; BDIA Board Minutes, April 17, 1962, in Operation New Birmingham files, Birmingham City Hall; Alabama Council on Human Relations, Quarterly Reports, December, 1961–February, 1962, and March–May, 1962, Frank Dukes (student body president, Miles College) to Birmingham merchants, March 6, 1962, Norman Jimerson, memo to U.S. Commission on Civil Rights, August 31, 1962, all in SRC Papers.
27   LaMonte, "Politics and Welfare in Birmingham," 313; Alabama Council on Human Relations, Quarterly Report, June–August, 1962, in SRC Papers.

The initial contact between the white and the black leaders was made through Lucius Pitts of Miles and Norman Jimerson, executive director of the Alabama Council on Human Relations, a local biracial affiliate of the Southern Regional Council. Pitts and Jimerson met with Smyer on September 16, about a week before the SCLC conference was scheduled. They told him that the demonstrations could be postponed only if the merchants made visible concessions, and they suggested the removal of "colored only" signs from water fountains and rest rooms, and a public commitment to a "status-backed" interracial committee. Smyer replied that these suggestions were "reasonable" and that the signs could be removed "in forty-eight hours." In addition, Smyer indicated that a public announcement regarding an interracial committee would be forthcoming since such a group had been planned for some time. A few days later, Smyer and some of the white merchants met with Shuttlesworth and agreed to remove the offensive signs. On the basis of this important concession, the SCLC agreed to delay demonstrations for sixty days.[28]

Even before this moratorium period had ended, however, black rights leaders again were seriously considering demonstrations. Soon after the merchants had taken their signs down in September, Bull Connor began to harass them systematically by sending building and fire inspectors into their stores. These inspectors readily found "unsafe" elevators and stairs, as well as other violations of building or fire codes. Thus, when the harried merchants began putting the Jim Crow signs back up, black leaders felt betrayed. At about this same time, white business leaders themselves became embittered when the blacks rejected their apparently sincere offer to raise funds for legal fees and court costs if the blacks wished to test the city's segregation ordinances in court. The Negroes reportedly had replied that "the store owners ought to be arrested and fight their own case." In such an atmosphere of distrust and recrimination, renewed plans for demonstrations were almost inevitable. King and local

28   Paul Rilling, "Field Report, Birmingham, Alabama," September 18, 1962, in SRC Papers; interview with Rev. Fred L. Shuttlesworth, (Transcript in Civil Rights Documentation Project Papers, Manuscript Division, the Moorland-Spingarn Research Center, Howard University, Washington, D.C.), 55–58; Lee Edmundson Bains, Jr., "Birmingham, 1963: Confrontation over Civil Rights" (Honors thesis, Harvard College, 1977), 10.

civil rights leaders had pledged only that demonstrations would not occur until after the runoff election for the new mayor and city council, which was set for April 2, 1963. King wanted to make certain he would not give any ready issues to Bull Connor, who was trailing in a tight race for mayor behind the candidate of the moderates, Albert Boutwell. Boutwell won the runoff with 57.8 percent of the vote, but the moderates' victory was dimmed the next day when King ignored their pleas for more time and began demonstrations with sit-ins at downtown lunch counters. Within a few days, street marches had also begun.[29]

As King was certainly aware, the demonstrations could not have come at a worse time for the city's commercial and civic leaders. Connor and the other commissioners were challenging the validity of the law which would permit the new government to take office on April 15, and this dispute remained unresolved throughout the period of the demonstrations. In addition, although a number of King's demands were already on the agenda of reform, business leaders were reluctant to make any binding commitments to black leaders that might later be overturned by a legally rejuvenated city commission. Predictably, too, the white leaders who had worked to change the government and improve race relations were deeply disturbed by the street demonstrations, which they regarded as ill-timed and inappropriate. They were, therefore, loath to reach any agreement while demonstrations continued for fear that they would appear to have capitulated under pressure. Primarily for these reasons, then, the informal negotiations which Smyer had initiated with Shuttlesworth on April 9 were abruptly halted on April 16 after only three meetings.[30]

As the demonstrations continued unabated into May, tensions mounted. Merchants became increasingly concerned as their retail sales plunged downward, the result of black boycotts and white fears. The threat of violence also arose, as King, in an unprecedented maneuver, used school children in the street marches, and Bull Connor responded with fire hoses and dogs.

29 LaMonte, "Politics and Welfare in Birmingham," 296–97; Bains, "Birmingham, 1963," 10, 19, 22–23; Jimerson to Rilling, October 25, November 19, 1962, in SRC Papers.
30 Bains, "Birmingham, 1963," 35–36, 71; Alabama Council on Human Relations, Quarterly Report, March–May, 1963, in SRC Papers; and "Outline of negotiations . . ." (Undated typescript in David Vann Papers, BPL Archives).

Deeply concerned that matters would soon reach a violent breaking point, the merchants appointed David Vann and Sidney Smyer on May 5 to resume negotiations with local black leaders. Vann and Smyer were assisted in getting discussions under way through the mediating efforts of Assistant U.S. Attorney General Burke Marshall, who had been sent to Birmingham by President Kennedy the day before. Once a tentative settlement was reached, however, the merchants were reluctant to approve it without the support of the prestigious Senior Citizens Committee. Therefore, on May 7, that group sent its representatives with Smyer to the final negotiating session. The discussions continued well into the early morning of May 8, and finally, that afternoon, the full Senior Citizens Committee met and approved the settlement with only scattered dissent. On May 10, the terms of the agreement were announced by King and Smyer at separate news conferences.[31]

In retrospect, this agreement, worked out against the backdrop of disruptive demonstrations, was remarkably modest in its scope. In fact, every substantive point of the agreement had been under serious consideration among white leaders for nearly a year. For example, the settlement desegregated lunch counters, rest rooms, fitting rooms, and drinking fountains, but most of these reforms had been implemented in 1962 and had been reversed only because of pressure from the recently ousted Connor. It also called for the hiring and upgrading of black clerks and sales personnel, but this proposal was already on the agenda of moderate merchants before the demonstrations. Finally, the agreement provided for the establishment of a biracial committee, which had been the goal of several white moderates since 1961 and which would in effect simply reopen the old lines of communication employed by the Interracial Committee.[32]

31   Bains, "Birmingham, 1963," 30, 73; interview with Burke Marshall by Anthony Lewis, June 20, 1964 (Transcript in John F. Kennedy Library, Waltham, Massachusetts), 99–102; LaMonte, "Politics and Welfare in Birmingham," 309–10; "Outline of negotiations . . ." in Vann Papers; Carl M. Brauer, *John F. Kennedy and the Second Reconstruction* (New York: Columbia University Press, 1977), 234–36. Throughout the negotiations, the role of Marshall and other members of the Kennedy administration remained one of encouragement for continued bargaining. There was apparently no effort by Marshall or others to impose the actual terms of the agreement.
32   Bains, "Birmingham, 1963," 31–32; LaMonte, "Politics and Welfare in Bir-

Yet, despite the modest scope of the agreement itself, it had far-reaching implications for the city and its leaders. Since 1950, except for the brief period between 1956 and 1961, white business leaders in Birmingham had been involved in an unsuccessful quest for racial harmony. Before 1963, they had always been restrained by the limitations imposed by segregation. But the negotiations to end the demonstrations in that spring of 1963 finally freed them from the bonds of segregation, and thus liberated their search for racial order. Significantly, too, moderate business leaders, who had been isolated and intimidated since the death of the Interracial Committee, were able once again to speak freely without fear. Finally, biracial communication, which had been almost totally broken off in 1956 and had only been intermittent since 1961, was now formally and fully restored, and was pursued with enthusiasm.

Birmingham's racial problems, of course, were far from solved in 1963. Vital and difficult issues such as school desegregation, black police, and job equality still remained to be grappled with during the remainder of the decade. But community leaders faced these problems with a new determination and a new realism, confident that the first and most important step toward eventual solutions—the establishment of racial peace— had already been taken.

The Senior Citizens Committee, the Birmingham Downtown Improvement Association, the Young Men's Business Club, and the other white business and community leaders who effected this momentous change in Birmingham's race relations represented a broad spectrum of the city's commercial elite, ranging from the downtown merchants through the real estate developers and lawyers to the board members and executives of the city's largest banks and industrial firms. Each member of this elite group since 1961 had been confronting the prospect of continued racial unrest and had now decided, in several cases with some reluctance, that in 1963 the time had finally come for Birmingham to move beyond its blind and destructive devotion to segregation.

To be sure, these white leaders were not suddenly converted to the cause of black civil rights, nor did they act solely for rea-

mingham," 313; *Wall Street Journal*, May 14, 1963; James A. Head to Albert Boutwell, April 5, 1963, in Albert Boutwell Papers, BPL Archives.

sons of economic self-interest, although some admitted that their businesses were suffering financially. On balance, most business leaders instead viewed Birmingham's racial problems in terms of community stability and social order. In the past, as with the Interracial Committee, these leaders had hoped to control black discontent and channel it into constructive paths, while at the same time maintaining segregation. But by 1963, the blacks' demands for desegregation had reached the point where they threatened not only the economic vitality of Birmingham, but its social order as well.

Some leaders, such as Smyer and Vann, recognized before 1963 that a more moderate and flexible approach to the city's racial difficulties was required. Therefore, they not only led the drive to remove Connor from office, but they also attempted to alleviate racial tensions through a series of secret meetings with local black leaders. These early ameliorative efforts ultimately failed, however, for two reasons: local black leaders did not feel that they could trust the white elite to fulfill their promises of change; and moderate white leaders were unable at the same time to forge a consensus for changing the racial status quo.

King's demonstrations in the spring of 1963 provided the catalyst both for change and the restoration of harmony. Although the groundwork had already been laid by the change in government and the previous biracial bargaining, the end of segregation in Birmingham was dramatically hastened because King and his demonstrators threatened chaos in a city whose leaders were now desperate for order. When the settlement was finally reached, both blacks and whites could claim some measure of victory. The blacks had won pledges of desegregation in the most segregated city in the South, and the white leaders had won what they had really been seeking all along—racial harmony.

GEORGE C. WRIGHT

DESEGREGATION OF PUBLIC ACCOMMODATIONS IN LOUISVILLE

A LONG AND DIFFICULT STRUGGLE IN A "LIBERAL"
BORDER CITY

On February 1, 1960, four black college students in Greensboro, North Carolina, held a sit-in at the local Woolworth store to protest its policy of not serving blacks at lunch counters. The action of the four students sparked a wave of protests by young blacks throughout the South. Sit-ins at lunch counters and in department stores led to some immediate results: by August, 1960, lunch counters in twenty-eight cities had been integrated, and other downtown facilities were open to blacks as well.[1]

Interestingly, Louisville, Kentucky, a border city that prided itself on being liberal in the field of race relations, was not one of the twenty-eight cities to desegregate downtown eating establishments fully or to allow blacks access to downtown facilities. Furthermore, blacks in Louisville had started their drive to desegregate downtown before the sit-ins began in Greensboro, and they met such stern opposition that it took three and one-half years of demonstrating and negotiating before blacks received equal access to downtown facilities. The long, but ultimately successful, desegregation of downtown Louisville can be attrib-

---

1 Louisville *Courier-Journal*, August 7, 1960.

uted to several factors: black demonstrations and an economic boycott which affected the numerous white establishments that relied on black customers; black voting which helped elect candidates sympathetic to desegregation; and a desire by white civic leaders to see an end to demonstrations and to maintain Louisville's reputation as a liberal and progressive city.

Louisville has always boasted of having good race relations and has pointed to numerous advances blacks have made in the city. Since the 1930s, blacks received political patronage and even party support for black office seekers. In 1936 Charles W. Anderson, a local black attorney, was elected to the Kentucky state legislature, thereby becoming the state's first black to serve there. All told, Anderson served six consecutive terms in the legislature (1935–1947). In fact, he ran unopposed in 1945. Anderson resigned from the legislature in 1947 to accept a position as the first black assistant commonwealth's attorney for Jefferson County. Beginning in the 1940s, both the Democrats and Republicans regularly chose a black to run for a seat on the city's board of aldermen. The city's mayors and aldermen responded to pleas by blacks in the 1940s and eliminated a number of Jim Crow practices in Louisville. In 1941, for example, black teachers received a 15 percent increase to equalize their salaries with those of white teachers, and in that same year black nurses started receiving training at General Hospital. A decade later, the city closed Louisville Municipal College for Negroes and admitted blacks to the University of Louisville. Also in the early 1950s, blacks achieved two goals that they had sought for years: admission to all branches of the Louisville Free Public Library System and to the city's parks, swimming pools, and amphitheaters.[2]

Louisville's reputation in race relations was further enhanced in 1956 with the smooth desegregation of the public schools. That year the Louisville Public School System (with 27 percent black enrollment) was not only the largest school system in the nation to desegregate but it did so without any serious racial incidents. Louisville's desegregation plan, with its emphasis on "freedom of choice" for students, became a model

2 Kentucky Commission on Human Rights, *Kentucky's Black Heritage* (Frankfort: Commonwealth of Kentucky, 1971), 97.

of peaceful school integration. School superintendent Omer Carmichael received praise throughout the nation for his guidance of the Louisville school system. The national media, television networks, and magazine and newspaper columnists focused on Louisville as a city where progressive leaders were eliminating racial problems without turmoil.[3]

But after all the praises had been said, a close look at the Louisville public schools revealed that very little desegregation occurred in 1956. When initiating school desegregation, Superintendent Carmichael wanted desperately for the white community to approve his actions. Therefore, his scheme relied on "permissiveness," which meant that the school system would oppose both compulsory segregation and integration. Carmichael's plan rested on a freedom of choice in attending school, and not surprisingly, most whites chose to keep their children in all-white schools. Token integration developed under the Louisville Board of Education's desegregation plan with no whites enrolling at all-black Central High School and with only a handful of blacks transferring to the five formerly all-white high schools.[4] In the black community it was widely believed that the board of education discouraged blacks from transferring to white schools. Lyman Johnson, a well known and highly respected Louisville black educator and civil rights activist, explained that the only blacks fully accepted at the white schools were the gifted black students with high grade averages or the black athletes who could enhance the athletic programs of the white schools. "The white schools would show off . . . [the gifted black students and athletes]. The average Negro student would not be accepted there and [many] would be back in the black schools." Also, under Carmichael's plan black teachers were not allowed to teach in white schools. Carmichael explained on nu-

3   See Darlene Walker, "Preparation for the Desegregation of the Louisville School System," (M.A. thesis, University of Louisville, 1974). For laudatory views of Louisville and especially race relations in the city, see Omer Carmichael and James Weldon, *The Louisville Story* (New York: Simon and Schuster, 1957); Ben Muse, "Louisville" (Paper presented to Southern Regional Council, 1964), in Southern Regional Council Archives, Atlanta, Georgia; Fred Powledge, "Profiles," *New Yorker*, September 9, 1974, pp. 42–83, explains that the "people of Louisville and Jefferson County have been under no pressure to champion segregation."
4   Walker, "Preparation for Desegregation," 15–32, 130.

merous occasions that black teachers were inferior to white teachers. The city's black leaders, appalled at the superintendent's assessment of black teachers, conducted studies that completely refuted his claim. Nevertheless, black teachers taught only at black schools until the 1960s.[5]

In the late 1950s, the illusion of desegregation was not limited to the school system. Blacks had always lacked adequate housing in Louisville and this condition remained unchanged. On one occasion a black man, Andrew Wade, had a white couple, Carl and Ann Braden, purchase a home for him in the Louisville suburb of Shively. The residents of Shively, upon learning that Wade owned the home, demanded that he sell it and leave the area. Wade refused to do so, and his house was bombed. The police failed to apprehend the bombers. But Braden, who had purchased the home for Wade, was arrested and convicted and sent to prison for sedition. Wade and his family never returned to the house after the bombing and eventually sold the property.[6]

Black Louisvillians also encountered discrimination in employment. Most companies hired them for menial jobs only, excluding them from white-collar jobs, skilled positions, and apprenticeship programs. Labor unions, for the most part, remained closed to blacks. With little room for advancement in employment, blacks earned only 4 percent of the wages in Louisville even though they comprised 16 percent of the working population. Segregation and discrimination existed in the police department as well, with black policemen being assigned to the city's all-black districts and no black officer commanding whites. In the juvenile delinquency department black probation officers handled only black juveniles.[7]

Blacks encountered discrimination when attempting to spend what little money they earned in Louisville. "All Louisville theaters are completely segregated and make no provisions for Negro citizens even on a segregated basis with the exception of the Rodeo, Crescent, and possibly the Westend Theater," a report from the Urban League's executive secretary noted in 1959.

5   Kentucky Commission on Human Rights, *Kentucky's Black Heritage*, 105–106; interview with Lyman T. Johnson by the author, March 16, 1978.
6   Ann Braden, *The Wall Between* (New York: Monthly Review Press, 1958).
7   Interview with Dr. Maurice Rabb by Dwayne Cox of the University of Louisville Archives, August 15, 1977; interview with Charles Tachau by Cox, July 6, 1977.

Other places of amusement—bowling alleys, skating rinks, and Fountaine Ferry Amusement Park—completely excluded blacks. The local hotels varied in their discriminatory policies toward blacks. The Brown and Kentucky hotels refused blacks overnight lodging. Three hotels, the Seelback-Sheraton, the Watterson-Sheraton, and the Henry Clay, accepted blacks as guests on a limited basis. None of the hotels served blacks in the public dining rooms. All five hotels, however, would serve blacks in private dining rooms when they attended meetings held by predominately white organizations. All of Louisville's major restaurants and cafeterias, with the notable exception of Sears, had strict exclusionary policies. Finally, there was a widespread practice in downtown Louisville of not allowing blacks to try on clothes or shoes before purchasing them.[8]

Black leaders, realizing that discrimination existed in virtually every area of life in Louisville, decided to make their first goal equal access to all public accommodations. They firmly believed it would be easier to desegregate downtown facilities than housing or employment, and that a successful movement in that area would be a lever to other racial advances. In 1956 the Louisville NAACP chose Lyman Johnson, Andrew Bishop, and Mrs. Jewel Rabb to lead the Youth Division of the NAACP in demonstrations to protest segregation in the city's downtown area. Lyman Johnson, who had been active in Louisville in civil rights since 1933, emerged as the leader of the demonstrations. He first led the young people in marching and picketing against Louisville dime stores which refused to serve blacks at their lunch counters even though these stores depended heavily on black customers. By mid-1957, after almost six months of weekend demonstrations by blacks, the dime stores succumbed and began serving blacks.[9]

Encouraged by its success, the NAACP Youth Council next sought to desegregate drugstores. The drugstores eagerly accepted the patronage of black doctors and their patients at the

8   Charles Steele, "Status of Desegregation in Places of Public Accommodation" (Report prepared for Mayor's Advisory Committee on Human Rights, February 4, 1959), in Archives Department, University of Louisville; interview with Mrs. Murray Walls by Cox, July 27, 1977.
9   Patrick McElhone, "The Civil Rights Activities of the Louisville Branch of the National Association for the Advancement of Colored People, 1914–1960" (M.A. thesis, University of Louisville, 1976); Johnson interview.

prescription counters but excluded blacks from their lunch counters. As a black physician noted with disgust, Taylor Drugs gave him a discount on the purchase of supplies and medicine but refused to serve him a cup of coffee. The Youth Council picketed the drugstores for more than a year without any success. But in December, 1958, the struggle ended very quickly and dramatically: the mayor of Kingston, Jamaica, Mrs. Iris King, while visiting in Louisville was denied service at Walgreen Drugstore and protested the treatment she received. Walgreen's management, embarrassed by the bad publicity the incident caused, ended all racial restrictions at its lunch counters and the other drugstores followed Walgreen's example.[10]

In 1959, with desegregation achieved in dime stores and drugstores, the NAACP prepared to launch an all-out movement against discrimination in hotels, theaters, restaurants, and cafeterias in downtown Louisville. Frank Stanley, Jr., one of the student leaders of the demonstrations, argued that various groups from the black community had to lend assistance to the NAACP Youth Council if it hoped to succeed. Stanley pointed out that all of the civil rights groups had strengths that could aid the movement. The Interdenominational Ministers Council, comprised of black ministers, could get masses of people together very quickly. The adult division of the NAACP had financial resources and legal talent that would be important if arrests resulted from the demonstrations. And most important, the Louisville NAACP with its long history in the field of civil rights (since 1914) brought credibility as well as attention to any activity in which it became involved. Even the usually conservative Urban League would have an important role, Stanley pointed out. Urban Leaguers were personally acquainted with the city's white leaders and were adept at negotiation. Stanley also explained that the Congress of Racial Equality (CORE) could train large numbers of people in nonviolent demonstration techniques. Finally, Stanley made an appeal to the city's white civic leaders to aid blacks in their attempt to desegregate downtown Louisville. But unfortunately, except for the few whites involved with CORE, none came forward.[11]

10   Rabb interview; Louisville *Courier-Journal*, December 11, 1958; McElhone, "The Civil Rights Activities of the Louisville NAACP," 154.
11   Interview with Frank Stanley, Jr., by the author, March 7, 1978.

From the numerous strategy sessions held, four men emerged as the leaders of the demonstrations: Lyman Johnson, Frank Stanley, Jr., Rev. C. Ewbank Tucker, and Rev. W. J. Hodge. Lyman Johnson was a logical choice since he had led the activities of the NAACP Youth Council, had been involved in every important interracial movement in Kentucky since the 1930s, and had served as NAACP president more times than anyone could remember. Tucker, the leader of CORE, had been active in Louisville for decades as a civil rights attorney. He was also a bishop in the African Methodist Episcopal Zion Church, a position he used to rally supporters for civil rights ventures. Hodge, a newcomer to Louisville, having moved from Virginia in the mid-1950s, was president of the NAACP and pastor of the Fifth Street Baptist Church, the most prestigious black church in Kentucky. Frank Stanley, Jr., whose father owned the Louisville *Defender*, Kentucky's only black newspaper, was the youngest of the four leaders. Nevertheless, he quickly became the spokesman for the demonstrators. A close friend of Rev. Martin Luther King, Jr., Stanley consulted constantly with King on what measures to take and persuaded King to come to Louisville on several occasions to give encouragement.[12]

Widespread demonstrations started in downtown Louisville in late 1959 with special attention devoted to the exclusionary policy of the theaters. As fate would have it, during the Christmas season the Brown Theater presented the Gershwin-DuBose Heyward classic, *Porgy and Bess*. Black demonstrators made much of the fact that the Brown Theater denied blacks the right to see the all-black play. To give a clear picture of the wrongs and inconveniences caused by discrimination, the NAACP chartered a bus and traveled to Indianapolis to see *Porgy and Bess*. As they left for Indianapolis, Louisville's civil rights leaders let it be known that the 1960s would witness changes in downtown accommodations.[13]

As part of their strategy, blacks stopped their demonstrations in the downtown area after the Christmas season and

12   Johnson interview; Stanley interview; interview with Rev. W. J. Hodge, by Charles C. Staiger of the University of Louisville Archives, December 14, 1977; Louisville *Courier-Journal*, September 14, 1960.
13   Louisville *Defender*, February 4, 1960; Hodge interview; Johnson interview.

turned to negotiation. A black group went to city hall January 4, 1960, and urged Mayor Bruce Hoblitzell to support desegregation and to put the weight of his office behind a law to end discrimination in public accommodations. The mayor's response, though disappointing, was not unexpected. He explained that, although segregation was morally wrong, a law of "non-selectivity was ridiculous." Hoblitzell outlined his position, a view he would not budge from during his term as mayor and one that the aldermen supported: desegregation should be voluntary and a public accommodation ordinance would be unjust.[14]

After the mayor refused to endorse a public accommodation ordinance, black leaders turned to William Beckett, the only black alderman, and pressured him into introducing a desegregation bill. Beckett was reluctant to introduce any civil rights legislation, for he knew that the other aldermen would not only vote against a public accommodation ordinance but against all legislation he proposed thereafter. But the city's black leaders wanted a bill put before the board of aldermen so that the elected officials would have to state publicly how they felt about desegregation. A black committee went to Beckett's Funeral Home and threatened to lead a boycott of his business unless he introduced a public accommodation bill. Beckett, at the next meeting of the board of aldermen on February 9, 1960, introduced a bill that called for complete integration of downtown restaurants, hotels, and theaters and a fine of twenty-five to a hundred dollars for any business that refused to do so.[15]

The board of aldermen defeated Beckett's bill by a vote of 11–1. On March 8 Beckett introduced a second public accommodation bill, a bill which differed slightly from the first one. Nevertheless, the board of aldermen rejected the second bill by the identical vote of 11–1. The white aldermen then went on the offensive and passed a resolution declaring, "We the Board of Aldermen of the City of Louisville are opposed to any ordinance which takes away the right of an owner of a private business to select his customers or clientele." The resolution, which caught Beckett and the city's black leaders by surprise, was designed to

14 Louisville *Defender*, January 7, February 4, 1960.
15 Johnson interview; Louisville *Courier-Journal*, February 10, 1960; Louisville *Defender*, February 11, 18, 1960.

head off further attempts to legislate black admission to theaters, restaurants, and hotels.[16]

In the ensuing weeks, the board of aldermen took additional steps to curtail the black civil rights movement. The aldermen passed an ordinance to arrest anyone for picketing and demonstrating in downtown Louisville. They defeated an ordinance proposed by Beckett to create a city human relations committee. Under Beckett's proposal, the human relations committee would encourage and promote better race relations through education, persuasion, and conciliation. The committee would have no authority to force desegregation. But, the aldermen rejected Beckett's ordinance by the same 11–1 vote.[17]

After realizing that the board of aldermen were adamant in their opposition to desegregation, Louisville's black leaders made plans to reassume the initiative in the public accommodation struggle. But unfortunately, CORE and the NAACP differed over which method should be used: CORE, led by Tucker, called for direct action through demonstrations while the NAACP called for a series of meeting with white business leaders. Much to the dismay of Lyman Johnson and the NAACP, Len Holt, a CORE representative from Norfolk, Virginia, journeyed to Louisville and held sit-in workshops. The NAACP had assured white businessmen that there would be no demonstrations during their negotiations. CORE, distrustful of the city's business leaders, resumed demonstrations, an act that led to much bickering in the civil rights camp. Even though CORE and the NAACP occasionally assisted each other throughout the remainder of the public accommodations drive, relations between them were cool from this point on. As Lyman Johnson explains, members of the NAACP doubted the sincerity of CORE and viewed the organization as a "band of white radicals" and economically affluent blacks. "What did they have in common with us [the black masses]?" The disagreement took its toll on the struggle for civil rights. Very little desegregation of public accommodations occurred in Louisville in 1960. In fact, from May, 1960, to the end of the year only a few scattered demonstrations

16   Louisville *Courier-Journal*, February 25, March 8, 9, 1960; Louisville *Defender*, February 25, March 10, 24, 1960.
17   Louisville *Defender*, April 21, 28, 1960; Louisville *Courier-Journal*, April 27, 1960.

were conducted by Tucker and his followers. The NAACP, meanwhile, held a series of fruitless talks with city leaders.[18]

Sit-ins and picketing resumed in January, 1961, after several months of negotiations failed. Black high school students, without the leadership or approval of the adult organizations, started the demonstrations. As Hodge, then president of the NAACP, explains, "Seven students, without the knowledge of the NAACP and other groups, sat-in at Stewart's. They were arrested. The movement grew from there." Black Louisville youths "took the initiative, seized the headlines, and bypassed the older organizations" just as black youths were doing throughout the South. Frank Stanley, Jr., applauded the actions of the students, noting that "our expectations of desegregation in Louisville are not unrealistic when you consider that in a three-week period St. Louis desegregated 200 downtown restaurants, Kansas City 121, and Oklahoma City 116. But here in Louisville, working on the problem for 7 weeks, only 10 restaurants have integrated."[19]

With the high school students leading the way and with CORE and the NAACP hurrying into the action, public accommodation demonstrations peaked from mid-February to early May, 1961. The largest of the demonstrations, held on March 14 and 15, attracted well over four hundred participants and extended over four blocks as the marchers walked from Fourth Street (the center of downtown shopping) to Broadway. Special targets of the demonstrators were Kaufman's and Stewart's restaurants and the two Blue Boar cafeterias, whose owner, L. Eugene Johnson, served on the Louisville Board of Education. For months Johnson had refused all overtures from civil rights leaders, stating that no Negroes would be served in the Blue Boar. But unknown to him, Frank Stanley, Jr., had persuaded several light-skinned women—who could easily pass for whites—to eat at the Blue Boar on several occasions. On April 24, while four Negro women were in the Blue Boar, Stanley informed Eugene Johnson that Negroes were indeed being served in his restaurant and were not causing any problems. "How inconsistent

18   Louisville *Courier-Journal*, July 26, September 14, 1960; Johnson interview; Louisville *Defender*, June 16, 1960.
19   Hodge interview; August Meier and Elliott Rudwick, *CORE: A Study in the Civil Rights Movement, 1942–1968* (New York: Oxford University Press, 1973), 105; Louisville *Courier-Journal*, April 16, 1961.

can the policy of segregation be? Negroes are Negroes and only by the difference of color, some were served and other refused," Stanley informed an irate Johnson. Blacks also held demonstrations at city hall and at board of aldermen meetings. In late March over 350 young people paraded through downtown to Mayor Hoblitzell's office, and on Easter Sunday a prayer pilgrimage at city hall attracted over 3,000 people.[20]

Numerous blacks were arrested during the mass demonstrations. The NAACP responded by conducting a series of rallies to raise bail money. One such rally attracted 2,800 blacks who contributed $2,100 to the public accommodation struggle. All of the money raised came in very handy since more than 600 demonstrators were eventually arrested, including 177 people during a large demonstration on March 14, "as the police hauled away vanload after vanload of young people." According to the *Defender* of April 27, 1961, "The police attained a dubious record . . . in the arrests of juveniles and adults conducting 'stand ins' and 'squat ins' protesting segregation in public accommodations by bringing the total number to 685—the highest in the nation—since the demonstrations were intensified on February 20." And on one occasion three of the four civil rights leaders, Hodge, Tucker, and Frank Stanley, Jr., were arrested.[21]

During the height of the demonstrations, Louisville's civil rights leaders announced an economic boycott of downtown stores. They had been encouraged by Rev. Martin Luther King, Jr., to conduct a nonbuying campaign to protest discrimination in public accommodations. "If 50,000 blacks in Montgomery can walk in dignity for a year surely 75,000 Negroes in Louisville can stop buying in protest for one month," King pointed out in a telegram to civil rights leaders. The "Nothing New for Easter Campaign" started February 28 and was to have ended on April 3, but since it proved so effective it was extended through the

20   Louisville *Courier-Journal*, March 13–18, April 25, 1961; Louisville *Defender*, April 6, 1961.
21   Louisville *Courier-Journal*, February 20, 24, March 12–18, April 21, 22, 1961; Louisville *Defender*, February 9, 16, March 16, April 27, 1961; Stanley interview. Charles Tachau, who served as a police judge in the early 1960s, noted that juvenile judge Henry Triplett found black juveniles guilty for taking part in the civil rights demonstrations, but then he filed the charges away. Triplett was, Tachau explained, clearly in sympathy with the demonstrators. Tachau interview.

entire month of April. The campaign, according to Louisville's black leaders, was supported by 98 percent of the black population as only a handful of blacks ventured into department and dime stores to make purchases. The economic boycott forced at least one store that depended heavily on black trade out of business. The *Defender* quoted a white storekeeper as saying that the boycott hurt business: "We are off 25–50% in sales. Even some of our white trade has fallen off."[22]

With the mass arrests of juveniles occurring and the economic boycott disrupting business, Kentucky's Governor Burt Combs became personally involved in Louisville's desegregation struggle and encouraged other whites to do likewise. As governor, Combs had aggressively pursued changes in the racial status quo in Kentucky. Under his guidance the Kentucky General Assembly of 1960 created a new state merit sytem which was designed to ensure that state agencies did not discriminate against black employees. Also, under his leadership the general assembly created a Commission on Human Rights "to encourage fair treatment for, to foster mutual understanding and respect among, and to discourage discrimination against any racial or ethnic group or its members." Governor Combs traveled to Louisville to hold a series of meetings with Mayor Hoblitzell, and he finally convinced the reluctant mayor to form an emergency committee to work with the white business community and black civil rights leaders. The mayor named the following civic leaders to the emergency committee: Dillman Rash, president of the Louisville Tile Company; Thomas Ballantine, vice-president of Glenmore Distillers; William Henderson, head of Taylor Drugs; George Norton, president of WAVE Broadcasting Inc.; Berry Bingham, editor of the *Courier-Journal* and the Louisville *Times*; John Hennessy, Jefferson court clerk; Henning Hilliard, a local broker; John Acree, president of Lincoln Income Life Insurance; Archibald Cochran, president of Anaconda Aluminum; and Henry Offut, president of Kentucky Trust. These men, all active in community affairs, expressed

22   Stanley interview; Hodge interview; Johnson interview; Louisville *Defender*, February 9, 16, 23, March 23, 1961; Louisville *Courier-Journal*, March 10, April 2, 21, 1961. Hodge explained that the boycott was being held not only to open all public accommodations to blacks but to acquire more jobs for blacks as well. About "98 percent of the stores do not employ Negroes in clerical or sales capacities."

their concern about the disruptions caused by demonstrations and the negative image a segregated downtown area brought to Louisville. In their very first policy statement these community leaders put their "moral weight" behind desegregation, saying that "it is desirable that the inevitable action [desegregation] take place before the generally good atmosphere of the Louisville community deteriorates."[23]

The mayor's emergency committee appealed to both sides for cooperation. Committee members sent letters to all restaurant, hotel, and theater owners, urging them to desegregate their facilities by May 1, 1961. They also urged black leaders to end their demonstrations. On May 1 blacks found mixed results in downtown eating establishments: of the fifty-seven restaurants blacks entered, thirty-two restaurants refused to serve them. The emergency committee sent telegrams to the thirty-two holdouts, pleading with them to join the other restaurants and make desegregation complete. Even though downtown integration was not unanimous, the mayor's committee informed blacks that they should be encouraged by the number of restaurants that had desegregated (including such strong holdouts as the Blue Boar, whose owner, L. Eugene Johnson, had vowed that he would never allow blacks in his establishment) and pointed out that since February, 1961, eighty-eight eating establishments in the downtown area had desegregated, which represented more than 80 percent of the downtown restaurants. "Under these circumstances," the mayor's emergency committee informed blacks, "[we] would strongly urge that there be no more mass demonstrations as we feel that this very probably would hurt rather than help the cause of integration by creating resentment and by tending to alienate some of those who to date have been strong supporters of the local integration movement." Black leaders responded by ending their nonbuying campaign and announcing a halt to their demonstrations on May 6 (so as not to interfere with the events surrounding the Kentucky Derby) even though thirty-two restaurants and most of the theaters and hotels remained segregated.[24]

23 Kentucky Commission on Human Rights, *Kentucky's Black Heritage*, 113; interview with Burt Combs by the author, April 4, 1978; Louisville *Courier-Journal*, February 25, 26, March 5, 1961.
24 Louisville *Courier-Journal*, May 6, 9, 1961. See the following sources at the University of Louisville Archives: Mayor's Papers on Desegregation; telegram

To the dismay of blacks, the mayor's emergency committee supported integration but on a voluntary basis only. Black civil rights groups and high school students, upon ending their demonstrations, urged the emergency committee to use its influence and get the board of aldermen to pass a public accommodation ordinance so that all establishments would be desegregated. Black leaders explained that until desegregation was complete, blacks had attained only a partial victory and would still be subjected to discrimination. But on May 24 Mayor Hoblitzell and his committee formally refused to press the aldermen to adopt an ordinance banning segregation. Furthermore, the mayor announced that the emergency committee had dissolved itself "since most of the city is desegregated." The committee did not want to force integration on anyone, Mayor Hoblitzell concluded.[25]

In retrospect, it is obvious that Mayor Hoblitzell and the civic-business leaders of the emergency committee were more concerned with ending the demonstrations and mass arrests than with desegregating downtown Louisville. Before starting their demonstrations, black leaders had appealed in vain to the white business community to take part in the public accommodation struggle. It was the prodding of Governor Combs and the bad image the mass arrests of black juveniles gave Louisville that led to the formation of the emergency committee. The actions of the emergency committee reveal that the members of that organization had mixed feelings about public accommodation desegregation: instead of using their influence to have a public accommodation law passed they merely wrote letters and made a few telephone calls urging reluctant businessmen to voluntarily desegregate their businesses. Furthermore, after the mass demonstrations and mass arrests stopped, the emergency committee disbanded itself even though downtown desegregation was far from complete.

The attitude of the mayor and his special committee encouraged the aldermen to remain firm in their opposition to a desegregation ordinance. The aldermen met several weeks after the

from Mayor Bruce Hoblitzell to thirty-two restaurants, May 4, 1961; Integration Steering Committee, "Official Results of Sit-ins, Testing, and Re-Testing" (June 1, 1961).
25. Louisville *Courier-Journal*, May 25, 1961.

disbanding of the emergency committee and passed another resolution (by 11–1) "opposing any ordinance that would impose enforced desegregation," and secondly, they remained firm in their disapproval of a human relations commission.[26] So despite mass demonstrations, mass arrests, an economic boycott, and persuasion from the governor, Louisville's Democratic board of aldermen—led by William S. Milburn—had not budged in their view of desegregation of public accommodations.

Black leaders soon discovered that they had made a tactical error by halting their mass demonstrations in early May. It was extremely difficult to resume marching and picketing on a large scale. The large marches and the publicity received from the mass arrests had drawn new groups, such as white professionals and older blacks, to the downtown struggle and had the students—the backbone of the marches—more involved than ever, only to see all of their energies halted on May 6. Discontinuing the demonstrations in early May sapped the momentum that had been built up since February. Demonstrations started again in midsummer, but for the remainder of 1961 only a handful of people participated. Moreover, the demonstrations were poorly coordinated. CORE and the NAACP held marches independently of each other. CORE even ventured out and started picketing at Fountaine Ferry Amusement Park, but accomplished nothing in the way of desegregation. By late 1961, with the demonstrations dying down and with the board of aldermen still refusing to act, a few downtown establishments actually began discriminating against blacks again while other places that had nearly relented during the spring demonstrations resumed segregative practices. For example, Stewart's Dry Goods Store, a focal point during the spring marches, had desegregated its restaurant but still prohibited blacks from trying on garments at the store.[27]

While the mass demonstrations continued in 1961, black leaders also pursued a political settlement. The political effort actually began in 1960 during the standstill in the public accommodation drive. A few black leaders formed the Non-Partisan Registration Committee to register all eligible blacks and

26   Ibid., June 14, 1961; Louisville Defender, June 15, 1961.
27   Louisville Courier-Journal, September 26, 1961; Louisville Defender, November 30, 1961.

pointed out that elections for mayor and the board of aldermen would be held in November, 1961. Woodford Porter, a local funeral director, served as chairman of the registration committee and Frank Stanley, Jr., was the cochairman. Before the registration drive began only twenty thousand out of fifty-one thousand eligible blacks were registered to vote. The committee's battle cry was "fifty-one thousand registered voters can totally desegregate Louisville." The Non-Partisan Registration Committee's effort resulted in increased black voter registration, and by November, 1960, more than fifteen thousand blacks had registered. The registration drive picked up more steam in February, 1961, after William Milburn, the president of the board of aldermen and the leading opponent of desegregation of public accommodations, announced his candidacy for mayor. Milburn headed the Democratic ticket while the Republicans chose William Cowger, a businessman. The *Defender* and a few black leaders explained that as far as black efforts to desegregate downtown Louisville were concerned, Cowger and Milburn were "cut from the same cloth." As the *Defender* explained, "The only difference between the two on the question of civil rights is that Cowger says that if the Board of Aldermen pass a public accommodation ordinance he will not veto it, Milburn says he will." Cowger did promise that if elected he would establish a human relations commission to promote integration. But Frank Stanley, Sr., for the first time in the history of his newspaper, did not endorse a mayoral candidate: "Both [Milburn and Cowger] have failed to display sufficient positive leadership required to advance the cause of human dignity so sorely needed in our community." Nevertheless, most blacks, and this included such leaders as Hodge, Tucker, and Lyman Johnson, opposed Milburn because of his opposition to a public accommodation ordinance. As Johnson explained in a recent interview, Milburn offended the black community with his arrogant attitude and adamant opposition to integration. Hodge said that Milburn did nothing to hide the fact that he was "an outright, first-class, super segregationist."[28]

28   Louisville *Times*, September 30, 1960; Louisville *Defender*, August 11, 1960, March 2, May 25, June 29, November 2, 1961; Louisville *Courier-Journal*, August 24, 1960, February 25, March 9, June 16, October 21, 1961; Hodge interview; Johnson interview; interview with William S. Milburn by the author, March 28, 1978.

On November 7, 1961, the Republican party won a stunning victory in Louisville as Cowger became the city's first Republican mayor in twenty-eight years and the Republicans swept the seats on the board of aldermen for the first time in fourteen years. Two blacks, Russell Lee and Mrs. Louise Reynolds, won seats on the aldermanic board while William Beckett, who had endorsed Milburn, lost. It is unclear just how big a factor the civil rights issue ultimately played in the outcome of the election. Milburn stated that losing the sizable Catholic vote cost him the election. (Milburn had won the Democratic primary in a bitter campaign with the city's leading Catholic politician. After the primary the Catholics bolted the Democratic party and supported the Republicans.) Members of the Non-Partisan Registration Committee proclaimed loudly that black voters (over forty thousand out of fifty-one thousand eligible black voters were registered) had brought about Milburn's defeat. The *Defender* found satisfaction in Milburn's stunning loss even though the paper had not endorsed either candidate. The paper pointed out that between 60 and 75 percent of the black vote went to the Republicans compared to 54 percent in 1957. For example, in the twenty-first precinct, which had gone Democrat in 1957, Milburn received 141 votes to 314 for Cowger.[29] Blacks were confident that the new Republican administration, upon taking office, would ensure desegregation of public accommodations.

But the Cowger administration disappointed the black community with its slow pace in ending discrimination in downtown Louisville. In January, 1962, Cowger met with a black delegation and pleaded with them not to resume demonstrations but to allow him to establish a human relations commission that would negotiate with white businessmen. In March the aldermen passed an ordinance establishing a human relations commission, but it was not until June that commission members were chosen and the board finally met. The human relations commission spent the remainder of 1962 organizing subcommittees to investigate discrimination in Louisville and in meeting with various white and black groups. Its efforts, however,

29   Louisville *Courier-Journal*, November 8, 1961; Louisville *Defender*, November 9, 1961; Johnson interview; Stanley interview; Kentucky Commission on Human Rights, *Kentucky's Black Heritage*, 117.

seemed like stalling tactics to some black leaders, and they began pressing the mayor and the aldermen to pass a desegregation ordinance. On December 28, 1962, Bishop Tucker and CORE went a step further and announced that they would march on city hall unless definite steps were taken within thirty days to pass an ordinance outlawing racial discrimination in public accommodations.[30]

One positive result of the year-long negotiation between the human relations commission and various white and black groups was general agreement on the need for a public accommodation law. Those white businessmen who had already desegregated wanted a law that would compel all businesses to desegregate. S. J. Switow, owner of the Westend Theater, explained that such a law would put all businesses on an equal footing without subjecting any business to unfair competition because of racial policies. Secondly, he and other white businessmen pointed out, a law would enable businessmen to say to their white customers, "We had no choice but to integrate because of the ordinance." The civic leaders who had served on Mayor Hoblitzell's emergency committee now agreed on the need for a public accommodation ordinance. With their eye on the city's image, they noted that other cities, many without Louisville's reputation for good race relations, had enacted ordinances ensuring equal treatment for all citizens.[31]

In early 1963 the NAACP, CORE, the human relations commission, and white civic leaders called for the passing of a public accommodation ordinance. Noting that 1963 marked one hundred years of black freedom, the *Defender* adopted the theme that without a public accommodation law, "Emancipation is not yet achieved." The *Courier-Journal*, in a series of editorials early in 1963, came out strongly for a desegregation law. In its call for a public accommodation ordinance, the human relations commission said, "We recognize the failure of this community by voluntary means to ensure equal treatment for all citizens. We are grateful for those who have voluntarily put into practice such convictions. Nevertheless, we believe that law is an honorable instrument for translating moral principle in the frame-

30   Louisville *Defender*, May 24, 31, 1962; Louisville *Courier-Journal*, March 26, December 29, 1962.
31   Louisville *Courier-Journal*, August 3, 1962; Stanley interview.

work of human relations." The commission presented its proposed ordinance to the board of aldermen on April 10, 1963.[32]

Those groups and individuals who desired a nonexclusionary law put intense pressure on the aldermen to adopt the public accommodation ordinance. CORE and the NAACP not only lobbied for the ordinance but threatened to resume demonstrations if the ordinance was rejected, a step neither the mayor nor the aldermen desired. Mayor Cowger, fearful of a return of mass demonstrations to downtown Louisville, now changed from being for voluntary desegregation to favoring the passage of the accommodation ordinance. A jam-packed crowd attended the board of aldermen meeting on May 14, 1963. The public accommodation ordinance was first on the agenda; and as the *Courier-Journal* proclaimed in the next morning's edition, "The Louisville Board of Aldermen . . . passed by voice vote the ordinance to prohibit racial discrimination in public business places."[33] Louisville's public accommodation ordinance, the first of its kind in Kentucky, made it unlawful for any public place that provided food, shelter, entertainment, or amusement to refuse services to anyone on the basis of race, color, or religious belief. The ordinance provided fines up to one hundred dollars for each violation and after three violations the city would seek an injunction against the violator. Failure to obey the injunction would result in a jail sentence.[34]

Louisville's civil rights leaders, though elated that desegregation of the downtown area had finally been achieved (many of them, in fact, celebrated by going "out to dinner" on May 15), said that the battle for equality was far from over. They explained that Louisville blacks still faced discrimination when traveling to other Kentucky towns, and that Kentucky needed a statewide antibias law. Governor Combs, who had long been active in civil rights, agreed; and he urged the general assembly to pass a law that would desegregate public accommodation facilities everywhere in Kentucky. The leaders of the state senate and house, however, informed the governor that an antibias law

32 Louisville *Defender*, January 3, 17, 24, 31, February 21, 28, April 11, 1963; Louisville *Courier-Journal*, January 8, 10, 12, February 27, April 10, 1963.
33 Louisville *Courier-Journal*, May 10, 15, 16, 1963. The vote on the ordinance, according to the *Defender* of May 16, 1963, was either 7–4 or 8–3.
34 Louisville *Courier-Journal*, May 15, 1963.

stood no chance of passing in the general assembly. Even though he knew that public opinion in Kentucky still favored discriminatory policies in public accommodations, Governor Combs was convinced that ending discrimination was the morally right thing to do (though not necessarily a wise political move). On June 26, 1963, he issued an executive order ending racial discrimination in all establishments and by all professions licensed by the state. This broad ordinance covered virtually every area of secular activity in Kentucky "outside the private homes of citizens."[35]

Civil rights organizations fought long to desegregate downtown Louisville. Accomplishing that goal did not lead to complacency on their part, for they were aware that desegregation of public accommodations was merely an early stage in the civil rights struggle. After all, they reasoned, if it was difficult to gain the right to eat in fine restaurants, stay in the hotels, and attend the theater, surely it would require a supreme effort from civil rights groups and concerned civic leaders for blacks to make breakthroughs in employment and housing. Indeed one discouraging note was evident after the public accommodation struggle in Louisville: without the full support of white civic leaders and city government officials it would be extremely difficult for blacks to end racial injustices. In Louisville blacks would continue to find discrimination in housing, employment, and even in equal access to all facilities because the city's white leadership never completely committed itself to the ending of racial injustices. Gains would be made by blacks only when they convinced city fathers that discrimination hurt Louisville's liberal image.

35   Combs interview; Louisville *Courier-Journal*, May 16, June 27, 1963.

DAVID R. COLBURN

THE SAINT AUGUSTINE BUSINESS COMMUNITY

DESEGREGATION, 1963–1964

With the conclusion of World War II the United States entered into an age which would see a fundamental change in the social and economic condition of its people. No region remained isolated from this metamorphosis, especially the South. Southerners left the farms in record numbers to enjoy the economic opportunities offered by their cities. Northern industry flocked into the South seeking to take advantage of tax incentives, cheap labor, and expanding markets. Northerners frequently joined their departing industries. Socially, the South gradually abolished the accouterments of a segregated society. By 1971 public schools were integrated, and blacks voted in party primaries and held public office.[1]

The dramatic socioeconomic changes that have occurred in the South since World War II have yet to be fully explained or understood. In particular, the reasons for the evolution in the South's racial traditions are not altogether clear. Did the changes result, for example, primarily from pressures exerted on the South by the federal government and the federal courts? Or

1   For an elaboration of these social, economic, and political developments see Kirkpatrick Sale, *Power Shift: The Rise of the Southern Rim and Its Challenge to the Eastern Establishment* (New York: Random House, 1975).

were the changes effected by forces at work within the southern communities? This essay examines one community in the South, Saint Augustine, Florida, and the response of its businessmen to the pressures for change occasioned by the civil rights movement.

In analyzing a 1963 racial disturbance in Cambridge, Maryland, reporter Claude Sitton of the New York *Times* observed that although political, social, and moral considerations entered into the controversy's resolution, "the effective pressure to end the crisis came from within the business community." Sitton was personally convinced that similar developments had occurred in Little Rock, Birmingham, Atlanta, and several other southern communities. He concluded that "economic self-interest frequently leads to racial change in situations where other factors seemingly have little influence."[2]

Sitton's findings were endorsed three years later by Reed Sarratt, who observed that in Little Rock and New Orleans, "when controversy developed into public disorder and violence," businessmen "began to act in their accustomed role as community leaders." He also found that in Dallas and Atlanta "businessmen successfully exerted their influence to prevent disorder before it developed."[3]

On the surface, the racial attitudes and economic desires of the businessmen in Saint Augustine appeared little different from those found elsewhere in the South. They joined with their white neighbors in supporting the segregation barriers which had been erected in the city during the 1890s. Unlike most southern communities, however, Saint Augustine was a city that depended heavily on tourism for its economic vitality. Over 85 percent of its income was generated by tourism with the vast majority of visitors coming from the Northeast and Midwest. In this economic setting, the business community down-played racial extremism to avoid alienating their northern guests. As one historian and former resident commented, the business community consistently sought "to keep social order and peace" and avoid exciting passions.[4]

2   Quoted in Kenneth K. Bailey, *Southern White Protestantism in the Twentieth Century* (New York: Harper and Row, 1964), 148.
3   Reed Sarratt, *The Ordeal of Segregation: The First Decade* (New York: Harper and Row, 1966), 285, 286.
4   Interview with Michael V. Gannon by the author, May 3, 1977; interviews

During the post-World War II period Saint Augustine remained a relatively stable society in a state that was experiencing rapid socioeconomic changes. Prosperity accelerated due to a resurgent tourist trade but otherwise the community seemed little changed from the prewar era. The leadership still came from the oldest and most respected families and tended to be lawyers, bankers, or businessmen, most of whom were involved only indirectly in the tourist industry. The majority of newcomers who arrived seemed to come chiefly to retire. According to local observers, they generally accepted the prevailing values of the community without dissent. "It was still a small town and everybody knew everybody," a local clergyman commented. It was also a society "not terribly interested in change," the same man noted, and "not terribly interested in being disturbed." Despite the cosmopolitanism fostered by tourism, racial traditions remained remarkably unchanged throughout the twentieth century. In contrast to the conditions James Silver found in Mississippi, however, there was no constant beating of the drums on behalf of white supremacy in Saint Augustine. Supremacist views were much more subtly presented but nonetheless firmly believed.[5]

Living in the nation's oldest city, Saint Augustinians were especially conscious of their past. According to one historian who spent several years studying the city's early history, the postwar white leadership exhibited a craze "for genealogy." Several Saint Augustinians took pride in tracing their ancestry back to the period of British and even Spanish occupation.[6] These people lived in particular neighborhoods in the city where they practiced very formal social customs modeled upon those

with Frank Upchurch, Hamilton Upchurch, and Douglas Hartley by the author, January 27, 1978; *Wall Street Journal*, June 19, 1964, p. 1.

5 Interviews with Gannon, Hamilton Upchurch, Frank Upchurch, and Hartley; U.S. Bureau of the Census, *Census of the Population: 1950, Vol. II, Characteristics of the Population, Part 10, Florida* (Washington, D.C.: Government Printing Office, 1952), 10–28; U.S. Bureau of the Census, *Census of the Population: 1960, Vol. I, Characteristics of the Population, Part 11, Florida* (Washington, D.C.: Government Printing Office, 1963), 11–29; interview with the Reverend Stanley Bullock by the author, January 17, 1978; interview with the Reverend Charles Seymour by the author, August 16, 1978; New York *Times*, July 5, 1964, Sec. 6, p. 30. See also James W. Silver, *Mississippi: The Closed Society* (New York: Harcourt, Brace and World, 1964).

6 New York *Times*, July 5, 1964, Sec. 6, p. 30; Gannon interview; Bullock interview.

conducted by the very rich from New York and New England who had visited Saint Augustine during the late nineteenth and early twentieth centuries. Here then was a very stable, personally close, and structured society with strong ties to the past on the verge of being confronted by a civil rights crisis of considerable magnitude.

In this oldest of American societies, black citizens, who constituted 21 percent of the population, held a distinctly subservient role. Census data disclosed that black economic activity clearly meant waiting upon whites and the tourist trade reinforced this subservient status. A total of 60 percent of all black female employees were engaged in domestic or service work and 80 percent of all male employees worked in service or blue-collar positions. The black family median income stood at $3,500 in 1960, $1,500 less than white family income. The future seemed to offer faint promise to black children as they averaged only 7.4 years of schooling compared to 11.2 years for white children.[7]

Despite the pervasiveness of segregation and their economically inferior status, blacks generally "thought things were good" in Saint Augustine. While blacks were expected to defer to whites, relations between the races were cordial and, in many cases, friendly. No social interchange took place, but blacks and whites exchanged pleasantries on the street and often sat in discussion on the park benches in the plaza. Blacks were allowed to register and vote in the Democratic primary following *Smith* v. *Allwright* (1944) although only a small minority of black residents exercised this privilege. Black citizens also served on grand juries but this occurred very infrequently.[8]

Outside observers who visited Saint Augustine for extended periods of time considered race relations there to be "above the average." "Less segregation, less animosity" existed there, ac-

7   Bureau of the Census, *Census of the Population: 1950, Vol. II*, 10–28, 58, 67; Bureau of the Census, *Census of the Population: 1960, Vol. I*, 11–29, 127, 129, 204, 210.

8   Interview with Henry Twine, president of the Saint Augustine Branch of the NAACP, by the author, September 19, 1977; interview with Clyde Jenkins by the author, September 19, 1977; interview with John D. Bailey by the author, August 11, 1977; "Presentment of the Grand Jury, Fall Term—1963, in the Circuit Court, Seventh Judicial Circuit of Florida, In and For St. Johns County," in folder labeled "Governor's Statements, Legal Matters, St. Augustine," Governor Farris Bryant Papers, Florida State Archives, Tallahassee.

cording to reporter and native Floridian Hank Drane, "than in many communities in Florida." Historian David Chalmers noted in a similar vein that Saint Augustine permitted a greater degree of racial intermingling than "hundreds of other Southern towns." Even local blacks observed, "You really weren't too conscious at that time of the difference that existed." Black Assistant Superintendent of Schools Otis Mason portrayed it as "an harmonious thing."[9]

But all was not racial bliss in this southern town, and some leaders envisioned difficulty for black citizens should they seek to improve their lot. "Racially, there was no concern on the part of most of the white people there as to the black," the Episcopal minister commented. "They were servants. They were kept in this position and there was no attempt . . . to help them except . . . to the extent that you would keep them in their place."[10]

Following the *Brown* decision in 1954 and the efforts of a few local citizens, two of whom had just moved to the city, black Saint Augustine began to assert itself. Under the leadership of the Reverend Thomas Wright, blacks requested that the city commission provide additional recreational facilities and funding for a community library in the late 1950s. Since neither request threatened the maintenance of a segregated society, both were approved. The commitment of white Saint Augustinians to segregation, however, was apparent for any who wished to challenge it. In the summer of 1961 a young black student from Howard University, Henry Thomas, who had just returned home from a workshop on sit-ins, decided to seek service at Woolworth's lunch counter. Thomas was quickly carried off to jail once the waitress realized what he was attempting to do. The police transferred Thomas to the hospital during the night, seeking to have him ruled insane and committed to a mental institution. Only Thomas' screams for help and his reputation in the community, as well as the apparent reluctance of the doctors, prevented police from having him locked away.[11]

9   Jenkins interview; interview with Hank Drane by the author, January 31, 1978; interview with Otis Mason by the author, June 13, 1978; David Chalmers, *Hooded Americanism: The First Century of the Ku Klux Klan* (Chicago: Quadrangle, 1968), 378.
10   Seymour interview.
11   Interview with the Reverend Thomas Wright by the author, October 6, 1977; Twine interview.

Thomas' personal example and that of the North Carolina A & T students in Greensboro encouraged local black teenagers and students at Florida Memorial College, a black school in the city, to conduct additional sit-ins. Sporadic demonstrations began in 1962 under the direction of Wright and continued until Dr. Robert Hayling, a recently arrived black dentist in the community, took over the leadership of the Youth Council of the local National Association for the Advancement of Colored People in 1963. Hayling developed a Youth Council agenda and coordinated daily demonstrations during that summer aimed at ending segregation in places of public accommodation. Civil rights forces relied heavily on young people in Saint Augustine apparently because many old people were either afraid or satisfied with the way things were. Claude Sitton noted in the New York *Times* that "the Negro community here is generally poor, apathetic over the civil rights drive."[12]

The struggle proved to be difficult for Hayling and his young assistants. Hayling was waylaid at a Ku Klux Klan meeting and severely beaten. His home was also shot into several times and the family's dog was killed while sitting in the living room. Four black teenagers (two boys and two girls), who took part in the demonstrations, were placed in state reform schools for over four months by the county judge when their parents refused to keep them from participating in future sit-ins. They remained in jail until January when the state Correctional Institutions Board released them.[13]

During these early days of the desegregation drive, the civil rights forces achieved a few breakthroughs, persuading Howard Johnson's, Woolworth's and McCrory's, three national concerns, and Del Monico's Restaurant to desegregate. But these gains did not represent a trend in the business community. Indeed, they would be the only victories by the civil rights forces in Saint Augustine until the passage of the Civil Rights Act in July, 1964.[14]

The more typical response by the business leadership came in July, 1963, when three black men were fired from their jobs

12   Wright interview; New York *Times*, May 31, 1964, p. 50.
13   St. Augustine *Record*, February 9, 1964, p. 1; *Florida Times-Union* (Jacksonville), July 30, 1963, p. 20; Pittsburgh *Courier*, January 25, 1964, p. 1.
14   *Florida Star News* (Jacksonville), October 12, 1963, p. 1; "Along the NAACP Battlefront: Florida Breakthrough," *Crisis*, LXX (November, 1963), 553.

for participating in the demonstrations. Shortly after these firings the shop steward at the Fairchild Stratos Corporation, an
aircraft manufacturing plant, called a meeting of all black
workers and, with the apparent support of company officials,
threatened them with the loss of their jobs if they took part in
the sit-ins. Women and wives of men who were involved in the
civil protests, and who worked in motels or as domestics, were
also intimidated by employers. The business community seemed
determined to stop the demonstrations before they spread further. No conspiracy existed among white businessmen to intim-
idate black residents. Segregationist attitudes were sufficiently
widespread, however, that business leaders responded almost
uniformly to civil rights demonstrations. This economic retaliation continued into 1964.[15]

The opposition of the businessmen to racial accommodation
reflected their personal prejudices as well as those of their
friends in the community. Typifying the views of many businessmen in Saint Augustine, Herbert E. Wolfe, president of the
town's major bank and generally recognized as the most influential man in the community, regarded blacks as racial inferiors
and opposed any equality between the races. A story he occasionally recounted to close friends reflected his personal prejudices: As a young man he was preparing his father's land for
planting when an old black man, who was whiling away his
time on a fence overlooking the land, told young Wolfe he was
doing the plowing all wrong. The old-timer then proceeded to
tell him how to do it correctly. Wolfe listened for a moment then
dropped the plow and walked off, deciding he would never do
anything again "that a nigger could do better."[16]

Businessmen were encouraged to resist the pressures to de-

15   Local Chapter of the Southern Christian Leadership Conference to Dr. William Sanders, Organization of American States, n.d., 7, in private papers of Professor David Chalmers, University of Florida, Gainesville; *Florida Star News*
(Jacksonville), July 13, 1963, p. 1; *Andrew Young* v. *L. O. Davis, et al.*, #64–
133–Civ–J, and pamphlet entitled "St. Augustine, Florida: 400 Years of Bigotry
and Hate," 4, both in Judge Bryan J. Simpson Papers, P. K. Yonge Library of
Florida History, University of Florida, Gainesville; interviews with Gannon,
Hamilton Upchurch, Bullock, and Seymour.
16   Gannon interview. David K. Bartholomew in "An Analysis of Change in
Power System and Decision-Making Process in a Selected County" (Ed.D., University of Florida, 1971), 42, ranked Wolfe as one of the two most influential men
in the county.

segregate by the recently established John Birch Society. In fact, a large segment of the business community either belonged to or sympathized with the Birch Society. According to state senator Verle Pope from Saint Johns County: "There was a very active group who might be said to be of a John Birch variety, who were very prominent and very strong. They were the leaders in the Kiwanis Club and Rotary Club. They were on the vestries in the churches. Wherever you turned it was the same group of people who were in power in the various organizations." They also "tended to associate socially."[17]

Saint Augustine maintained a very active right-wing chapter called the Saint Johns Chapter of the Florida Coalition of Patriotic Societies. The organization brought together the community's right-wing organizations and maintained an office and reading room on Saint George Street in the heart of the old Spanish quarter. The chapter, headed by prominent local physician Dr. Hardgrove Norris, sponsored weekly lectures by right-wing speakers. The women who kept the room told a reporter that "the Communists are behind all this integration business." The anticommunist appeal of the Birch Society received widespread support from civil rights opponents in the community who perceived the civil rights movement as part of the Communist menace. Norris' views were shared by his many prominent friends in the community, including Mayor Joseph Shelley, Herbert Wolfe, newspaper editor A. H. Tebault, county school superintendent Douglas Hartley, city attorney Robert Andreu, police chief Virgil Stuart, county sheriff L. O. Davis, and county judge Charles Mathis.[18]

The support the John Birch Society received from the community made it very difficult, if not impossible, for those who wanted to compromise with the demonstrators in 1963 and 1964. Hamilton Upchurch, president of the Chamber of Commerce in 1965, noted: "Anything you proposed even . . . at a

17   Robert W. Hartley, "A Long, Hot Summer: The St. Augustine Racial Disorders of 1964" (M.A. thesis, Stetson University, 1972), 93; interview with Judge Richard O. Watson by the author, January 9, 1977; Hamilton Upchurch interview; Gannon interview; Bartholomew, "An Analysis of Change in Power System," 63, 64. The Birch Society regarded the civil rights movement as having "been deliberately and almost wholly created by the Communists." St. Augustine *Record*, August 22, 1965, p. 7A.
18   New York *Times*, June 14, 1964, p. 50; anonymous source; interviews with Bullock, Gannon, and Hartley.

cocktail party that was in any way conciliatory . . . you were ostracized by this extreme right wing. They said this thing is bigger than your pocketbook." Businessmen were also reluctant to take an independent position because the community was relatively small and close-knit. Upchurch observed that "every job had a name and a face."[19]

With progress at a standstill during the summer of 1963, leaders of the local NAACP, including Dr. Hayling, asked the city commission to establish a biracial committee. Mayor Shelley, a physician, and his fellow commissioners, all businessmen, opposed the idea. Shelly declared: "We have no biracial committee here because it could do nothing we have not already done." Dr. Norris, head of the local John Birch Society, opposed the creation of a biracial committee because "the negotiating table has been the chosen battleground by the Communist conspiracy for world conquest." Shelley was in great sympathy with this view. He pointed out that integration existed in all city-operated facilities. He was not being entirely truthful since the city's library was still closed to blacks. Shelley also contended that the commission "has no legal or moral right to tell any merchant how to operate his business."[20]

Local leaders argued that they had gone more than halfway in meeting the NAACP demands. Shelley noted repeatedly that the county school system had agreed voluntarily to desegregate its schools by admitting six black children to previously all-white schools. This was done, however, under the Florida Pupil Placement Law which had been designed to circumvent the Supreme Court's decision of 1954. While Saint Johns County had integrated its schools of its own accord, a suit by the NAACP was pending in federal district court asking for complete integration of the county schools. County school officials appear to have taken this first step to demonstrate some compliance with the *Brown* decision and thereby avoid massive court-ordered integration. In short, the school integration could not be said to demonstrate the city or county's racial progressivism as suggested by Shelley.[21]

19   Hamilton Upchurch interview.
20   St. Augustine *Record*, July 7, 1963, p. 1B.; interview with Dr. Joseph Shelley by the author, September 6, 1977; New York *Times*, July 3, 1964, p. 8.
21   Minutes of the Saint Augustine City Commission, June 28, 1963, pp. 4410–11, in City Hall, Saint Augustine; St. Augustine *Record*, May 10, 1963, p. 1,

Business leaders found additional support for maintaining the status quo in race relations from Governor Farris Bryant. Bryant had expressed his opposition to the civil rights bill while appearing before the United States Senate Commerce Committee. He argued that a motel owner, for example, should have the right to refuse service: "That's simple justice. The wonder is really that it can be questioned."[22]

The business community in Saint Augustine was thus under no pressure from the political leaders at the state or local level to ease the racial barriers that existed. In addition, the demonstrations had not caused any economic difficulties; tourism figures for the summer were above those for 1962. As a consequence, only the national chain stores which feared problems elsewhere modified their stance against serving blacks at lunch counters. The remaining members of the business community experienced no such pressures in this direction and opted instead to maintain racial barriers.[23]

In mid-August, 1963, the Florida Advisory Committee to the United States Commission on Civil Rights, which had been visiting several strife-ridden cities in the state, arrived in Saint Augustine. During the one day the committee received testimony on race relations in the community, not one member of the city commission, county commission, or any of the "invited business leaders" appeared as witnesses. White leaders stayed away from the meeting in the belief that the committee was not an impartial body and would only stir up more racial problems in the community. Many whites also felt that the problems in Saint Augustine were not the concern of any outside group. The committee noted that "in none of the other cities [in Florida] . . . has there been such a boycott." After hearing the testimony of several black leaders, their report concluded that "St. Augustine was a segregated super-bomb aimed at the heart of Florida's economic prosperity and political integrity, and the fuse is short."[24]

September 3, 1963, p. 1. Saint Augustine was not in the forefront of school desegregation in Florida; nearly two thousand black students attended white schools in Florida in 1964. Joseph Aaron Tomberlin, "The Negro and Florida's System of Education: The Aftermath of the *Brown* Case" (Ph.D. dissertation, Florida State University, 1967), 199.

22   *Florida Times-Union* (Jacksonville), July 30, 1963, p. 1.

23   New York *Times*, July 29, 1963, p. 9.

24   Florida Advisory Committee to the United States Commission on Civil Dis-

In December, 1963, a grand jury, which had been meeting for several weeks in an effort to head off the growing violence in the city—one white man was killed in the fall and several blacks beaten and their homes damaged—warned local leaders that unless they sat down and discussed black demands 1964 would see additional acts of racial violence.[25]

City leaders chose to ignore the warning of both groups and refused to negotiate with black leaders. Instead they laid the blame for Saint Augustine's racial difficulties on "outsiders," the Klan, and black militants. One leader commented, businessmen "attributed their problem [in 1963] to a pushy nigger [Hayling]." As a consequence, the city council, supported by the business community, refused to meet with black leaders. State Attorney Dan Warren from Daytona Beach viewed this decision by the white community as crucial for the future of race relations in Saint Augustine. In his eyes, by ignoring the grand jury's suggestion "the only remaining voice of moderation was smothered."[26]

During the late fall of 1963, after being approached by Dr. Hayling and other black leaders from Saint Augustine, the Southern Christian Leadership Conference decided to commit its resources to the desegregation drive in the city. The decision by the SCLC seems to have been based in part on the conditions in Saint Augustine and in part on its own needs and concerns. SCLC felt it needed publicity in 1964 to pressure Congress into passing the civil rights bill, to combat the growing militancy among blacks in America, and to raise money for its other campaigns. Since Saint Augustine was on the eve of its four hundredth anniversary, making it the oldest community in America and already the object of considerable nationwide interest, it had

orders, "Report on the Opening Meeting in St. Augustine, Florida, August 16, 1963," p. 3, and *Young* v. *Davis, et al.*, both in Simpson Papers; anonymous source; Hamilton Upchurch interview.

25   Reprint of article in Daytona Beach *Sunday News Journal*, February 21, 1965, in Simpson Papers.

26   Upchurch interview. Arrest records for 1963 and 1964 show rather clearly, however, that the majority of those arrested were Saint Augustinians and not outsiders. *Young* v. *Davis*, in Simpson Papers. The white attitude toward the demonstrators in 1963 was an old one—"These are our niggers—we can handle them." Pat Watters, *Down to Now: Reflections on the Southern Civil Rights Movement* (New York: Random House, 1971), 97; reprint from Daytona Beach *Sunday News Journal*, February 21, 1965, in Simpson Papers.

symbolic as well as practical value as a target. In addition to the desegregation of public accommodations, the SCLC also sought the employment of black policemen, firemen, and office workers by the city; establishment of a biracial committee; dropping of charges against demonstrators; and employment of people in the business community on the basis of merit, not race.[27]

The first wave of demonstrators arrived during Easter week, 1964. Led by Mrs. Malcolm Peabody, mother of the governor of Massachusetts, and accompanied by several prominent women and clergymen from the Boston area and a retinue of college students, the demonstrators transformed the situation in Saint Augustine from a rather insignificant local racial disturbance into a national civil rights crusade. In the process, the white community was further alienated. Mayor Shelley, speaking for many whites, declared that the trouble in the city was due to northern "scalawags" and that matters were well in hand until northerners "came down here with the idea of getting in jail."[28]

The intervention of northerners generated a deep-seated hostility among white Saint Augustinians who were personally insulted by these northern "do-gooders," especially the white college hippie and the "uppity" northern "nigger." Now the struggle took on the added appearance of a clash between cultures, and white southerners in Saint Augustine, very proud of their heritage, refused to accept criticism of their cultural traditions. Of additional concern to local residents was the view spread by the Birch Society that the Communist-led civil rights movement threatened the basic fabric of Saint Augustine society.[29]

27   Twine interview. Twine was a member of the Saint Augustine delegation that first approached the SCLC. Interview with the Reverend Fred Shuttlesworth by the author, September 13, 1978. See also John Herbers, *The Lost Priority: What Happened to the Civil Rights Movement in America?* (New York: Funk and Wagnalls, 1970), 68.

28   St. Augustine *Record*, March 29, 1964, p. 1. A variation of this view was expressed in 1963 by a businessman who told a northern correspondent: "Why don't you stay up North where you are really having trouble with Negroes." New York *Times*, July 29, 1963, p. 9.

29   For an elaboration of this point see Watters, *Down to Now*, 97. Interviews with Gannon and Shelley; interview with Dr. Hardgrove Norris by the author, September 15, 1978.

The Easter demonstrations were the highly publicized phase of the movement, designed to draw national attention to the problems in this historic city. In that they were very successful. Now, in late May, 1964, there began the second phase of the movement led by Dr. Martin Luther King, Jr., and aimed at bringing an end to segregation in Saint Augustine.

To facilitate this phase of the struggle, black leaders called for an economic boycott. Because the community was so economically dependent on tourism, civil rights leaders were confident that they could force the business community to abandon segregation. As Harry Boyte, a top King aide, pointed out: "This is the first time we've been able to put things on such a firm economic basis. In Birmingham the downtown merchants were hurt but we couldn't shut down U.S. Steel. Here it's a total community effort." A major part of this effort involved demonstrations to keep the city's problems on the front page of the nation's newspapers and on the evening television news. The daily sit-ins followed by the evening marches and the ocean wade-ins kept the press's attention, particularly when white mobs, spurred on by the rhetoric of J. B. Stoner of the Ku Klux Klan and the Reverend Connie Lynch, assaulted the demonstrators.[30]

The demonstrations were carefully planned in advance. Local black leader Henry Twine noted that strategy meetings were held every night to determine "whitey's reaction." One reporter observed that the demonstrators "always came up with something new that would cause the whites to trigger some violence and so it would get the headlines." The goal of SCLC was to keep the nation's attention riveted on Saint Augustine and in this manner to bring outside pressure to bear on the community as well as to point out the need for the civil rights bill.

Commenting on the movement in Saint Augustine, King observed, "Even if we do not get all we should, movements such as this tend more and more to give a Negro the sense of self-respect that he needs. It tends to generate courage in Negroes outside the movement. It brings intangible results outside the community where it is carried out. There is a hardening of attitudes in situations like this. But other cities see and say, 'We don't want to be another Albany [Georgia] or Birmingham,' and they make

30 *Wall Street Journal*, June 19, 1964, p. 1.

changes. Some communities, like this one, had to bear the cross."[31]

The use of the boycott seemed to make business leaders only more adamant in their opposition to desegregation, however. When Harry Boyte approached Herbert Wolfe and asked him to use his influence to stop the mounting violence, Wolfe refused. He told Boyte he saw nothing wrong with the status of Negroes in Saint Augustine. Wolfe said he agreed with a local editorial which accused King of being a troublemaker who was turning the city into a battleground. Two other business leaders who opposed any compromise argued that "the sole reason for this movement is that local public officials will not force owners of private businesses to integrate their facilities in direct opposition to the 13th Amendment to the United States Constitution which outlaws involuntary servitude."[32]

The motel and restaurant owners, who bore the brunt of the demonstrations, followed the lead of James Brock, manager of the Monson Motor Lodge and president of the state and past president of the local hotel and motel managers association. Brock refused to serve any blacks unless "a federal court orders us to." But, significantly, Brock was not unyielding in his position, for he later declared, "If a representative group of St. Augustine citizens appeals to us, in the interests of community welfare, we might consider it [integration]."[33]

Brock and his colleagues in the motel, restaurant, and tourist trade were desperately looking for help from other community leaders. Tourism had fallen off dramatically by the early weeks of June. One motel owner complained, "I've gotten as many cancellations as reservations this week. I just want all this to end." James A. Kalivas of Chimes Restaurant claimed his business was off 60 percent. Capt. Francis F. Usina, who ran a sightseeing vessel, grumbled that business was running 50 percent behind a year ago. "If Martin Luther King doesn't stay away, the whole summer will be lost," he said. Perhaps the most accurate barometer of the tourist trade was the daily attendance record kept by the Castillo de San Marcos, an old Spanish fort

31   Interviews with Twine and Drane; Herbers, *The Lost Priority*, 70.
32   Pittsburgh *Courier*, June 6, 1964, p. 4; New York *Times*, June 7, 1964, p. 48; *Florida Times-Union* (Jacksonville), June 14, 1964, p. 22.
33   Miami *Herald*, June 5, 1964, p. 8A; New York *Times*, June 7, 1964, p. 48.

administered by the National Park Service, whose attendance had fallen a full 30 percent behind the previous year's total. The fort's historian commented: "If it keeps up, there's no doubt the decline will get bigger."[34]

The business leaders who were only indirectly tied to the tourist trade and the professional leaders appeared largely unmoved by the growing problems of the tourist economy, however. Racial traditions, pressures from friends in the Birch Society, and the belief that the community was being used by outside forces for other purposes, made these business and civic leaders resistant to change or compromise. The sense of being beleaguered and embattled also created a "fortress mentality" in which the leadership turned increasingly inward. A reporter, who had covered the city since 1959, observed that "all of a sudden it became leaderless."[35]

The unwillingness of the business community, the most influential group in the city at this time, to assume the mantle of leadership enabled the Klan and local white militants to become spokesmen for the community. It also allowed city police chief Virgil Stuart and Saint Johns County sheriff L. O. Davis, both of whom opposed the efforts of the civil rights movement, to enforce the law selectively. Davis was generally recognized to be in league with the white militants. Hoss Manucy, their spokesman, maintained his office on a chair in front of the sheriff's office and appeared to have free access to the sheriff's office. Chief Stuart was alleged to be an "extreme right winger" who not only thought there was "a communist behind every bush . . . he saw one."[36]

The SCLC was clearly surprised by the unbending attitude of the community leaders and the violence it encountered on the street. Many members of the SCLC, including Dr. King and Andrew Young, had thought that a great deal could be accomplished in Saint Augustine since it had widespread residential integration and was so dependent on tourism. They now realized in mid-June that they were in for a long fight which would

34   Wall Street Journal, June 19, 1964, p. 1; New York Times, June 7, 1964, p. 48.
35   Drane interview.
36   Ibid.; interview with Judge Bryan Simpson by the author, June 24, 1964; Upchurch interview.

be every bit as arduous as the Birmingham struggle. King was moved by the hostility of business and civic leaders and the mounting violence in Saint Augustine as well as by a desire to elicit federal assistance to say that "we have never worked in . . . [a city] as lawless as this."

The night marches and the wade-ins by the civil rights forces generated the most violence. Whites responded by throwing bricks, acid, firecrackers and physically assaulting any black or white they could get their hands on. Cameramen who tried to film these events were also badly beaten and their cameras broken. After a few weeks of this violence, several cameramen and reporters asked for new assignments.[37]

By the third week in June as the violence continued unabated and business continued to fall off, the motel owners met, with Edward Mussallem, owner of the Caravan Motel, acting as chairman. The assembly also included representatives from the Chamber of Commerce, the Florida East Coast Railroad, Wolfe, and owners of restaurants and entertainment facilities. But rather than suggesting a compromise, the businessmen, through their spokesman state senator Verle Pope, denounced the role of outsiders for desecrating Saint Augustine "for some unknown reason." They only agreed "to continue to operate their businesses in accordance with present and future laws." The implication was that they would abide by the civil rights bill when it was passed by Congress.[38]

Without offering a concrete proposal, the merchants did announce that they were interested in a peaceful settlement of the crisis. They refused, however, to meet with Dr. Robert Hayling. The Reverend Fred Shuttlesworth of the SCLC characterized the statement as "segregationist" and declared that it did "not show much evolution." He promised "to keep up our present program."[39]

But SCLC was tiring of the violence and the cost of the struggle, and, with the passage of the civil rights bill imminent,

37 Drane interview. See also Miami *Herald* and New York *Times*, May 28–June 4, 1964. The residential desegregation was misleading. It was a result of geographic limitations as well as a carry-over from antebellum days when slaves lived in the rear quarters of their master's residence. New York *Times*, June 6, 1964, p. 10.
38 New York *Times*, June 18, 1964, p. 25; Tampa *Tribune*, June 18, 1964, p. 8A.
39 New York *Times*, June 18, 1964, p. 25.

decided to keep the lines of communication with the business community open. Dr. King said he would consider the necessity of including Hayling at such meetings. To add encouragement to the voices of moderation in the business community, he observed that he had heard that several business leaders were willing to desegregate, hire blacks, and drop charges against the demonstrators if a compromise could be arranged. Adding to King's initiatives, a special grand jury had just completed its hearings and was expected to recommend a cooling-off period of thirty days during which time a biracial committee would attempt to alleviate the crisis. Moreover, Herbert Wolfe had privately initiated discussions with civic and business leaders in an attempt to effect a compromise.[40]

Just when it appeared a settlement might be possible, the SCLC staged its most spectacular demonstration. Seven demonstrators jumped into the swimming pool at the Monson Motor Lodge. Brock, the manager of the motel and a moderating force in the community up to that time, lost his composure. Shouting at the swimmers to get out, Brock told them he was pouring acid into the pool (it turned out to be muriatic acid, a harmless cleaning detergent for the pool).[41]

This incident was followed by a series of marches, sit-ins, and wade-ins at the ocean which further alienated the white community and ended efforts to bring about a compromise. Verle Pope told reporters: "Well, we are through. We can't understand why they hit us like this when we were working sincerely on this thing. The jury was working on a really worthwhile report. Now it's all gone."[42]

Despite the improved chances for peace, SCLC had decided to continue the demonstrations because Dr. King and his aides felt the white leadership had not developed an adequate desegregation plan. King also believed the grand jury's thirty-day cooling-off period was much too long and would cripple the desegregation drive. It was back to the barricades for the organization.[43]

40   *Ibid.*, June 25, 1964, p. 19; Miami *Herald*, June 18, 1964, p. 1A, June 28, 1964, pp. 1A–2A; *Young* v. *Davis, et al.*, and notes of Judge Bryan Simpson, Box 1, both in Simpson Papers.
41   *Florida Times-Union* (Jacksonville), June 21, 1964, p. 22.
42   Miami *Herald*, June 28, 1964, pp. 1A–2A.
43   *Ibid.*

At the end of June, Florida Senator George Smathers informed his close friend and former campaign finance chairman, Herbert Wolfe, that President Lyndon Johnson was anxious for a cessation of the crisis before he signed the civil rights bill into law. Smathers asked Wolfe to see if he could establish a biracial committee to ease tensions and satisfy one of King's demands. Wolfe called together twenty-five civic and business leaders and informed them of the president's wishes. Mayor Shelley immediately expressed his opposition to the idea telling Wolfe, "You're going to sell the community out and give Martin Luther King a victory." The others agreed completely with Shelley and called Governor Bryant, who had also been contacted by Smathers and the president, to inform him of their decision.[44]

To the chagrin of these men, Bryant announced to the press on the following day, June 30, the formation of a biracial commission in Saint Augustine to end the crisis. Shelley called Bryant and asked him what had happened. Bryant replied that the "truth of it is, I haven't formed a committee in Saint Augustine." Bryant, who was under considerable pressure from President Johnson, decided to go ahead with his announcement as a concession to the president. King called off further demonstrations, praising Bryant and white leaders for taking "a first important step" toward peace, although he surely must have known that the commission was a fraud. Nevertheless, King also realized that the governor's proposal placed the state on the side of the civil rights movement and when combined with the signing of the Civil Rights Act on July 2 assured SCLC of achieving most of its goals in Saint Augustine.[45]

The crisis appeared to be at an end. At a meeting in which eighty of the town's one hundred businessmen were present, a vote was rendered to comply with the public accommodation sections of the new law. James Brock commented that his col-

---

44 Shelley interview.
45 *Ibid.*; St. Augustine *Record*, July 1, 1964, p. 1. Federal pressure was not confined to Governor Bryant. Hamilton Upchurch noted that he represented a group of men in 1964 who were trying to obtain a federal charter to establish a savings and loan association. The charter was rejected. Upchurch was informed some years later by the federal hearing officer that "St. Augustine could not have gotten the Red Cross if they had been wiped off the map in 1964." Upchurch interview.

leagues unanimously opposed the measure in principle but, with only "a few dissenters," agreed to abide by it.[46]

The racial problems were not over yet, however. No one had taken into consideration the response of the Klan members and their sympathizers. Allowed to assume a leadership position in the community when a power vacuum was created by the unwillingness of business and civic leaders to deal with the racial crisis, these elements were not now ready to step aside and permit the community to comply with this hated law. Carrying picket signs proclaiming DELICIOUS FOOD—EAT WITH NIGGERS HERE, NIGGERS SLEEP HERE—WOULD YOU, and CIVIL RIGHTS HAS TO GO, white militants paraded in front of the desegregated establishments. One businessman complained: "We have been caught in a dilemma." Under federal law "we are forced to serve Negroes although it hurts our business. If we serve them, then white pickets run the rest of the business away."[47]

The activities of the Klan and their supporters were not confined to demonstrations alone. When restaurant and motel owners continued to serve blacks, they began receiving telephone calls threatening their lives and their businesses. On the evening of July 24 two whites threw a molotov cocktail into Brock's restaurant, badly damaging the interior. The following day, those businessmen who had not begun turning blacks away now did.[48]

State Attorney General James Kynes, who viewed most of the crisis from Tallahassee but was periodically sent to Saint Augustine at the request of the governor, had little sympathy for the plight of the business community. Kynes felt the restaurant and motel owners wanted to have it both ways. When Negroes were conducting sit-ins, he observed, merchants allowed young white toughs to set the mood of the town with little or no resis-

46   Florida Times-Union (Jacksonville), July 2, 1964, p. 18; Lucille Plummer, et al. v. James E. Brock, et al., #64–187–Civ–J, and Simpson's Notes, both in Simpson Papers.

47   St. Augustine Record, July 16, 1964, p. 1.

48   Testimony of James E. Brock, Lucille Plummer, et al. v. James E. Brock, et al., #64–187–Civ–J, p. 56, in Record Group 21, Accession No. 73A377, FRC No. 1E15823, Agency Box 13, Federal Records Center, East Point, Georgia; St. Augustine Record, July 24, 1964, p. 1. Louis Connell of Santa Maria Restaurant told Judge Simpson, "I was scared; I don't mind admitting it." New York Times, July 23, 1964, p. 15.

tance to this takeover. Now, Kynes declared, the businessmen found they could not take back control when it no longer suited their purpose to have gangs of whites roaming the streets.[49]

Perhaps more significantly, a number of businessmen, who were angered by having to accept new racial patterns, hoped these militants might yet resurrect segregation. This attitude was further reflected during an abortive effort to establish a genuine biracial committee. In early August, 1964, a grand jury nominated several members to such a committee to head off the renewed violence. Only one of the white members appointed to the committee agreed to serve. Andrew McGhin, president of the Chamber of Commerce, said he could not serve "due to pre-existing business and a community commitment." Three of the remaining four whites named also spoke of more pressing concerns. The grand jury had erred in naming the committee without first informing these individuals. Nevertheless, after these four whites declined to serve, no other white leaders in the community could be found to replace them. Another opportunity to bring the community together had been consciously rejected by the white leadership.[50]

While SCLC leaders received little support from businessmen, they found a powerful ally in Federal Judge Bryan Simpson of the district court of appeals in Jacksonville. Simpson ordered the police department to enforce the laws equitably and made the businessmen abide by the new Civil Rights Act. In a series of decisions he blocked the resegregation of motel and restaurant facilities and forbade the segregationists from threatening or coercing owners. Furthermore, when he ordered a deputy sheriff to turn in his badge for intimidating a local black citizen, he made it demonstrably clear that he would not allow race relations to return to their pre-1963 state.[51]

Simpson's intervention was critical, for it led to the removal of outside militants from the community and enabled the more moderate forces to reestablish political control. This did not

49   St. Petersburg *Times*, July 26, 1964, p. 16.
50   Newspaper Scrapbook on the Saint Augustine Civil Rights Movement, August 7, 1964, Saint Augustine Historical Society, Saint Augustine; St. Augustine *Record*, August 14, 1964, p. 15B.
51   St. Augustine *Record*, July 20, 1964, p. 1, August 5, 1964, p. 1; New York *Times*, August 6, 1964, p. 16; *Plummer, et al.* v. *Brock, et al.*, Transcript of Oral Findings, August 19, 1964, p. 10, in Simpson Papers.

bring about an immediate reconciliation between the races nor a permanent end to the violence. Many white businessmen were still incensed over the intervention of outside forces into "their peaceful community." The restaurant association, for example, adopted a resolution reluctantly agreeing to integrate but also deploring "the action of the Congress and the Courts in enforcing integration" and stating "that integration of places of accommodation is obnoxious to us." Several restaurant owners put signs above their cash register stating that all money spent by integrationists in their establishments would be used to aid Barry Goldwater's 1964 presidential campaign. In a speech before a local civic group, Harold Colee, head of the state Chamber of Commerce and a native Saint Augustinian, reflected the views of many when he remarked derisively how the recent racial crisis could be marketed to attract more tourists: "You may interestingly point out just where a certain prominent New England lady—a professional bleeding heart—was standing when she posed for cameramen of the national news media, working from a prepared script, in the year 1964."[52]

By the middle of 1965, blacks were still unsure about their place in Saint Augustine and few were willing to dine in white restaurants or register at white motels. One black citizen who could afford to eat at such restaurants commented: "You can be pretty sure that if you eat at a white restaurant and they know who you are, your boss will be told that you're trying to stir up trouble. If they don't know you, you might be arrested after you leave so they can find out about you." Sporadic violence continued through the fall of 1964 and winter of 1965, as blacks were assaulted often for no apparent reason.[53]

Despite such circumstances, the business community had substantially altered its racial policies if not its racial attitudes by the spring of 1965. The impact of the racial crisis on the tourist industry in Saint Augustine had gradually awakened business leaders to the economic consequences of their actions during the past year. By the end of 1964 tourism was off by 40 to 60 percent from the 1963 levels in virtually all businesses. No

---

52   St. Augustine *Record*, August 11, 1964, p. 1; Pittsburgh *Courier*, September 26, 1964, p. 4.
53   *Wall Street Journal*, August 6, 1965, p. 1; *Florida Star News* (Jacksonville), September 18, 1964, p. 1, April 17, 1965, p. 1; St. Augustine *Record*, August 26, 1964, p. 6, July 21, 1965, p. 1.

one in the community, not even those whose businesses were only indirectly tied to the tourist trade, could afford a repetition of the economic decline experienced in 1964.[54]

With the four hundredth anniversary about to be celebrated in September, 1965, and the SCLC promising renewed demonstrations if the violence did not cease, businessmen organized to block further resistance. When racial incidents recurred in the spring of 1965, City Manager Charles Barrier, at the urging of Wolfe, and business leaders deplored the violence. In a front-page story in the city's newspaper, Barrier warned whites who committed such acts that they would be arrested and vigorously prosecuted. In a similar statement a few days earlier, Sheriff Davis let it be known that his department would not permit the fighting and rock throwing of last year. Reporter Hank Drane of the *Florida Times-Union* observed that "once the community decided they wanted to get rid of it [the Klan], it was amazing how speedily . . . they got the Klan out."[55]

If this decision to alter the racial policies of the past was not sufficient, Judge Bryan Simpson stood in the background having made it apparent to all that Saint Augustinians must abide by the Civil Rights Act of 1964 and accept a biracial society. Leon Friedman called Simpson "one district judge who has excelled all others in his speed in enforcing the law and in his willingness to embark on new legal territory to protect Negro rights." The community thus no longer had recourse even to southern justice.[56]

Finally, recently elected Governor Haydon Burns refused to challenge the judicial findings of Judge Simpson as Governor Farris Bryant had done on one occasion. If Saint Augustinians wanted to continue the struggle to preserve their segregationist society, they would have to do so alone. This they were unwilling to do.[57]

54   St. Augustine *Record*, January 22, 1965, p. 5. Chamber of Commerce manager H. B. Chitty estimated the economic loss at from eight to ten million dollars of the city's annual tourist income of twenty-two million dollars. Atlanta *Journal and Constitution*, July 5, 1964, p. 80.

55   St. Augustine *Record*, July 23, 1965, p. 1, July 21, 1965, p. 1; Drane interview. Blacks were also given token representation on all quadricentennial committees and encouraged to participate in all activities.

56   Leon Friedman, *Southern Justice* (New York: Random House, 1965), 193.

57   Bryant attempted to stop the night marches by the civil rights forces. Simpson ruled against Bryant's position and then threatened him with contempt

In many respects the business community's response to the racial crisis in Saint Augustine had a great deal in common with that found in such " 'Old South' cities as Charleston [and] New Orleans." Numan Bartley observed that "tradition, respect for old wealth, concern for the style of social life, and an elitist outlook acted as barriers to changes in social and ideological outlook." While this observation appears applicable to the Saint Augustine experience, a distinctly non–Old South organization, the John Birch Society, added a new variable to the racial picture in this community making it much more difficult for civil rights leaders to change racial traditions. An Episcopal clergyman found the businessmen in the city to be "independently minded" and "sufficiently committed to what they believed . . . to jeopardize their businesses." The pressures of an influential John Birch organization and a relatively small, interpersonal society whose leaders shared the anti-Communist views of the Birch Society thus tended to suppress dissent and discourage moderation as the community rallied to ward off the civil rights movement's frontal assault.[58]

The businessmen in Saint Augustine had to be forced to abandon the racial traditions of the past by civil rights forces, the federal courts, and the federal government. Only when the business leaders realized there was no turning back, and their economic viability and the celebration of the town's four hundredth anniversary were tied to the amelioration of the crisis did they oppose the reemergence of racial violence.

In marked contrast to the era of Reconstruction, the federal pressure to desegregate Saint Augustine remained unwavering throughout the 1960s. Responding to the moral suasion and

---

when the governor indicated he would ignore the decision. Bryant then reversed his position. St. Augustine *Record*, June 10, 1964, p. 1. The business committee seems to have opposed completely Judge Simpson's decision overturning Governor Bryant's ban on the night marches. Businessmen felt these marches were largely responsible for the violence. The testimony before Judge Simpson clearly revealed, however, that the violence was fostered not by the marchers but by the white onlookers. Transcript of Hearing, June 13, 1964, *Andrew Young* v. *L. O. Davis, et al.*, #64–133–Civ–J, Record Group 21, Accession No. 73A377, FRC No. 1E15887, Agency Box 9, Federal Records Center. See also Arguments of Tobias Simon and William Kunstler in same location.

58   Numan V. Bartley, *The Rise of Massive Resistance: Race and Politics in the South During the 1950's* (Baton Rouge: Louisiana State University Press, 1969), 313; Bullock interview.

activism of the civil rights movement, the federal government abolished racial discrimination in public accommodations,
schools, and voting. A social revolution did occur in Saint Augustine, but it did not emanate from the white leadership in the
community as suggested by Claude Sitton and Reed Sarratt.
Time, a dogmatic civil rights leadership, the constant threat of
federal intervention, and a decline in influence of the Birch Society gradually brought about an acceptance of a biracial society
by the city's businessmen in the 1970s. If Saint Augustine's response is typical of other tradition-bound, Birch-influenced
southern communities, then such places did not willingly accept the racial developments of the 1950s. On the contrary, a
federal government, encouraged to act by the courts, civil rights
groups, and a sympathetic North, mandated these social changes.

Significantly, the change in white attitudes and in the political and social condition of black Saint Augustinians had very
little impact on black economic standing. Because of the heavy
tourist orientation of the economy, black residents continued to
work in largely unskilled, service-oriented positions during the
1970s. The closing of the Fairchild-Hiller aircraft plant in 1972
further reduced employment opportunities for blacks outside
the tourist industry. One black leader described the job opportunities as basically "pick and shovel." Hamilton Upchurch observed in 1978 that there were still "no blacks in responsible
jobs." Black parents were particularly concerned about the departure of their children to other cities where greater employment opportunities existed.[59]

Jobs which offered more than menial wages and limited opportunity for advancement thus became the major concern of
black leaders in the decade of the 1970s and into the 1980s.
They have focused their demands on the city, seeking more jobs
in government, especially in the police department and fire department. Presently, only one black is employed by the police
department, where Virgil Stuart still serves as police chief, and
none are employed by the fire department. Black employment
has increased steadily in city government during the 1970s, but
the jobs have been almost exclusively in the blue-collar and sec-

59   Twine interview; Hamilton Upchurch interview; interview with Mrs. Cath-
erine Twine by the author, September 19, 1977.

retarial ranks. Only in the school system have blacks been able to obtain white-collar positions in large numbers.[60]

Businessmen largely removed themselves from the civil rights debate after 1965. The rapid decline of the civil rights movement with the final departure of SCLC and the decision by Dr. Hayling to move to south Florida in 1967 facilitated the withdrawal of business leaders from racial deliberations. With the racial crisis at an end, businessmen readily returned to their chief concern, their own enterprises.

In recent years, businessmen have avoided becoming involved in civil rights developments. Black leaders have concentrated their efforts against the city in an effort to improve job opportunities and public services for black neighborhoods. Never anxious to be in the limelight on social issues which did not directly affect their economic enterprises, businessmen have been content to stay in the background and ignore recent racial concerns. Without the involvement of this most influential group, however, real economic opportunity for black Saint Augustinians has not been possible and black gains since 1965 have been largely limited to the social and political arenas.

60   Henry Twine interview.

CHARLES SALLIS AND
JOHN QUINCY ADAMS

DESEGREGATION IN JACKSON MISSISSIPPI

Jackson, Mississippi, founded in 1822, is the state's capital and largest city. Its 1950 population was over ninety-eight thousand, of whom approximately 41 percent were black. Only recently has Jackson approached the progressive outlook of many other southern cities. Most of the migration to Jackson came from the surrounding countryside. Both city and state lacked a cosmopolitan tradition, and attitudes toward race and modernization, which might be expected to improve with urbanization, did not change readily. Nonsoutherners who became residents of the city either sympathized with local customs or did not interfere. Nor did Jackson have newspapers which molded public opinion in a constructive way. In 1954 white Mississippians, wedded to the past and resistant to change, were not ready for the revolution in race relations that began that year.

Response to the decision in *Brown* v. *Board of Education* on May 17, 1954, was immediate. The next day the Jackson *Clarion-Ledger* called it a "black day of tragedy," and the Jackson *Daily News* fumed that Mississippi "cannot and will not try to abide by such a decision." It would mean "racial strife of the bitterest sort. . . . Human blood may stain Southern soil in many places because of this decision but the dark red stains of that blood will be on the marble steps of the United States Supreme Court Building."

The state legislature began at once to implement "lawful means" to circumvent the decision. A constitutional amendment authorizing abolition of the state's public schools signaled the beginning of "massive resistance" to desegregation in Mississippi.

In July the militantly segregationist Citizens Council was organized in Indianola by Robert B. Patterson, a plantation manager, and fourteen business and community leaders from that delta town. Within a year, the organization had spread to sixty-five of Mississippi's eighty-two counties, enrolling some eighty thousand members. Composed of influential white Mississippians, the council reached the apex of its power during the administration of Governor Ross Barnett (1960–1964) and became "the almost unchallenged arbiter of state politics." Barnett appointed them to key governmental positions; they advised him, wrote speeches for him, and "comprised a kind of Cabinet extraordinary for racial affairs."[1] The Jackson chapter kept files on certain individuals' racial views. Their 1958 "freedom of choice" survey of every white family in Jackson revealed that 98 percent of those responding supported school segregation and Citizens Council policies.

Vehicles for the council's massive propaganda campaign were its magazine, the *Council*, and its radio and television series, "The Citizens Council Forum," which preached the virtues of segregated society and the dangers of integration. After Barnett took office and until 1963, the State Sovereignty Commission funneled $193,500 of public funds to the council. The morning *Clarion-Ledger* and evening *Daily News*, both owned by the powerful Hederman family, ardently endorsed the council. Slanted editorials and inflammatory journalism from the Hederman press reinforced the council position. According to Professor James Silver of the University of Mississippi, "To read

---

1   Neil R. McMillen, "Development of Civil Rights, 1956–1970," in R. A. McLemore (ed.), *A History of Mississippi*, (2 vols.; Hattiesburg: University and College Press of Mississippi, 1973), II, 159–60. See McMillen's *The Citizens' Council: Organized Resistance to the Second Reconstruction* (Urbana: University of Illinois Press, 1971) for a full account.

the Hederman press day after day is to understand what the people of the state believe and are prepared to defend."[2]

The Jackson *State Times* called for moderation. Lacking subscriptions and advertising, however, the *State Times* ceased publication after seven years. The Hedermans then had a monopoly of the Jackson daily press. Only Hazel Brannon Smith's weekly *Northside Reporter* offered Jackson's readers an alternative to the Hedermans' extremism.

After the Supreme Court's May, 1955, mandate to implement desegregation "with all deliberate speed," forty-two blacks signed a Jackson NAACP chapter petition calling on the Jackson school board to comply with the Supreme Court decisions. This movement halted when names and places of the petitioners' employment appeared in the Jackson papers. After that, direct civil rights activity in Jackson and in Mississippi was sporadic.

Jackson's first nationally publicized experience with civil rights activity came in 1961 when Freedom Riders set out from Washington to test compliance with ICC regulations regarding interstate bus terminals. Out-of-state newsmen covering the trip arrived in Jackson to see if the Freedom Riders' brutal treatment along the way would be duplicated here. One of Jackson's leading bankers, concerned about the image of the city, hosted a party for journalists at the city's largest hotel where they could meet select prominent citizens who would dispel any preconceived notions of hostility and backwardness about Jackson. The next day, when the Freedom Riders arrived, they were arrested as expected, although police did prevent the crowd from attacking them. The incident energized Mississippi's blacks. The marches and demonstrations that took place throughout the state that year were accompanied by violence; there were twenty-four documented instances of brutality in 1961.[3]

When native black Mississippian James Meredith gained admission to the University of Mississippi after an eighteen-month legal delay, further obstructions were climaxed by Governor Barnett's "interposition proclamation" of September 13, 1962, televised statewide, pitting the state against the federal govern-

2   James W. Silver, *Mississippi: The Closed Society* (New York: Harcourt, Brace and World, 1964), 30.
3   Neal R. Peirce, *The Deep South States of America* (New York: Norton, 1974), 180; Lester A. Sobel (ed.), *Civil Rights: 1960–66* (New York: Facts on File, Inc., 1967), 66–69.

ment. Silver reported an attempt, of which most people were unaware, to forestall the inevitable confrontation. "Frantic wires
were dispatched and telephone calls . . . hurriedly made, meetings . . . arranged, resolutions and petitions . . . drawn up, as
the elite among the state's business and professional men tried
desperately to stave off disaster. The effort came too late, was
too meager, and failed miserably."[4] Jackson, two hundred miles
from the Ole Miss campus, was the scene of the final frenzied
rally to support the governor's obstinacy. Barnett spoke at half-
time during an Ole Miss football game in Jackson and brought
the hysteria to a peak. No voice of moderation was heard in the
city. The next day, Meredith was admitted and the infamous Old
Miss riot ensued.[5]

In the spring of 1962, a suit had been filed to desegregate
Jackson's libraries, parks, and swimming pools. Later that year,
Jackson blacks, led by John Salter, a white sociology professor
at Tougaloo College, undertook a boycott effort of downtown
stores. They sought nondiscriminatory hiring of personnel; an
end to segregated fountains, rest rooms, and seating; and use of
courtesy titles for all people. By May, 1963, with Birmingham
on everyone's minds, a nonviolent, direct-action campaign was
planned under the direction of Medgar Evers, Mississippi field
secretary for the NAACP. (Among the objectives sought were the
integration of stores, public facilities, and schools; the removal
of segregation signs in public buildings; the hiring of black policemen, black school-crossing guards, and black city employees; and the establishment of a biracial committee to deal with
Jackson's racial problems.[6] Telegrams were sent to most of Jackson's businesses and to heads of national chain stores with Jackson outlets.[7]

On May 27 Mayor Thompson met with local black represen-

---

4   Silver, *Mississippi: The Closed Society*, 117.
5   See Silver's *Mississippi: The Closed Society*, and Walter Lord, *The Past That
Would Not Die* (New York: Harper and Row, 1965), for background material.
6   See John R. Salter, Jr., *Jackson, Mississippi: An American Chronicle of
Struggle and Schism* (Hicksville, N.Y.: Exposition Press, 1979), for a graphic
account of the grass-roots Jackson movement of 1962–63. He writes movingly
of its "betrayal" by the national NAACP and the "liberal experts" in Washington
who favored voter registration drives rather than direct-action campaigns. He
also writes convincingly of the harassment, threats, and physical danger which
faced civil rights workers in Jackson.
7   Jackson *Daily News*, June 12, 1963.

tatives. Thompson told them that "Economic boycotts, civil disobedience, and mass marches designed to disrupt the normal
business activities and create mass hysteria . . . can only lead to
distrust and ill-will. . . . Those who participate in such ill advised activities . . . run the risk of loss of job, of family disruptions, and may assume the serious role of law violators."[8] Most
of the blacks walked out when Thompson finished. When the
board of directors of the Chamber of Commerce, the Junior
Chamber of Commerce, the Exchange Club, and the North Jackson Lions Club went on record as supporting the mayor, the
stage was set for direct confrontation.

At 11:16 A.M. on Tuesday, May 28, 1963, Mississippi's first
sit-in was staged at F. W. Woolworth's segregated lunch counter
in the Capitol Street store. Three black Tougaloo College students, all native Mississippians, made small purchases and then
took their seats at the lunch counter. Waitresses refused to wait
on them and all but two of the seven whites who were eating left
immediately; the three blacks were jerked from their stools and
harassed. Outside, five demonstrators for a biracial committee
were arrested and charged with blocking the sidewalk. A crowd
of some two hundred whites gathered at Woolworth's as other
Tougaloo students and Professor Salter joined the sit-in. Cursed,
slapped, splashed with mustard, catsup, sugar, and salt, they
were arrested and charged with violating a 1960 breach-of-the-
peace law.[9]

The next day eleven demonstrators were jailed for picketing
Capitol Street stores. Despite a temporary injunction by Chancery Court Judge J. C. Stennett, demonstrations continued. On
May 30, four hundred black students demonstrated in a school
yard; police barricaded streets. The next day, there was a massive demonstration downtown. City policemen, reinforced by
sheriff's deputies and the state highway patrol, arrested some
six hundred demonstrators, loaded them onto trucks (with the
help of black prison trusties), and took them to a compound at
the nearby state fairgrounds. During a march on June 1, the
one hundred demonstrators arrested included Medgar Evers

8   *Ibid.*, May 28, 1963.
9   One of the students was Anne Moody of Centreville, who later wrote of her
involvement in the civil rights struggle in *Coming of Age in Mississippi* (New
York: Dial Press, 1968).

and NAACP Executive Secretary Roy Wilkins. That day Mayor Thompson and the city commissioners agreed to consider desegregating city water fountains and rest rooms and hiring black policemen, school-crossing guards, and city employees. On Sunday, June 9, blacks were refused admission to six white Protestant churches. Two days later Federal District Court Judge Harold Cox formally delayed a verdict on the NAACP petition to have Judge Stennett withdraw his ban. In municipal court that afternoon, fifty-two persons were convicted on charges stemming from the demonstrations: thirty-five were fined a hundred dollars each for parading without permits and seventeen drew five-hundred-dollar fines and six-month jail sentences for obstructing sidewalks.[10]

At a mass rally that night black leaders talked of setting aside demonstrations to work on a massive voter registration campaign. After the meeting adjourned shortly after midnight, Medgar Evers drove home. He stepped from his car, was shot in the back from ambush, and fell mortally wounded in his driveway. Mayor Thompson, who hurried home from vacation, professed Jackson's citizens as "shocked, humiliated and sick at heart." The city offered a five-thousand-dollar reward for information leading to the arrest and conviction of Evers' killer.[11] Blacks took to the streets in a mass demonstration; 158, including several ministers, were arrested. Evers' funeral on June 15 led to more arrests when young blacks left the mourning march and confronted police. Other arrests followed the next day; by now, over a thousand demonstrators had been arrested.

Telephone calls from President Kennedy and Attorney General Kennedy on June 18 prompted Mayor Thompson's agreement to hire six black policemen, eight black school-crossing guards, and to promote seven black sanitation workers to drivers. In return, demonstrations were suspended on June 20. Two days later, Byron de la Beckwith of Greenwood, a fertilizer salesman and Citizens Council member, was arrested and charged with Evers' murder (later, two hung juries resulted in his release).

During the winter of 1963–1964, the city fathers, knowing

10 Jackson *Daily News*, June 10, 12, 1963.
11 *Ibid.*, June 12, 1963.

they soon would have to comply with the court's declaratory judgment regarding the use of public facilities, including swimming pools, decided to close the pools permanently. The NAACP did not go to the courts over the pool closing during the summer of 1964, probably because it was already involved in the school suit, the implementation of the public accommodations section of the pending Civil Rights Act, and "Freedom Summer."

Mississippi's continued resistance sparked a concerted effort in the summer of 1964 by the four major civil rights organizations in the nation—SNCC, NAACP, CORE, and SCLC—to ally with several Mississippi organizations. This coalition, known as the Council of Federated Organizations (COFO), sponsored hundreds of summer volunteers to promote black community development, challenge segregation practices, operate Freedom Schools, conduct voter registration drives, and raise the morale of downtrodden black Mississippians. The State Sovereignty Commission, the Citizens Council, and segregationist newspapers, especially in Jackson, condemned this "massive attack" by "outside agitators." While most of the projects were located outside Jackson, some of the statewide coordination was done in the city. More important, those in the movement quickly became aware that outside legal assistance would be necessary to prevent false arrests and convictions.[12]

The advent of Freedom Summer prompted the Lawyers' Committee for Civil Rights Under Law to send volunteers on two-week assignments to Mississippi and to seek some formal liaison with the Mississippi State Bar. At the same time, differences over tactics and strategy resulted in the formation of the Lawyers' Constitutional Defense Committee (LCDC), which set up an office in Jackson. Attorneys from both groups were harshly received by Jackson lawyers and local judges. Problems were smoothed somewhat when representatives of the Lawyers' Committee and several leaders of the Mississippi Bar (including a prominent Jackson attorney) negotiated a formal recognition of the Lawyers' Committee by the Bar. Thus the involvement of the outside lawyers was legitimized. A year later, the Lawyers' Committee established a permanent office in Jackson.[13]

12   See Len Holt, *The Summer That Didn't End* (New York: Morrow, 1965).
13   See John Honnold, "The Bourgeois Bar and the Mississippi Movement," *American Bar Association Journal*, LII (1966), 228, and Richard Hammer, "Yankee Lawyers in Mississippi Courts," *Harper's*, November, 1966, pp. 79–88.

On July 2, in the midst of "Freedom Summer," a strong civil rights bill became law, despite the longest filibuster in the nation's history. Governor Paul B. Johnson, Jr., called on Mississippians not to comply with the act until it was tested in the courts. In a significant move breaking with state leadership, the board of directors of the Jackson Chamber of Commerce urged compliance, although the Jackson Chamber had officially opposed the passage of the act and many members continued to oppose it in principle. The Chamber explained, "The citizens of Jackson have earned a reputation as a law-abiding community, and the business and professional leadership of the city, and our elected city officials, have always encouraged all of our people of both races to abide by the law of the land. We may not be in sympathy with all of the laws of the land, but we must maintain our standing as a community which abides by the law." Editor Hazel Brannon Smith hailed the Chamber statement as "wise and needed, the first indication of responsible leadership in some time."[14] Bishop Richard O. Gerow of the Natchez-Jackson Diocese of the Catholic Church in Mississippi urged Mississippians to "reject the spirit of rebellion."[15]

When eight NAACP officials came to Jackson to study the effects of compliance with the new law, they registered at local hotels and a motel and were served in the coffee shops. Four black youths attended a previously all-white movie theater. Other than one motel's closing its swimming pool to guests because of "insufficient chemicals," there were no incidents. Rather than integrate, the Robert E. Lee Hotel temporarily closed its doors.[16]

A legislative resolution condemned the Civil Rights Act as unconstitutional and urged Mississippians to resist its enforcement "by all legal means." A state senator from Hinds County charged the Jackson Chamber of Commerce with supporting "left-wing radicals" and of adhering to "the dollar mark rather than principle." As expected, the Jackson Citizens Council branded the Civil Rights Act an unconstitutional "force bill" and urged citizens to refuse "to eat, swim or sleep under integrated conditions. . . . If Negroes enter a restaurant, swimming pool, hotel or motel to force themselves into mixed social situations

14   Jackson *Northside Reporter*, July 9, 1964.
15   Jackson *Daily News*, July 3, 1964.
16   *Ibid.*

(which the many self-respecting Negroes of Jackson will not do), then the whites can protest effectively—and in a peaceful, lawful and non-violent manner by vacating the premises immediately." It condemned the "surrender statement" of the Chamber and called for a boycott of all white businesses which complied. "Integration cannot be imposed upon an unwilling white majority by the business community in Jackson, or anywhere else. Businessmen cannot play both sides of the street; they must ultimately choose whether to serve white or negro customers, especially in social or semi-social institutions." The statement closed with the admonition: "We can buy white—we can vote white!"[17]

Some Jackson restaurants closed after passage of the Civil Rights Act. A few later were issued "charters" by the secretary of state designating them "private clubs" whose patrons paid one dollar in "membership dues." The Robert E. Lee Hotel reopened as a "private club" for those members who paid a twelve-dollar annual "membership fee." Most businessmen in Jackson operated normally, however, serving clients of both races.

On July 9, Mayor Thompson endorsed the Chamber of Commerce stand saying he personally opposed the Civil Rights Act and "federally-forced integration," but that Jackson was a "law-abiding city" and was "going to do what the law says about facilities." City officials had to prevent the current racial situation from exploding into "riot, insurrection and violence" because "the federal government would move troops in."[18] Thompson's stand, which directly contravened that of the legislature and Governor Johnson, also marked his split from the Citizens Council and its resistance posture, followed for so long by Mississippi and Jackson officialdom. It was a turning-point in Mississippi's history.

In the first full week after passage of the Civil Rights Act, segregation barriers tumbled all over Mississippi, mainly in the larger towns and cities, as well as throughout the entire South. Although there were some trouble spots elsewhere in the state, such as Laurel, initial compliance was encouraging. In September, schools in Jackson, Biloxi, Clarksdale, and Carthage were

17   *Ibid.*, July 7, 1964.
18   *Ibid.*, July 9, 1964.

tokenly desegregated without incident. Mississippians for Public Education, organized in Jackson in April to promote the peaceful and orderly continuation of the public schools, played no small role in preparing the way for compliance.

Throughout Freedom Summer and the succeeding fall, there were reports that Mississippi's industrial progress was faltering because of the state's image. WLBT-TV in Jackson featured a program in which leading industrialists noted that prospects for new industries in the state had cooled noticeably. Although several reasons were given for the slump, a number of prospective newcomers to Mississippi were reported to have been afraid of the racial situation.

In February, 1965, the Mississippi Economic Council denounced lawless activity in the state and declared that "order and respect for the law must be maintained. . . . We recognize that the Civil Rights Act of 1964 has been enacted by Congress as law. It cannot be ignored and should not be unlawfully defied." The council further stated that Mississippians should adjust to the act's impact "regardless of personal feelings and conviction" and called upon citizens to take "positive action" to achieve "justice, harmony and continued development." Governor Johnson, changing his stand, gave the statement his support calling it "a good, sound and strong position."[19]

Other business groups throughout the state endorsed the stand of the Mississippi Economic Council. Attorney General Joe T. Patterson spoke to the Mississippi Sheriffs' and Peace Officers' Association in emphatic terms: "We must . . . recognize that we are part of the Union . . . and that we are bound by the laws of the United States and the decisions of the United States Supreme Court." Adding to the more favorable climate, Millsaps College in Jackson became the state's first private college voluntarily to open its doors (in February, 1965) to black students. All these developments, according to Hodding Carter, were part of the "creeping realism" which was taking hold in Mississippi.[20]

How can one explain the sudden switch to moderation in Mississippi? There are several factors associated with compliance. First, there was the Civil Rights Act itself. Heretofore,

19   *Ibid.*, February 4, 1965.
20   McMillen, "Development of Civil Rights," 165.

Mississippians had gone along with state law and local custom; now there was a federal law that demanded compliance and there were federal officials to enforce it. In the face of this, local patterns of segregation had to give way. Conduct or behavior had to change whether opinions did or not.

There was also the growing realization that the measures identified with the "defiance-at-all-costs" stand taken by the Citizens Council and state and local politicians were no longer viable. Even Senator Stennis, who had opposed the civil rights bill and who voted against it, gave this advice: "The bill passed and is now enacted into law. Under our system of government, it is the law and where applicable, must be complied with until repealed or modified by the Congress or held unconstitutional by the Courts."[21]

The course taken by Atlanta and other southern cities in opening public accommodations without incident before the Civil Rights Act became law encouraged moderates in Jackson to speak out. They were supported by a few clergy who, for the first time, were able to counsel obedience to the law without themselves becoming the objects of retaliation. The climate had changed, albeit slowly, so that churches were no longer forced to support the status quo.

The overwhelming bipartisan support in Congress for the Civil Rights Act and the swift action of the Federal Bureau of Investigation and the Justice Department in investigating the three Philadelphia murders impressed upon reasonable Mississippians that the resolve of the federal government remained unshaken in upholding the rights of black people. The overwhelming defeat of Republican Barry Goldwater in November, 1964, despite his getting 87 percent of the vote in Mississippi, lessened the chances of the repeal of civil rights legislation.

The impact of the Ole Miss riot of 1962, the violence in Birmingham and elsewhere in the South in 1963, and Freedom Summer of 1964 in Mississippi made many Mississippians realize that the state was getting an infamous reputation for its intransigent posture on race. Defiance of federal law by state officials, beatings, murders, the failure of local law enforcement in the state were all covered by the national media. "Mississippi

21   Jackson *Northside Reporter*, July 30, 1964.

Goddamn" was a popular cry of civil rights demonstrators all over the country. Most important, many businessmen realized that continued resistance, racial unrest, and violence (or the threat of it) projected the image of a lawless state and would retard economic development. Local boycotts and a threatened national boycott of Mississippi goods heightened this concern. The difficulty Little Rock had in getting new industries to locate there after the school crisis in 1957 and the stagnating industrial development of Bogalusa, Louisiana, where there was continuing racial turmoil, made vivid impressions upon Jackson businessmen and industrialists. One businessman, entertaining a prospective Ohio manufacturer who was looking at Jackson as a possible site for relocating his plant, was quoted as saying, "We had to reassure this man we could and would maintain the law." As one observer of the Jackson situation put it, "Mississippi business opinion generally came to believe that the state's economic development would be hurt by racial disorder. When they reached this conclusion, the weight of their influence moved toward easing the conflict through compliance with the federal law."[22]

Thus, Mississippi business interests, seeing business hurt in other southern cities by social disruption and feeling pressure from both the black protesters and the federal government, decided to comply with the law. When businessmen became convinced that sustained racial upheaval would imperil economic development, they provided a climate for change in southern customs by taking a stand on upholding "law and order."

A very important economic factor was federal assistance to Mississippi. The Justice Department notified all public agencies that federal aid would be jeopardized unless pledges ensuring compliance were forthcoming. In 1964 federal aid to Mississippi totaled some $1,225,500,000 while taxes collected amounted to only $341,000,000. Clearly the federal government was a powerful coercive force as well as an essential element in Mississippi's continuing economic growth.

Even though business played a key role in this period, most Mississippi businessmen were segregationists. Even northern

22 Quoted in Jack Patterson, "Business Response to the Negro Movement," *New South*, XXI (Winter, 1966), 69.

managers who had come South went along with the status quo
and "native customs." Businessmen supported segregation and
states rights, yet they feared extremism. There were, of course,
dissenters in the business community, but they were few and far
outnumbered by segregationists. During the 1950s and the
early 1960s the business community in Jackson vacillated—
they left racial issues to the politicians and the Citizens Council.
Most believed white supremacy and economic progress could go
hand in hand. Not until the Ole Miss crisis was this attitude
seriously questioned. The business leaders made no commitment, however, to solve the basic needs of the black community.
As one authority stated: "In Mississippi, and elsewhere, businessmen have thought more in terms of stilling the bad publicity and improving the state's 'image' rather than searching out
root causes. To establish peace, to quiet troubled waters, businessmen have been willing to pay the price of some desegregation, some concessions; rarely has business showed willingness
to give more than was required."[23]

The "bad publicity" and poor state image were in part
caused by the role of local newspapers and television stations.
There were two network television stations in the city then.
WJTV (CBS) was partly owned by the Jackson newspaper publishing family; WLBT (NBC) had absentee owners. The management and news departments of both stations reflected the thinking of the general white Mississippi public, so that prominent
blacks on network shows were bleeped out, derogatory statements were made without rebuttal, and so forth. The licenses of
both stations were challenged in 1964 at renewal time. WJTV
negotiated a settlement, but WLBT did not and lost its license in
a protracted battle through the FCC and the courts. A nonprofit,
biracial, public-service-oriented interim licensee ran the station
until July 1, 1980, when integrated applicant groups, representing the entire business and political spectrum, merged into
one which got the permanent license.[24]

During the late 1960s, there were both setbacks and progress in race relations. In May, 1967, and May, 1970, the issue
of traffic through the Jackson State campus was escalated into

23   *Ibid.*, 72.
24   Peirce, *The Deep South States of America*, 220–21.

nationally publicized confrontations between students and other young blacks, and state and local police. Three blacks were killed in these two incidents. A black-led boycott in 1967, protesting the continuation of pool closings and the lack of meaningful integration in both public and private employment, affected the Jackson business community. The reappearance of KKK bombings in Jackson in the fall of 1967 increased the tension. Matters came to a head after demonstrations occurred following the assassination of Martin Luther King in 1968. The stalemate in making significant progress in race relations led over 250 business, civic, educational, and religious leaders to take out full-page ads in the Jackson papers calling for equality of treatment in law enforcement, employment, education, and public facilities. This bold statement marked the beginning of a favorable climate for the continuing resolutions of many problems.

This favorable climate was strengthened by the results of Freedom Summer and the Voting Rights Act of 1965, which spurred a slow but steady increase in black registration and voting participation in Jackson and elsewhere. Black political involvement became organized, and issues affecting blacks forced the business community and other city leaders to work with (or at least communicate with) the new black leadership. One of the first manifestations of the new black political role occurred in the 1969 municipal elections. After the retirement of twenty-year incumbent Allen Thompson, the mayor's race was open. Russell Davis, a businessman and a moderate who had served in the legislature, ran on a progressive platform, and, with the help of black votes, won.

All of the developments discussed above overlap in time one of the major civil rights issues in Jackson: public school integration. Not until almost a decade after the famous *Brown* case had there been any effort to desegregate public schools in Mississippi, and Jackson's dual system was one of the first challenged. NAACP Field Secretary Medgar Evers filed federal suit on March 8, 1963, on behalf of his daughter to enter her into an all-white elementary school. During the next six years, the plaintiff's name became Singleton, the case went back and forth to the Fifth Circuit Court of Appeals, freedom of choice was reluctantly adopted, business leaders and the mayor urged peace and calm—but only token integration resulted.[25] A U.S. Supreme Court ruling on January 14, 1970, that the fifth circuit's timetable was too slow caught Jackson unprepared for the decree that the schools were to be completely integrated by the beginning of the second semester in early February, just three weeks hence! The high court's ruling included no specifics, and District Judge Dan Russell had to fashion a plan for immediate implementation. The judge's plan, while making a giant stride toward compliance, had several features concerning the elementary schools which led plaintiffs to appeal to the fifth circuit. On May 5, 1970, the appellate court made changes and also ordered that a biracial committee be appointed by the district court to assist in the process of perfecting the plan. This marked the first time that the judicial system recognized the need for community involvement in the Jackson school case.

One week later twelve prominent Jacksonians were named to the biracial committee by Judge Russell from lists submitted by the parties. Its chairman was J. Herman Hines, president of Jackson's largest bank, and its vice-chairman was Jack Young, Sr., one of the few black attorneys predating the civil rights movement. The white members were a "who's who" of the business community: the president of the second largest bank, the president of one of the two largest electrical utilities in the state, the president of a large business who also happened to be chairman of the board of the state's leading liberal arts college, and so forth. Among the blacks was a long-time leader during the stormy period of Jackson's desegregation struggle, the Reverend R. L. T. Smith. This committee was called upon to submit an alternative to the existing elementary school integration plan, which it did in mid-June, 1970.

While the plaintiffs and defendants, the biracial committee, HEW, and the courts wrestled with the differences still preventing unanimity among the parties, an unexpected announcement in late July revealed the further involvement of the city's leadership. A few months earlier, Congress, at the urging of

25 *Evers* v. *Jackson Municipal Separate School District*, 328 F.2d 408 (1964). See also *Singleton* v. *Jackson Municipal Separate School District*, 348 F.2d 729 (1965), 355 F.2d 865 (1966), 404 F.2d 353 (1968), 419 F.2d 1211 (1969), 425 F.2d 1211 (1970), 426 F.2d 1364 (1970), 432 F.2d 927 (1970), 332 F. Supp. 984 (1971), 509 F.2d 818 (1975).

President Nixon, enacted a $75 million Emergency School Assistance Fund to help school districts facing problems stemming from school integration orders. School superintendent John Martin, Henry Hederman, and newly appointed and widely respected Jackson State President John A. Peoples went to Washington during the spring to investigate the possibilities of obtaining a grant for Jackson. Assisting in promoting the Jacksonians' interest was Fred LaRue, a White House aide who had formerly been a Jackson businessman (and who was subsequently convicted for his part in the Watergate scandal). LaRue's connections and the additional support of Dr. Gilbert Mason of Biloxi, long-time civil rights leader and vice-chairman of the Mississippi Advisory Committee to the U.S. Commission on Civil Rights, gave strong impetus to HEW's unusual funding of $1.3 million to the school district four days before the formal application was received by the government! The grant, largest in the nation, was later said by critics to have little relevance to the act's purpose: "The Jackson application defines its emergency not as making desegregation work, but as saving the city from the effects of it." Half the grant was used to upgrade the quality of teaching in the school system. Finally, three days prior to the official transmittal of the $1.3 million, about eight hundred state-owned textbooks were transferred to a newly opened segregationist academy under the state program of furnishing free texts, using public schools as a conduit, to all private schools. This seemed to make a mockery of the school district's promise that it had not engaged "in the gifts, lease, or sale of property or services, directly or indirectly" to private schools set up to avoid desegregation, and after a week of national as well as local publicity, the transfer was rescinded.[26]

The suddenness of the February, 1970, district court order requiring complete integration resulted in a 600 percent enrollment increase in private schools (from five hundred to three thousand). The influence of the Citizens Council was waning, however, for their strident message was too much at odds with the progressive image being developed by the city's business and professional leadership. Thus, a desire to provide a more sophisticated way out of public school integration led some well-to-do

26 New York *Times*, September 5, 1971.

conservatives to encourage their large church congregations to create elementary schools as a facet of "Christian" education. To provide for secondary education, a large tract of land was acquired just outside the city and a crash building program began for Jackson Preparatory School. To finance these endeavors, the two largest banks, whose presidents served on the court-appointed biracial committee, loaned six hundred thousand dollars to support the development of these new schools.

As white flight began, enhanced by increasing opportunities for private education, the student ratio in the Jackson schools switched from sixty-forty white-black to sixty-forty black-white. Fear that white flight would lead to a resegregated, mostly black public school system beside lily-white private schools prompted two leading organizations in the city to file a joint brief in October, 1970, as amicus curiae in the pending U.S. Supreme Court case, *Swann* v. *Charlotte-Mecklenburg County Board of Education.* The *Swann* case, although a North Carolina suit, was expected to bring forth a definitive ruling on the use of busing to achieve integration.[27] The Jackson case, though not directly a part of the *Swann* proceedings, would certainly be affected by its outcome, since the unresolved elements in the ongoing *Singleton* suit could be dealt with through a busing order. The unusual alliance between the Chamber of Commerce and the Urban League in filing the brief took place because both groups feared that proposed school assignments under the court plan then in effect, shuffling many pupils as often as six times in the course of their twelve grades, would drive whites out of the public schools and leave them largely all black. The brief, among other things, asked that neighborhood schools be kept as a mainstay of public education. Chamber of Commerce President Henry Hederman, who had vigorously opposed every implementation of desegregation in Mississippi since 1954, had now come to see the negative impact that community recalcitrance had upon the economic growth and prosperity of the city and state. The black leaders of the Urban League, too, knew that business stagnation could only damage the economic prospects for blacks in the community. The brief

27   *Swann* v. *Charlotte-Mecklenburg County Board of Education,* 402 U.S. 1 (1971).

took note of the need for stability in the public schools, pointing out that the current situation was preventing a major manufacturer from building a new, large plant in the Jackson area. The reference was to the Allis-Chalmers Corporation (now with the multinational name of Siemens-Chalmers), a heavy electrical equipment manufacturer seeking to build a branch operation in a good locale.[28]

It had been too many years since the last appearance of new industry in the Jackson area, and the Chamber of Commerce was most anxious to make a significant jump in the city's economic growth to avoid lagging behind other southern cities. The president of Allis-Chalmers had looked over Jackson, but the timing of his visit—shortly after the second incidence of violence at Jackson State—only served to accentuate his desire that there be stability in the community, including a general support for and commitment to quality public education.

Their arguments went unheeded. The Supreme Court ruling in *Swann*, handed down in April, 1971, unanimously permitting busing to achieve integration, gave implicit approval and direction to the district court and fifth circuit to include busing in the final plans for the Jackson schools. At this point a fortuitous circumstance facilitated agreement on the final plans. In an action unrelated to the suit, the school board had sought the assistance of the Mississippi Research and Development Center (a state think-tank set up in 1963 to try to overcome the state's perennial fiftieth ranking on various indices). The R & D Center put school officials in touch with the management analysis branch of General Electric, the TEMPO Center for Advanced Studies, and a contract was entered into for a study of management, organization, and educational practices in the school system. Before this project got fully under way, the consultants were asked by the school board to establish communications with all segments of the community and then fashion an elementary school desegregation plan acceptable to all. After extensive local research, the analysts recommended a plan providing for quasi-neighborhood schools supplemented by noncontiguous zones and utilizing broad-scale busing. The plaintiffs, after convincing the district court to make a few mi-

28   Jackson *Clarion-Ledger*, October 4, 1970.

nor modifications, accepted the plan, and for the first time in seven years, blacks and whites had agreed on a comprehensive scheme to integrate the city schools. A massive publicity campaign was then begun to support both the plan and the public schools. A few months later, Allis-Chalmers announced it would build its plant on the outskirts of Jackson. The business community was further elated when city officials were successful in getting New York bond-rating firms to raise the classification of Jackson's municipal bonds, in apparent recognition of the good economic climate likely to stem from the peaceful end to the school controversy.

Businessmen were soon to be involved in another aspect of the civil rights struggle: housing. Black leaders had long wanted some form of public housing because of the dire needs of their community, but a referendum requirement that 60 percent approve public housing plus the negative attitudes of Mayor Thompson seemed insuperable. However, in 1971 an unusual opportunity occurred for the passage of a housing referendum. For some time downtown property owners and businessmen had been aware that the heart of the city needed revitalization. Federal funds were available to assist in this revitalization but a referendum had to approve municipal involvement. The white business community felt it had to have black support in the election, so a deal was struck between black leaders and white businessmen to work for the adoption of two referenda: public housing and downtown renewal. The black leaders held to the bargain and convinced the black community to vote for both. The white businessmen supported the two issues with considerable advertising and a fairly large budget, but the housing issue was defeated by white voters, with some commentators saying that the white leadership really didn't push hard enough. Later, a method was found to avoid holding a referendum, and about a thousand units of tokenly integrated public housing were established.

Private housing discrimination did not end until a few years later. Then, white realtors began blockbusting, and white-controlled lending institutions practiced red-lining (refusing to make mortgage loans in changing neighborhoods on grounds that property values were unstable). However, the availability of financing from a Jackson all-black savings and loan association plus scrutiny by federal officials soon curbed these means of preventing change. While this made it possible for blacks to buy houses in formerly all-white neighborhoods, resegregation quickly took place, and the number of integrated neighborhoods in Jackson today is very, very few.

Since the late 1960s racial progress in Jackson has been steady but slow. In August, 1973, a reporter for the New York *Times* found that Jackson, known in the 1960s as one of the South's "meanest" cities, "now treats blacks much the same as Northern cities in most crucial respects—and even better in some. . . . Racial inequality and the grinding poverty that goes with it still exists . . . but open, harsh discrimination has been eliminated."[29]

There has indeed been notable progress in four areas of concern: school desegregation, public accommodations, voting rights and participation, and, most important, dialogue between blacks and whites. In the early 1970s, a black was appointed to the Jackson School Board. For the first time in a dozen years, the city operated swimming pools without controversy or compulsion. As a result of lawsuits brought in 1973 and 1974, municipal hiring practices now opened up more city jobs for blacks, who are also regularly seen downtown and in suburban shopping centers as clerks, cashiers, and even as store managers. The black vote in Jackson cannot be overlooked by any candidate; it has served to nudge extreme conservative and racist politicians toward moderation. White flight from the public schools has ended, and some of the private academies have been forced to close as more white students return to integrated schools. All television stations have black cameramen (and camerawomen), black announcers, and black reporters. Programs dealing with issues of special interest in the black community are regularly aired.

Advances are impressive on the surface; underneath problems remain. Behavior and actions may have changed, but racial attitudes have not among the majority of Jackson whites. Blacks are still seen by many as inferior. Despite a growing middle class of blacks in Jackson, most blacks are still on the bottom rung of the economic ladder, holding menial and low-

29 New York *Times*, June 14, 1975.

paying jobs. Unemployment among blacks, particularly young blacks, is a major problem. Segregation in churches and in most social relations is evidence that racism among whites is still part of the "Mississippi way of life."

STEVEN F. LAWSON

FROM SIT-IN TO RACE RIOT

BUSINESSMEN, BLACKS, AND THE PURSUIT OF
MODERATION IN TAMPA, 1960–1967

Much of the literature concerning the civil rights movement and
race relations in the South has concentrated on their explosive
nature. Journalists and scholars alike have been fascinated with
confrontation and crisis resolution. Montgomery, Little Rock,
New Orleans, Greenwood, Birmingham, Saint Augustine, and
Selma dot a civil rights road map as signposts of heroic
struggles. The turbulent battles fought in such places generated enough publicity to shape a national consensus supporting
passage of five civil rights acts in the decade and a half after
Brown v. *the Board of Education*. Studies of race relations during this era also follow the headlines, particularly those that
attracted national attention for a prolonged period. Often left
unrecorded are the sagas of southern communities which labored to resolve racial conflicts calmly and out of the limelight.
In such a fashion, they often hoped to cast an image as part of
the progressive "New South."

In examining racial policy-making on the local level, attention has been focused on civic elites, particularly on businessmen who influenced the political process either formally through
participation in public agencies or informally by virtue of the

deference they commanded from elected officials. Social scientists have discovered that the character of controlling elites determined the quality of race relations in troubled southern cities. Influential whites, such as those in New Orleans and Saint Augustine during the 1960s, derived their social standing from old family backgrounds rather than from recently acquired wealth. Committed to a traditional ethic, they scorned efforts to promote new economic growth, and they usually abstained from providing leadership to avert racial crises that might scare away potential outside investors in their city's financial development. In contrast, in Atlanta, Houston, and Miami, elites composed of nouveau riche and recent arrivals espoused a progressive ideology. Welcoming new industry and culture, they had a stake in thwarting racial turmoil that might damage prospects for their city's booming future. Hence, modernizing elites threw their considerable influence on the side of racial moderation.[1]

However, business leaders who chose to identify with the brand of the "New South" did not automatically become unrestrained advocates of racial egalitarianism. C. Vann Woodward, drawing upon his vast historical insight, in the early 1960s warned that a previous generation of "New South" promoters had fostered segregation and disfranchisement in the first place as a means of luring capitalists with a "contented and docile" labor supply. Subsequent empirical research has demonstrated that although modern apostles of the "New South" lent a hand in dismantling some of the discriminatory barriers erected by their predecessors during the Age of Redemption, they accepted "only enough moderation as [was] necessary to oppose extreme measures such as violence."[2] Furthermore, white elites chose

---

1   Morton Inger, *Politics and Reality in an American City: The New Orleans School Crisis of 1960* (New York: Center for Urban Education, 1969), 82–85; Robert L. Crain, *The Politics of School Desegregation: Comparative Case Studies of Community Structure and Policy-Making* (Chicago: Aldine, 1968), 3, 302–305; Numan V. Bartley, *The Rise of Massive Resistance: Race and Politics in the South During the 1950's* (Baton Rouge: Louisiana State University Press, 1969), 313.

2   C. Vann Woodward, "New South Fraud is Papered by Old South Myth," Washington *Post*, July 9, 1961, p. E3; Richard Cramer, "School Desegregation and New Industry: The Southern Community Leaders' Viewpoint," *Social Forces*, XLI (May, 1963), 387.

conciliation, especially with respect to school desegregation, as a useful tool for implementing alterations in racial behavior patterns in the slow, orderly, and piecemeal manner. In this light, moderation can be seen as a strategy adopted by influential whites to maintain their social control over biracial community affairs.

Models of race relations must further take into account the role of black leadership. Without the rise and acceptance of direct-action protest to replace the old style of accommodation, the contemporary version of the "New South" would have departed little from its post-Civil War prototype. In southern municipalities two kinds of strategies helped blacks to achieve first-class citizenship. After demonstrators had dramatically challenged practices of segregation and discrimination, respected blacks, sympathetic with the protesters' demands and recognized as responsible spokesmen, steered a moderate course to resolve specific problems without violent conflict. Thus, the push for racial equality in the urban "New South" was initiated by militant protest and was subsequently moderated by the responses of white and black elites.[3] Tampa, Florida, a self-proclaimed "New South" city, provides fertile but unexplored ground for testing these generalizations about changes in race relations.

On February 29, 1960, the afternoon temperature in Tampa climbed to seventy-seven degrees under bright, sunny skies, highlighting the kind of winter day that delighted the Chamber of Commerce. The splendid weather, however, was slightly marred by a peaceful sit-in by blacks at Woolworth's lunch counter. Seven years later, on June 11, 1967, the thermometer soared to ninety-four degrees, ushering in another long, hot, muggy summer. In the twilight hours when the day should have grown cooler, it turned unusually torrid and uncomfortable for Tampans as a riot erupted in the black ghetto. Different in many respects, these two events produced a consistent response: the exercise of moderation to remedy racial ills. From 1960 through 1967, community leaders prescribed cooperation and the soothing power of rational persuasion to check extremism and end discrimination. The cure did not heal all the

3   Jack L. Walker, "The Functions of Disunity: Negro Leadership in a Southern City," *Journal of Negro Education*, XXXII (Summer, 1963), 227–36.

wounds inflicted by racism, but the treatment allowed Tampa in 1967 to reduce the fever of civil disorder.

Straddled upon the banks of the meandering Hillsborough River and tucked against a bay whose waters empty into the Gulf of Mexico on Florida's west coast, Tampa in 1960 was in the midst of an economic boom reminiscent of that of the 1920s. Since 1950, the population of the city had doubled to approximately 275,000 residents, 47,000 of whom were black; over 400 companies had moved into the area adding $25 million to annual payrolls; and along with its sister cities across the bay, Saint Petersburg and Clearwater, Tampa had risen in the ratings as a national sales market. Presiding over this economic advance was a new breed of businessmen—bankers, industrialists, and merchants—many of whom had migrated to the Suncoast after World War II. "Ten years ago," the Tampa *Tribune* recalled in 1960, "Tampa was just a cigar factory with a port. Today we have all sorts of new industry—and the town has woken up." A Chamber of Commerce official gloated that the city's growth had "reached snowball dimensions—we wouldn't stop it if we wanted to." Prospects for the future appeared bright. Plans for renovation of the downtown section, urban renewal, construction of a state university campus, and extension of two interstate highways through the city tickled a newspaper reporter who gleefully noted that the "Associated Press won't even have to tack 'Fla.' onto Tampa in the datelines of dispatches. People all over the United States will know Tampa is in Florida."[4]

There were other changes on the horizon in 1960. Although Tampa followed the color line faithfully in maintaining Jim Crow, preparations were being made within the segment of its population that was 17 percent black to assault the walls of segregation. In the vanguard were officials of black fraternal and labor associations, the NAACP, and the Young Adults for Progressive Action, a nonpartisan organization composed mainly of black teachers and professionals. Most of them were under forty years old and had received degrees from southern black colleges; some had served in the armed forces during World War II or the Korean War; nearly all had spent time outside of the South; and a majority were either self-employed, worked for a

4 Tampa *Tribune*, November 13, 1960, p. 1A, June 22, 1960, p. 4A, July 3, 1961, p. 6A.

black-owned enterprise, or taught in the school system. The Florida field director for the NAACP, one of its principal attorneys in the "Sunshine State," and the president of the State's Conference of Branches all lived in Tampa, a circumstance guaranteeing that civil rights' concerns would be voiced. Part of the black bourgeoisie, they considered racial separation in or exclusion from public accommodations as an affront to their dignity and a deprivation of their rights as tax-paying citizens. "Segregation has proved itself a badge of inferiority," the *Florida Sentinel-Bulletin*, a black, biweekly newspaper, protested.[5] Furthermore, Negro leaders stressed that full equality depended upon obtaining jobs previously denied on the basis of race.

As with their white counterparts, black leaders welcomed the economic changes coming to Tampa and used them as the basis of arguments for breaking down racial barriers. C. Blythe Andrews, Sr., publisher of the *Florida Sentinel-Bulletin*, endorsed the trend toward industrialization as a "noble idea." However, his support was conditioned on the premise that blacks be given equal opportunity to obtain skilled jobs. "When the Negro is paid more in wages," Andrews asserted in the language that businessmen best understood, "the cash registers of the merchants . . . 'will run hot.'" Blacks also pointed out that while increased employment opportunities improved profits, racial discrimination reduced them. In the early sixties, the president of the local NAACP chapter reminded white civic leaders who looked forward to the expansion of Tampa's tourist trade "that millions of dollars are being lost . . . because organizations are refusing to meet in cities where racial segregation practices limit the use of facilities to Negroes."[6]

5 This composite profile is based on the careers of Blythe Andrews, Sr., and Blythe Andrews, Jr., publishers of the *Florida Sentinel-Bulletin*, a black biweekly newspaper, and prominent figures in the inappropriately named Lily White Benevolent Association, a fraternal group that provided health and burial services—Perry Harvey, Sr., who was president of International Longshoremen's Association Local 1402; A. Leon Lowry, Robert Saunders, Francisco Rodriguez, Charles Stanford, and Robert Gilder, who spearheaded the NAACP; and James Hammond and Charles Jones, who guided the Young Adults for Progressive Action. *Florida Sentinel-Bulletin*, September 3, 1960, p. 4.
6 *Florida Sentinel-Bulletin*, September 3, 1960, p. 4, September 29, 1962, p. 5. See Tampa *Tribune*, July 20, 1960, p. 14, for expectations of increased tourism. A. Leon Lowry, interviewed by the author on September 5, 1977, stated that black leaders used the economic arguments in discussions with white civic leaders.

To facilitate contacts between black and white elites, in the fall of 1959 Mayor Julian Lane had created a twelve-member interracial advisory committee. At the time, the NAACP had pending in the courts a school desegregation suit against Hillsborough County, and it was preparing litigation to challenge the policy of barring Negroes from visiting Tampa's main recreational attraction. Lane created the committee to encourage racial conciliation and to foster a peaceful environment that would boost civic plans for conversion of the "Cigar City" into a major economic and cultural center in the New South. The six black appointees included respected business, labor, and religious leaders, as well as the president of the Florida NAACP, Rev. A. Leon Lowry. Among the six recruited from the white community were several businessmen, a minister, and one of Tampa's most prominent attorneys, Cody Fowler, who served as chairman. Fowler had been president of the American Bar Association in the early fifties, had provided legal counsel for the Tampa Chamber of Commerce, and was head of a rapidly growing savings and loan association.[7] Convinced that Florida could not avoid integration for very long, he wanted the committee to pave the way for changes to occur slowly and bloodlessly, controlled by common sense instead of emotionalism. Several of the white and Negro members had already cooperated on another venture, the construction of Progress Village for black homeowners displaced by urban renewal. "When men of good will sit down together to attack a common problem," the Tampa *Times* correctly summed up the attitude of all the committeemen, "the likelihood of an acceptable solution being reached is greatly enhanced."[8]

7   Interview with Julian Lane by the author, January 16, 1978; Tampa *Times*, October 14, 1959, p. 6; *Florida Sentinel-Bulletin*, October 10, 1959, p. 4, November 3, 1959, p. 4; "Uncle Fed's Notebook," January, 1960, in Cody Fowler Files, University of South Florida Library, Tampa (USFL); Cody Fowler to members of Biracial Committee, December 24, 1959, in Robert Thomas Files, USFL. Among the white businessmen selected to the committee were Robert Thomas, a port developer, and Sandy A. Moffitt, a supplier of building materials. Along with Fowler they provided the most sustained interest and leadership. Besides Lowry, the most important blacks were Blythe Andrews, Sr., and Perry Harvey, Sr.
8   Interview with Cody Fowler by the author, December 5, 1977; interview with Robert Thomas by the author, December 7, 1977; untitled manuscript on Progress Village, in Thomas Files; Tampa *Times*, October 14, 1959, p. 6. During the late fifties, Andrews and Harvey had cooperated with Fowler and Thomas in establishing segregated but upgraded housing in Progress Village in order "to

The white committeemen defined their primary mission as encouraging equal opportunity rather than imposing racial integration. "We must give to the Negroes," Cody Fowler remarked, "the rights to which they are entitled . . . the elimination of the practices which make them feel inferior." However, Fowler also noted that "Negroes [are] Negroes and will remain Negroes, and that whites are whites and will remain whites. They must be made to realize that the whites have a right to choose their own friends and those with whom they wish to associate. They must develop their own society, just as . . . other races have done." Nevertheless, white moderates recognized that degrading Jim Crow conditions would not long survive militant black challenges; thus they sought to minimize the possibilities of violence and repression. After all, the pragmatic Fowler pointed out, "the white population must realize . . . that . . . [millions of] Negroes cannot be kept under police surveillance."[9]

The views of the black members complemented those of their white colleagues. Although strongly endorsing integration, Negro leaders preferred to achieve it without inflaming racial passions. Holding these beliefs, Blythe Andrews, Sr., denounced the policy of segregation that "makes possible a dual system of inferior schools; encourages the provision of inadequate and often filthy eating places for Negroes . . . breeds slum housing . . . encourages inequalities of facilities in the areas of parks, swimming pools, and recreation centers." At the same time Andrews cautioned that while "we are grasping for our legal rights and better job opportunities, it is well and vitally important that we tarry long enough to teach our people that if we wish to be accepted as first class citizens, we must first act like first class citizens."[10] Whatever yardstick was used to measure racial advancement, both blacks and whites on the committee agreed that progress should come on a step-by-step basis without arousing bitter animosities.

Demonstrations to integrate Tampa's department store lunch

---

prevent racial friction . . . caused by invasion of white districts by Negroes." See Andrews, "So They Tell Me," *Florida Sentinel-Bulletin*, January 10, 1961, p. 1.

9   Cody Fowler, Address to the Empire Club, Toronto, Canada, December 10, 1964, in Fowler Files. Robert Thomas bluntly recalled that he was not an integrationist. Thomas interview.

10   *Florida Sentinel-Bulletin*, August 30, 1960, p. 4, June 28, 1960, p. 4.

counters furnished a major test of the committee's ability to defuse potentially explosive racial conflicts. Inspired by sit-in protests in Greensboro, North Carolina, in early February, 1960, Clarence Fort, a twenty-year-old barber and president of the NAACP Youth Council, made arrangements to bring similar activities to Tampa. He questioned why blacks were refused service at a lunch counter, but were invited to purchase items in the rest of the store. Intending to demonstrate against this injustice, young Fort planned with older NAACP officials to conduct a direct-action drive. Well briefed by Robert Saunders, the association's state field director, and accompanied by Lowry, on February 29, Fort and about fifty black high school students tried twice to integrate the lunch counter at Woolworth's downtown store. Denied service in each instance, the protesters quietly sat on the counter stools for nearly two hours until closing time when they departed.[11]

The next day, racial tempers flared briefly. Approximately one hundred black youths, not associated with the NAACP, marched for two hours through the downtown area, where they were refused service at nine stores. At one location, the Greyhound bus terminal restaurant, a well publicized fracas erupted between a black protester and an unsympathetic white customer. In addition, newspapers disclosed that the apparent leader of the second day's efforts had a lengthy juvenile police record. Upset by the unfavorable publicity, the NAACP quickly repudiated the "rebels" and moved to reassert its control. The following afternoon on March 2, Clarence Fort returned with approximately eighty Negroes wearing identification tags with the inscription "I am an American, Youth Council, NAACP" and staged an orderly but unsuccessful half-hour sit-in at the Woolworth and Kress stores.[12]

Neither white nor black opinion-shapers wanted a violent confrontation. The *Tribune* warned that "demonstrations of this kind rub against the thinly covered nerves of racial feeling, as a

11   Tampa *Times*, March 1, 1960, p. 4; Tampa *Tribune*, March 1, 1960, p. 1; *Florida Sentinel-Bulletin*, March 1, 1960, p. 16; interview with Clarence Fort by the author, January 29, 1978; interview with Robert Saunders by the author, September 17, 1977.
12   Tampa *Tribune*, March 2, 1960, p. 1, March 3, 1960, p. 1A; *Florida Sentinel-Bulletin*, March 5, 1960, p. 13.

wind-tossed tree branch scrapes against a high tension wire," and while the editors of the *Florida Sentinel-Bulletin* cheered the young people on, they also cautioned their elders "to restrain and police the rowdy of our race and demonstrate that we can handle an ugly situation—without violence."[13] Significantly, the police were not called upon to evict the demonstrators, and the only arrests, resulting from the incident at the Greyhound station, involved a black and a white. Throughout the three days, law enforcement officials were conspicuously evident on the scene and preserved order in an evenhanded manner.[14] After unknown assailants fired several shots into the Lowry's home in the early morning hours of March 13, the *Tribune* pleaded: "If Florida is to preserve good race relations, if it is to continue to enjoy peace and prosperity . . . then people in the middle must make their influence felt."[15]

In the meantime, the Biracial Committee prepared to mediate the dispute. The day after the attack on his home, Lowry invited representatives of the Merchants Association "to discuss intelligently and sensibly the present situation." In extending this request, Lowry also alerted the merchants that what "has been custom must now be changed, if you expect Negroes to continue to patronize your establishments."[16] Aware that a black boycott was a possibility, store managers also worried about losing white customers if they integrated their lunch counters. Nevertheless, under pressure from the mayor and the Biracial Committee to work out an agreement, the Merchants Association, led by its executive vice-president Colby Armstrong, promised to participate in conferences to study how other cities approached the problem and to present recommendations. As a gesture of good faith, the NAACP declared a mor-

13   Tampa *Tribune*, March 2, 1960, p. 12; *Florida Sentinel-Bulletin*, March 5, 1960, p. 4.
14   Tampa *Tribune*, March 1, 1960, p. 1, March 2, 1960, p. 1, March 12, 1960, p. 9; Tampa *Times*, March 1, 1960, p. 1. However, there was a disparity in the outcome of the two arrest cases. Both youths were convicted for disturbing the peace, but the Negro was sentenced to eighty days in jail and given a six-hundred-dollar fine. The white man received a one-hundred-dollar fine and fifty days in prison.
15   Tampa *Tribune*, March 22, 1960, p. 14.
16   A. Leon Lowry to Merchants Association, March 14, 1960, in Thomas Files. See also Cody Fowler to Members of Biracial Committee, March 7, 1960, in Thomas Files; Lowry interview; Tampa *Tribune*, March 10, 1960, p. 8A.

atorium on sit-ins in order "to give the bi-racial committee a chance to solve racial problems in Tampa."[17]

Negotiations took place on both the municipal and state levels. Near the end of March, Governor Leroy Collins lived up to his reputation as a racial moderate by appointing a state biracial committee to settle the lunch counter issue fairly and harmoniously. Two of the six men selected came from Tampa and also sat on the city's biracial advisory board: Cody Fowler and Perry Harvey, Sr., president of the black longshoremen's union local. Throughout the spring and summer, the statewide commission chaired by Fowler met privately with Florida businessmen, urging them to adopt a new racial posture or suffer the consequences that prolonged resistance would bring. In typically cool-headed fashion, the Tampa attorney admonished that an "objective look at Little Rock will show us that such policies mean economic deterioration of a very substantial kind. It is our belief that thoughtful people do not want such a damaging effect on Florida's bright future."[18]

Fowler also delivered this message to Tampa. After several months of unpublicized sessions, the mayor's committee and the Merchants Association hatched a plan to desegregate lunch counters. The chain-store operators apparently had received word from their national headquarters to reach any accord acceptable to the local community. They listened carefully to reports that cities in Texas and North Carolina had integrated lunch counters without a loss in white trade. Convinced that the same pattern could prevail in Tampa, the merchants agreed to serve pairs of carefully selected black young adults on a prearranged date without prior public notice. By acting uniformly to drop the eating restrictions, the managers prepared to lessen the chance that any one of their stores would be singled out for reprisals by angry whites. They instructed waitresses to treat

17 Tampa *Tribune*, March 22, 1960, p. 7; Commission of Community Relations, "Historical Background of the Biracial Committee and the Commission of Community Relations," 3, n.d., in Thomas Files; Robert Saunders, "Monthly Report of Activities," March, 1960, in Robert Saunders Files, in Saunders' possession; Tampa *Tribune*, April 28, 1960. p. 11A. See also Robert Thomas to Cody Fowler, March 29, 1960, in Thomas Files.
18 "Statement by Cody Fowler, Chairman, Commission on Race Relations," press release, May 27, 1960, in Fowler Files; Tampa *Tribune*, March 21, 1960, p. 1, May 29, 1960, p. 1A.

Negroes courteously, and those who balked were given the day off. The committee tried to reduce the possibility of racial tension even further by scheduling black couples to patronize the stores when few whites diners would be present. In addition, Negro committeemen admonished black participants to conform to norms of proper middle-class behavior. Calling for an exertion of internal discipline, Blythe Andrews admonished that as "a race, we must show ourselves worthy of integrated service at the lunch counters."[19] Finally, on September 14, pairs of decorous Negroes were served at eighteen establishments without fanfare according to the carefully developed plan.[20]

Civic and business leaders interpreted this episode as a victory for moderation. Compared with Jacksonville, which had refused to form a biracial committee and had recently suffered through bloody clashes, Tampa voluntarily had talked over its difficulties until a calm settlement was reached between the races. "As long as men of reason and good will can sit down together," the *Tribune* boasted, "there is no racial problem which can't be diffused before it bursts into violence." Lowry commended businessmen "for their sensible attitude and realistic approach to problems." In this case, arbitration had succeeded because the position of stores in accepting blacks as shoppers but not as diners made little economic or moral sense. "A few years hence," the *Tribune* predicted correctly, "many citizens will look back at the yellowing headlines and wonder what the fuss was all about."[21]

Over the next six and one-half years the Biracial Committee implemented the "Tampa Technique," and segregation gradually disappeared while equal opportunity increased slightly with relatively little strife. The city quietly abandoned segregation in

19   Tampa *Tribune*, May 18, 1960, p. 31; interview with Melvin Stein by the author, January 13, 1978; "Proposed Method of Desegregation of Down Town Lunch Counters, Also Ybor City and Sears," August, 1960, in Thomas Files; *Florida Sentinel-Bulletin*, September 10, 1960, p. 4.
20   Tampa *Tribune*, September 15, 1960, p. 1A; *Florida Sentinel-Bulletin*, September 17, 1960, p. 1; Fort interview; Lowry interview. There was some minor opposition. Criminal Court Judge L. A. Grayson suggested a white boycott of the participating stores, and he turned in his credit cards. Tampa *Times*, September 15, 1960, p. 1; Stein interview.
21   Tampa *Tribune*, September 3, 1960, p. 10, September 15, 1960, p. 1A, September 16, 1960, p. 22A.

public buildings and facilities such as beaches, parks, and swimming pools. Although racial barriers fell at movie theaters, most hotels, and the annual Gasparilla Day Parade, most restaurants and bowling alleys did not open their doors to blacks until the passage of the 1964 Civil Rights Act. Even after the enactment of this landmark statute, hospitals continued to admit patients only on a segregated basis. When NAACP officials complained to Washington, the Biracial Committee intervened and persuaded the hospitals to operate in a nondiscriminatory fashion. At the same time, Tampa also phased out the existence of Clara Frye Hospital, a decrepit and neglected public institution for blacks.[22] Meanwhile the committee broke new ground along the employment front. In 1963 it had joined the Merchants Association, the Young Adults for Progressive Action, the Urban League, and the NAACP in setting up a retail training program involving eighteen department stores. Threatened boycotts and sporadic picketing marked some of these accomplishments, but in general black activists agreed to curtail their demonstrations and accept mediation. This happened largely because some of those associated with the protest groups sat as committee members alongside business and civic leaders whom they trusted.[23]

The Merchants Association's workshop provided a typical example of decision making involving blacks, businessmen, and white civic leaders. In late October, 1962, the Young Adults for Progressive Action (YAPA) informed Colby Armstrong of its intention to institute "selective buying practices" against retail stores that followed "outdated traditions in not employing Negroes in other than menial positions." Led by James Hammond, an electrical contractor and civil rights activist instrumental in

22   Robert Saunders to Blythe Andrews, Jr., June 26, 1962, in Saunders Files; *Florida Sentinel-Bulletin*, May 4, 1963, p. 4, June 8, 1963, p. 1, August 20, 1963, p. 1, November 16, 1963, p. 1, January 11, 1964, p. 3, February 11, 1964, p. 3, May 4, 1963, p. 4, May 22, 1965, p. 2; NAACP, "Report of Assignment," August 15–September 15, 1963, and Charles Stanford to Gene Diego, March 9, 1964, both in Saunders Files; Tampa *Times*, July 3, 1964, p. 1; Robert Thomas to Cody Fowler, January 13, 1964, and Commission of Community Relations, "Minutes," May 22, 1966, both in Thomas Files; Tampa *Tribune*, March 5, 1965, p. 2B, November 24, 1967, p. 1B.
23   On the committee during most of the 1960s was Leon Lowry of the NAACP and Jim Hammond of the Young Adults for Progressive Action. The business community was represented by Colby Armstrong, Robert Thomas, Leonard Hutchinson, regional manager of Sears, and Sandy Moffitt.

bringing about the integration of Tampa's municipal beach, the YAPA already had used the boycott as a weapon for obtaining job opportunities. Throughout the first eight months of 1961, members of the group had picketed a downtown grocery store heavily patronized by blacks "until Negroes are hired in all capacities." Halted by a court injunction in September, the boycott cost the grocery approximately $125,000. In the fall of 1962, when Hammond contacted the Merchants Association, he couched his demands in conciliatory language. Thus, he wrote Armstrong that the YAPA hoped to settle the issue through "peaceful negotiation" and keep the "city free from racial tension."[24]

With the Christmas shopping season approaching, Armstrong sought to avert the threatened boycott. He assured Hammond that the merchants desired an "amicable settlement," and the YAPA leader agreed to postpone the demonstration. At the time, Hammond served with Armstrong on the Biracial Committee; reflecting the philosophy of that group he had "no particular desire to disrupt the community, if our demands for employment can be met in a less spectacular fashion." In response to Hammond's olive branch offering, the Merchants Association created an Equal Job Opportunities Committee. For the first six months of 1963, Armstrong and representatives of Tampa's largest chain department stores conferred with Hammond, officials of the Urban League and the NAACP, and Perry Harvey, Sr., of the Biracial Committee. In April, twelve firms agreed to start interviewing black applicants and set September 9 as a target date for hiring at least one Negro at each store. Armstrong had cautioned that the process would be slow: "[We] at the present time are not interested in having 100 or 200 Negro persons apply for jobs at the same time, because certainly they are not all going to be hired. There is not going to be any great influx of colored employees." Furthermore, the Merchants Association insisted on giving the plan little publicity, because it did not want "to arouse extremists."[25] The merchants did not have to

24   James A. Hammond to Colby Armstrong, October 30, 1962, in Merchants Association Files, USFL; Tampa *Tribune*, September 13, 1961, p. 12B, September 14, 1961, p. 10A, September 18, 1961, p. 10A, September 20, 1961, p. 12A; interview with James Hammond by the author, September 12, 1977.
25   James Hammond to Colby Armstrong, November 24, 1962, and "Minutes," Equal Job Opportunities Committee, February 21, April 17, June 6, 1963, all in Merchants Association Files.

worry about being stampeded by black applicants, because not enough Negroes were recruited who could pass the standardized written tests given to prospective employees by the retailers.

Determined to fulfill its commitment to meet the September deadline, the Merchants Association decided to set up job-training workshops on a carefully monitored basis. To this end, the Equal Job Opportunities Committee instructed the Urban League to place in the *Florida Sentinel-Bulletin* an advertisement requesting applications for a variety of white-collar positions. After the announcement appeared on June 22, some 125 blacks responded promptly. From this group, 30 were selected to take a four-week course in "Basic Retail Salesmanship" scheduled to begin on July 16. In addition, 18 stores agreed to hire some of the black participants who successfully completed the training.[26]

In the meantime, racial confrontation in the city nearly halted the initiation of the program. On June 20, the NAACP Youth Council organized a march in front of two of the largest downtown movie theaters, protesting their policy of excluding blacks. Chanting freedom songs and carrying placards with such slogans as MY BROTHER DIED IN KOREA—SO AMERICAN COULD BE FREE, fifty black and white youths of high school and college age spent four hours picketing under the hot afternoon sun. The demonstrators apparently chose to march because they believed that the Biracial Committee was moving too slowly in eliminating segregation. In its customary manner, the committee had been negotiating quietly and behind the scenes with the theater operators. However, it did not keep the NAACP informed of the progress of the deliberations, and the youth leaders were dissatisfied. Thus, the decision to take to the streets was designed as a protest against the biracial establishment as well as the cinemas.[27]

The demonstration, although conducted peacefully, upset

26 Colby Armstrong to Joseph D. Kelly, August 6, 1963, in Merchants Association Files. Evidence about whether black graduates succeeded in obtaining employment is inconclusive. *Women's Wear Daily*, October 2, 1963, reported: "Some are known to have taken some of the positions in the stores." However, results of a survey conducted by the merchants immediately after the course indicated that participants enjoyed the training but most had not secured jobs.
27 *Florida Sentinel-Bulletin*, June 22, 1963, p. 24; Tampa *Tribune*, June 21, 1963, p. 1A; Tampa *Times*, June 22, 1963, p. 9.

civic leaders. Aware of the increasing level of racial confrontation in other parts of Florida and throughout the South, Mayor Lane called the NAACP's action "a mistake" that could "inflame more trouble." Lowry, whose influence within the NAACP was declining as his participation in the Biracial Committee grew, asserted that he was "very disappointed," preferring "to see integration of Tampa business facilities done . . . through negotiations rather than demonstrations." After meeting with Mayor Lane, Cody Fowler, and the Biracial Committee on June 21, the NAACP Youth Council leaders and their adult advisors consented to cease picketing in order to give city officials "sufficient time to adjust certain problems in employment and entertainment."[28] In the midst of delicate discussions over the job program, Colby Armstrong warned Jim Hammond "that if the type of trouble over the theatres . . . starts up again, I am certain you will not receive the full cooperation that we want to give."[29] With calm ensured, the Merchants Association soon began its workshop, and shortly after, the Biracial Committee persuaded the movie houses to admit blacks.

Throughout these difficulties, progressive business leaders supported moderation to avoid bloody clashes that might attract unfavorable national attention and bring intervention by the federal government. They considered the Biracial Committee an excellent instrument for regulating the pace of desegregation in a systematic manner and for retaining control of racial policy in the hands of Tampans. Thus, the Chamber of Commerce "appreciated the fine work" of the mayor's advisory board, while at the same time it went on record in opposition to federal civil rights legislation.[30]

After passage of the national Civil Rights Act of 1964, Tampa officials established a new agency to improve the mechanism for resolving conflicts locally. In order to develop a

28   Tampa *Times*, June 21, 1963, pp. 1, 7; Tampa *Tribune*, June 22, 1963, p. 2A; Fowler interview; interview with Francisco Rodriguez by the author, January 11, 1978. Rodriguez was an NAACP attorney who represented the Youth Council.
29   Colby Armstrong to James Hammond, June 27, 1963, in Merchants Association Files; Robert Saunders, "Report of Assignment, August 15–September 15, 1963," in Saunders Files.
30   Fischer Black to Colby Armstrong, August 14, 1963, in Merchants Association Files; Tampa *Tribune*, August 24, 1963, p. 1B.

"planned progressive program of nondiscrimination and equal opportunity for all [that] will give to this community an environment of good race relations and an area where industry and business growth will have an opportunity to move forward," Tampa created a Commission of Community Relations (CCR). The Biracial Committee had functioned without statutory authority as an informal, part-time group; in November, 1964, the city officially established the CCR with a full-time administrator, James A. Hammond. Leader of the Young Adults for Progressive Action and once arrested for participating in a civil rights demonstration at a drive-in movie theater, the thirty-five-year-old electrical contractor was a shrewd choice. Respected by blacks for his activism, he had also impressed whites by his willingness to discuss volatile issues around the bargaining table. "We would rather see Hammond stepping on a toe here and there," the *Sentinel-Bulletin* commented, "than to see him . . . launching demonstrations and boycotts . . . [that] do damage to the good name of Tampa which has enjoyed . . . the best race relations in the South."[31] Under his tenure, the CCR labored as a complaint bureau and as an initiator of innovative programs in compensatory preschool education and job training.

The creation of the CCR and the selection of Hammond to lead it heightened black aspirations of achieving economic and civil equality quickly. When the gap between expectation and reality continued to remain large, some civil rights leaders blamed the CCR. The NAACP applauded lunch counter and "twenty dollar a day hotel" desegregation, but charged that racial discrimination could "still be rigidly enforced through use of economic sanction." Guided by Robert Gilder, an outspoken black business executive, in 1965 the NAACP lambasted local government officials for perpetuating racial bias in public housing, municipal hospitals, and civil service employment, while spending "large sums of money on . . . a Commission . . . which . . . serves as a window dressing to give the City the appearance of having done a good job in the area of race relations." Unhappy with this situation, Gilder and the NAACP occasionally petitioned federal agencies to investigate the operation of Tampa's

31   Mayor's Biracial Committee to Nick Nuccio and Ellsworth Simmons, September 21, 1964, in Thomas Files; *Florida Sentinel-Bulletin*, November 27, 1965, p. 4; Tampa *Tribune*, January 29, 1964, p. 1B.

public facilities for violations of civil rights statutes. Nevertheless, despite such strident criticism by the NAACP, it usually chose to cooperate with Hammond and to give the CCR a chance to settle issues voluntarily and tranquilly at the local level before appealing to Washington or resorting to direct-action demonstrations. "Tampa enjoys wholesome race relations," the *Sentinel-Bulletin* proclaimed, stating the opinion of biracial leaders in mid-1966. "The lines of communication are kept open, and any problem can be solved without fanfare within a reasonable time."[32]

By 1967, biracial cooperation and vigilance on the part of the NAACP had achieved many of the goals of the civil rights movement without "angry polarization," but beneath the tranquil surface lay embers of discontent ready for a spark to ignite them. Segregation was officially dead, but discrimination persisted in subtle and powerful forms. With respect to municipal employment, civil service examinations obstructed blacks from obtaining all but the most menial jobs; and, those who did get hired often found that they were passed over for promotion by less experienced whites.[33]

Conditions were only slightly better in the private sector. Many firms paid lip service to the goal of hiring black employees, but maintained that they could not find enough Negroes who could pass the educational requirements for employment. Most businessmen did little more than call upon the public schools to upgrade their standards to satisfy the manpower needs of free enterprise. However, a shortage of skilled labor was not the sole barrier blocking advancement. Even when adult blacks had "a marketable skill and job openings are available," Jim Hammond insisted, "the person meets 'employer resistance,' and therefore does not get the job." The CCR administrator acknowledged that unskilled Negro labor posed a serious handicap, but he emphasized "on-the-job training and getting employers to cooperate in hiring these persons . . . rather than on testing of educational background." The Merchants Association, which had done more than any other business group along

32   Robert L. Gilder to Paul S. Walker, June 24, 1965, in Saunders Files; *Florida Sentinel-Bulletin*, July 19, 1966, p. 4.
33   *Florida Sentinel-Bulletin*, June 26, 1965, p. 3; Robert Gilder to Paul S. Walker, June 24, 1965, in Saunders Files.

lines sketched by Hammond, nevertheless admitted: "Our resulting efforts are pathetic."[34]

On another front, most adult blacks were registered to vote; yet, there were no elected black officials and only a handful of Negroes received government posts. Much of the difficulty stemmed from the use of multimember districts and at-large electoral procedures. A small fraction of Tampa's voters, blacks found it impossible to gain enough white backing outside of their residential districts to win political races. Black electors sometimes swung the outcome of close political contests, but more frequently they failed to take advantage of the potential strength indicated by their high registration figures. The problem of voter apathy was a complex one, and in Tampa a contributing factor was the absence of an effective, independent, political organization to educate and mobilize Negroes. Aware of this deficiency, the *Sentinel-Bulletin* repeatedly urged blacks to participate at the polls in order to achieve first-class citizenship. "We should walk proudly," the newspaper cajoled, "much like dedicated soldiers . . . and cast our ballot for our total freedom."[35]

In the area of education, moderates deliberately slowed down the rate of desegregation without violating the letter of the law. In 1960, faced with litigation by the NAACP, Hillsborough County School Superintendent J. Crockett Farnell had informed civic leaders of their choices: "token integration, mass integration, or the closing of the public schools." The first option was the favored one and became official policy in 1962 after a federal district judge ordered desegregation on a grade-a-year basis starting with the elementary schools. The *Tribune*, reflecting the attitude of influential Tampans, did not interpret the court's decision as ushering in a "social revolution" and cautioned against adopting massive resistance.[36] Hence, school officials with the support of business, civic, and religious leaders permitted Negroes to attend institutions with white pupils who

34   NAACP, "Report of Labor and Industry Committee," July 29, 1962, in Saunders Files; Florida Advisory Committee to the United States Commission on Civil Rights, *Report* (Washington, D.C.: Government Printing Office, 1963), 29–30; James Hammond to CCR, July 28, 1966, and "Continuing Employment Feeder Workshop," n.d. [*ca.* 1967], both in Thomas Files.
35   *Florida Sentinel-Bulletin*, February 22, 1966, p. 4. See also issue of June 4, 1966, p. 4.
36   Tampa *Tribune*, May 19, 1960, p. 1A.

lived inside the same attendance zone. Educational policy-makers did not panic, because they realized that residential segregation patterns would severely limit the scope of integration within the framework of the neighborhood school concept. The Tampa *Times* in 1962 correctly predicted that Hillsborough County would "be able to pick its way along a difficult path and achieve the goal of racial accord."[37] Thus by 1967, the moderate course had succeeded both in preserving peace and in confining integration to less than one-half of the system's schools.

Inadequate low-cost housing, a shortage of recreational facilities, the poor quality of police protection, and discrimination by white merchants in the ghetto completed the list of grievances. These complaints had reached alarming proportions by the end of 1966. Addressing local businessmen, the *Sentinel-Bulletin* noted that recent riots in the North "were really consumer revolts by the poor against exploitation in the marketplace in their neighborhoods." The newspaper warned white retailers to take corrective measures or face the consequences brought by "the winds of trouble and destruction." Already feeling the heat from the simmering racial cauldron, a prominent black attorney admonished the CCR that Tampa stood "on the threshold of the same riots that took place in Cleveland, Atlanta, and other cities."[38]

In the meantime, these danger signals did not go unnoticed by the CCR. In August, 1966, Hammond reported the "need for establishing necessary rapport and lines of communication with the youth element in our community."[39] Following up this suggestion, the administrator began visiting poolrooms and bars to hear directly the grievances of the most economically impoverished blacks. In the fall of 1966, as racial tensions mounted in West Tampa, the CCR staff subdued passions by persuading white merchants to hire blacks for other than servile duties. The

37 Tampa *Times*, August 23, 1962, p. 12A; Tampa *Tribune*, November 14, 1967, p. 11A. On school desegregation see United States Commission on Civil Rights, "Hillsborough County School Desegregation," March, 1976, Washington, D.C., staff report in possession of the author.

38 *Florida Sentinel-Bulletin*, October 15, 1966, p. 4; Tampa *Times*, September 23, 1966, p. 2.

39 Minutes, Commission of Community Relations, August 31, 1966, in Thomas Files; Administrator's Report, Commission of Community Relations, September 26, 1966, in Commission of Community Relations Files, CCR Office.

biracial group also convinced General Telephone Company to institute an affirmative action project to train and hire fifty-seven blacks for a variety of occupations. With the beginning of the new year, Hammond endeavored to win approval for expanding the CCR's personnel to include an industrial advisor, a job developer, and a vocational consultant. Endorsing this proposal, Cody Fowler remarked that the amount of money sought "is not so high when you consider what the cost of trouble here would be."[40] The city agreed to the request.

Despite these well-intended efforts, on Sunday, June 11, 1967, a major riot exploded in the black section adjacent to the downtown business district. Triggered by a white policeman's fatal shooting of an unarmed black robbery suspect, the disorder followed recent incidents involving charges of police brutality. Rioting first broke out in an area where over half of the families had an income under $3,000; the unemployment rate for black males was 10 percent, a figure double that for whites; 60 percent of the housing units were deteriorating or were dilapidated; and the median number of school years completed was 7.7.[41]

The civil rights struggles in Tampa, as elsewhere, had the paradoxical effect of both raising black expectations of full equality and intensifying the sense of disillusionment and despair. While official obstacles to integration crumbled, the races nevertheless remained segregated and unequal. Five months before racial violence erupted, the usually optimistic *Sentinel-Bulletin* grumbled: "Integration means nothing to the Negro if he is cast into the 'mainstream' without a job; into 'community affairs' if his family is starving in a rundown neighborhood. The word 'integration' has definite political and Jim Crow overtones

40   Quoted in Tampa *Tribune*, November 24, 1966, p. 2B; Administrator's Report, October 19, 1966, December 21, 1966, in CCR Files; Tampa *Tribune*, November 4, 1966, p. 2B, January 13, 1967, p. 16A; *Florida Sentinel-Bulletin*, February 11, 1967, p. 4; James Hammond to Commission of Community Relations, September 28, 1966, and James Hammond to Commissioners, Community Relations, April 21, 1967, including "Budget for 1967–68 as Proposed," both in Thomas Files.
41   National Advisory Commission on Civil Disorders, *Report* (New York: Bantam, 1968), 42–44; *Florida Sentinel-Bulletin*, October 11, 1966, p. 4, May 5, 1967, p. 4; Bureau of the Census, *Census Tracts Tampa-St. Petersburg, 1960* (Washington, D.C.: Government Printing Office, 1961), 72–97. On police brutality see *Florida Sentinel-Bulletin*, October 11, 1966, p. 4, May 13, 1967, p. 4.

to the Negro when already stiff qualifications are purposely set upward to deprive [him of] a job."[42] The violence in the ghetto was a form of spontaneous protest that publicized complaints neglected within conventional political channels. Moreover, it suggested that a shift was taking place away from the traditional civil rights goal of equal access and toward demands for a redistribution of economic and political power. For many black Tampans the legal victories of the 1960s did not convert into sufficient economic rewards. According to a report presented to the Biracial Committee less than a year before the riot, the "gains . . . are middle class advantages, the average Negro still remains untrained, unemployed, and unthought of." The *Sentinel-Bulletin*, which had scarcely missed an opportunity to praise Tampa's biracialism, admitted after the riot: "We have tended to support flowery talk about things getting better for a few."[43]

Nevertheless, in coping with the civil disruption, Tampa relied heavily on the channels of interracial communication built up over the years. Through four nights of burning, looting, and rock tossing, influential blacks and whites cooperated to restore order. The CCR dispatched Jim Hammond and his staff into the riot zone, where they joined popular community leaders to try to "keep the cool." It took several days to overcome the hostility of angry young rioters who voiced suspicion of the "cats who get respect downtown but not with their own people." Finally on Wednesday morning, after round-the-clock meetings, Hammond and other peacemakers convinced law enforcement authorities to withdraw their troops and allow black youth squads to patrol the strife-ridden neighborhoods. Assembled into paramilitary units, wearing white helmets, and accompanied by adult Negro advisors, young blacks, including a few who had

42   *Florida Sentinel-Bulletin*, January 21, 1967, p. 4.
43   *Ibid.*, September 24, 1966, p. 3, July 4, 1967, p. 4. Statistical evidence confirmed this assessment. Since 1960, little had improved for the residents of the Central Park Village neighborhood where the riot first broke out. In 1969, 48 percent of the families lived below the poverty level; median family income was around $3,000; and the median years of school completed was a little over 8.0. Bureau of the Census, *Census Tracts Tampa-St. Petersburg, 1970* (Washington, D.C.: Government Printing Office, 1971), 78. For a full discussion of riot causation and political ideology see Joe R. Feagin and Harlan Hahn, *Ghetto Revolts* (New York: Macmillan, 1973).

previously participated in the rioting, labored successfully to contain additional violence. They were particularly helpful in pacifying blacks outraged by an official exoneration of the policeman whose fatal shot originally had sparked the disturbance. By Thursday, June 15, as a result of tireless negotiations and alert vigilance on the part of the CCR staff, government officials, the "white hat" youths, and black civic leaders, the riots had ended.[44]

The costs of the riot were considerable. Although no one was killed, sixteen people received injuries. Estimated economic losses ranged in amount from $100,000 to over $1,000,000, and the city spent about $75,000 in overtime pay for police and firemen in addition to the money required to process and prosecute the 111 individuals arrested during the disturbances. Furthermore, the upheaval wounded the pride of smug city fathers who thought race relations were so good that "it couldn't happen here."[45] Colby Armstrong reminded them: "Local business is most affected by local civil unrest and the terrible cost of wasted human resources. We are soberly reflecting upon the unpleasant national publicity of June 1967, recognizing belatedly that it CAN happen in our city also."[46]

Before the smoke cleared, soul-searching had begun. While acknowledging that the riots had hurt the city's economy and record of racial harmony, Tampans searched for ways of relieving sources of black indignation. "Both in fairness and self protection," the *Tribune* argued, "the community must strive to correct conditions which create justifiable resentment and give

44   Gayle Everett Davis, "Riot in Tampa" (M.A. thesis, University of South Florida, 1976), 88; Commission of Community Relations, "Historical Background of the City Youth Patrol (White Hat Concept) 'Tampa Technique,'" June 27, 1967, in Thomas Files; Tampa *Tribune*, June 14, 1967, p. 8B; Tampa *Times*, June 16, 1967, p. 16; Hammond interview.

45   Tampa *Tribune*, June 13, 1967, p. 4B, June 16, 1967, p. 11C, June 18, 1967 p. 17A; Tampa *Times*, June 13, 1967, p. 14; National Advisory Commission on Civil Disorders, *Report*, 163; Permanent Subcommittee on Investigations of the Senate Committee on Government Operations, *Riots, Civil and Criminal Disorders*, 90th Cong., 1st Sess. (1967), Part 1, Insert, 14. The *Tribune* assessed the property losses at $1.5 million. Whatever the actual figure, Tampa escaped with fewer monetary damages, deaths, and injuries than did most of the eight cities— Buffalo, Cincinnati, Detroit, Milwaukee, Minneapolis, Newark, Plainfield, Tampa— which the Kerner Commission identified as having experienced major convulsions in 1967.

46   "Continuing Employment Feeder Workshop," in Thomas Files.

incendiaries a handy torch."[47] To work as trouble-shooters at the grass-roots level, the city hired five of the "white hats." In addition, money poured into the ghetto for recreational activities. The CCR and the Merchants Association organized another series of employment workshops and managed to line up some four hundred jobs for those who participated. At the same time, General Telephone Company invested three thousand dollars in a second job-training course. By the end of the year, the CCR, the Merchants Association, and the Chamber of Commerce had obtained a sixty-thousand-dollar matching grant from the William Donner Foundation to create a Young Adult Council. According to this plan, groups of fifty youths would be given an accelerated academic education along with on-the-job training for three months. Exhorting businessmen to raise their share of the funds, the president of the Chamber of Commerce justified the contribution on the basis of "hard cold business facts."[48] The CCR was also designing a similar project to cover civil service jobs.

In shaping their responses, Tampa's businessmen encouraged local initiative and voluntarism. The Merchants Association and Chamber of Commerce pointed out "the fallacy of dependency upon the state and national revenue as the panacea of all our community ills." The Donner Foundation conceived its grant as an "excellent opportunity to mount a program under private and local control contrasted with Washingtonian bureaucracy." However, businessmen lacked the dedication necessary to sustain an intensive drive to remove the vestiges of employment discrimination. Rhetoric outdistanced commitment, and Tampa business leaders soon retreated from implementing their lofty pledges uttered in the wake of the disorders. After an initial flurry of financial contributions to match the Donner Foundation grant, donations trickled off and never reached more than one-third of the expected amount. By the end of the decade, the experiment was scrapped.[49]

---

47   Tampa *Tribune*, June 14, 1967, p. 8B.
48   Davis, "Riot in Tampa," 99–101. Just in case these measures failed to snuff out the fires of insurrection, the city spent forty-five thousand dollars to augment its antiriot arsenal with the latest equipment. Davis, "Riot in Tampa," 104; Tampa *Tribune*, December 9, 1967, p. 2B, December 12, 1967, p. 4B.
49   "Continuing Employment Feeder Workshop," in Thomas Files; Frank Johnson to Cody Fowler, April 5, 1968, Cody Fowler to James Hammond, April 16,

Nevertheless, Tampa maintained a favorable image and salvaged a victory from a disastrous uprising. In November, 1967, the city gained national recognition for its work in race relations in general and curbing the riots in particular, when the CCR and Biracial Committee won a public service award of one thousand dollars bestowed annually by the Lane Bryant Corporation in New York City. In accepting the prize, Leon Lowry, chairman of the CCR, emphasized the key principles behind seven years of biracialism in Tampa: "To keep our city moving forward in wholesome racial relations is our objective. To keep violence and rioting away from our city is our sworn duty." Such policies, the *Tribune* commented enthusiastically, paid "high dividends to our community."[50]

From sit-in to race riot, Tampa's civic and business elites endorsed racial moderation. They preferred rational persuasion, voluntarism, and gradualism, instead of coercion, repression, and confrontation. A progressive Biracial Committee was certain that customs were about to change and sought to encourage an orderly and peaceful transition. Cooperation came from merchants and businessmen who calculated that ugly racial incidents did not make good dollars and cents. Little Rock, Birmingham, Jacksonville, and Saint Augustine offered vivid lessons for Chamber of Commerce and Merchants Association officials. "What new industry," the *Tribune* wondered in the early sixties, "would decide to go into a city which seethes with murderous racial conflict?"[51] Furthermore, the successful performance of the "Tampa Technique" owed much to the nature of black leadership, which blended militancy with restraint. Civil rights forces occasionally took to the streets and appealed to the federal government to redress grievances, but they usually chose to settle disputes locally around the conference table or quietly in the courts. This process did not benefit everybody, as it barely touched the lives of blacks trapped inside the poverty of slums after centuries of educational and economic depriva-

1968, both in Fowler Files; interview with Charles Jones by the author, January 9, 1978.

50 Tampa *Tribune*, December 1, 1967, p. 1B, December 2, 1967, p. 10A.

51 *Ibid.*, September 18, 1963, p. 4B; interview with Scott Christopher by the author, January 9, 1978; interview with Fred Learey by the author, January 20, 1978; *Florida Sentinel-Bulletin*, April 16, 1963, p. 4.

tion. Although from 1960 through 1967, the civil rights movement stormed the legal barricades of segregation, it had only begun to attack the unofficial remnants of racism still embedded in economic, social, and political institutions. As one assault gave way to another in Tampa, the Commission of Community Relations aptly remarked: "The end has not been reached, nor the beginning of the end, but perhaps the end of the beginning."[52] Moderation had provided a practical tool wielded by civic elites pushing for economic modernization with a minimum of political and social disruption.

52 "$1000 Lane Bryant Awards Group Winner," press release, November, 1967, in Fowler Files.

ANNE TROTTER

THE MEMPHIS BUSINESS COMMUNITY AND INTEGRATION

Located in the southwesternmost corner of Tennessee and named for the ancient Egyptian city on the River Nile, Memphis sprawls along a bluff atop the Mississippi River. *Memphis* means "city of good abode," but historically this has not been an apt description, for civic development has been shaped as often by disease and death as by harmony and foresight. Outwardly modern, with a population approaching seven hundred thousand in 1978, inwardly Memphis is "a city that wants never to change."[1] Both a product and prisoner of its history, Memphis has failed to develop the type of dynamic business leadership that has done so much for cities such as Atlanta and Houston. There is not and never has been a Chamber of Commerce or other business establishment group displaying the foresight to deal regularly with basic racial problems before they escalate into major crises. With the exception of business leadership in the opening up of public facilities during the early 1960s, integration in Memphis has been accomplished by pressure from the federal government and the growing cohesion of blacks who

1 New York *Times*, January 26, 1973, p. 27.

comprise some 40 percent of the population. Not until the late 1960s did these two forces coalesce to force long-range social and economic changes on the city. In order to understand why something more than token integration was so slow in coming and why the role of the business community was often so marginal, it is essential to look at the city's history, particularly the impact of the yellow fever epidemic.

Founded in 1819 by a small group of land speculators, Memphis was, by 1860, with a population of twenty-three thousand, the sixth largest southern city and a major economic competitor of New Orleans and Saint Louis. The dramatic growth and concurrent prosperity were based on an abundance of cotton, a good geographic position, and access to river and rail transportation. At least a third of its population were Irish and German, and for a time Memphis was a cosmopolitan metropolis complete with mercantile aristocracy, a thriving red-light district, and an infamous underworld. The Civil War dealt the city a temporary setback, but by 1866 it was again booming. The hardwood lumber and wholesale grocery businesses broadened the financial base and within a decade the population reached almost fifty thousand—more than double that of Atlanta or Dallas and almost twice that of Nashville.[2]

Then disaster struck. Three times in the 1870s Memphis was ravaged by yellow fever. As many as ten thousand died. The Irish, who were often too poor to flee, proved particularly susceptible and were almost wiped out. The well-to-do left town whenever the fever appeared and fewer returned after each outbreak. The Germans emigrated to Saint Louis; the wealthy settled wherever their fancy and finances took them. They left behind a city bereft of leadership, traditions, money, and drive. In fact the city ceased to exist between 1879 and 1893, becoming merely a special taxing district of the state.[3]

Quite simply Memphis would never be the same again. Yellow fever cost the city its numerical and economic ascendancy in the South. Although its economy was booming by 1900, Memphis was no longer a frontrunner and the citizenry knew

2   Gerald M. Capers, *The Biography of a River Town* (Chapel Hill: University of North Carolina Press, 1939), 205, 207. This remains the best history of Memphis.
3   *Ibid.*, 187–209.

it. It had lost its position to Atlanta.[4] The social impact of the fever was as devastating and perhaps more lasting, with the year 1880 considered as a transition date separating "old" from "new" Memphis. During the 1870s the population declined from about 40,000 to 33,000.[5] At least a third of the white population emigrated. They were rapidly replaced by people from the surrounding area. A special 1918 census showed that less than 2 percent of the 11,781 white parents residing in Memphis had been born there. Meanwhile the proportion of blacks had risen to half, some 7 or 8 percent more than in 1978.[6]

Historian Gerald Capers is not alone in concluding that as a result of the epidemic Memphis has "no aristocracy, no tradition, and little interest in its past." The old, pre-1880 Memphis was heterogeneous and cosmopolitan; the new became homogeneous and provincial. It did not readily adopt new ideas or admit nonsoutherners to the power structure. In general postfever residents were farmers from Arkansas, Mississippi, or Tennessee who were often simple, uneducated, prejudiced, and Protestant. Their values came from and were rooted in fundamentalism, southern patriotism, white supremacy, and a states-rights construction of the Constitution. The problem of provincialism was intensified by the newcomers' connection with cotton. Most had worked the land and were accustomed to being in debt and following unquestioningly the dictates of planters, merchants, and bankers. Power follows profits. Thus, although the well-to-do minority enjoyed a disproportionate influence in civic affairs, they tended to be more interested in parties and cotton prices than culture or urban affairs, and when they exerted themselves it was usually to help maintain the status quo.[7]

4   Memphis *Commercial Appeal*, June 20, 1978, p. 23. This is an interview with Dr. Charles Crawford, Memphis State University history professor, on the impact of yellow fever. See also Capers, *River Town*, 207–209. For an analysis of the economic situation in the 1970s see Bob Wallace, "State of the Economy: How Money Does—and Doesn't—Work in Memphis," *City of Memphis Magazine*, II (May, 1977), 5–8.
5   Capers, *River Town*, 207. Others such as Crawford think the figures on population loss and turnover are closer to thirty thousand.
6   *Ibid.*, 205.
7   *Ibid.*, 205–207. This view of Memphis was expressed by almost all commentators on the city and is a recurrent theme in all the interviews done for this essay. Memphis has never been a city providing an advanced system of social

The prosperity that returned in the late 1890s brought with it corruption in city government and an alarming increase in crime. By 1903 Memphis was the "murder capital of America." Into this situation stepped a young redhead from Holly Springs, Mississippi, Edward Hull Crump, whose father had died in the epidemic. In his own way Crump's impact was as great as that of yellow fever. Beginning as mayor, Crump cleaned up Memphis, initiated the commission form of government, and slowly came to exert influence over the entire state of Tennessee. Until his death at the age of eighty in 1954, Crump and his machine wielded inordinate influence over Memphis.

Simply stated, "Mr. Crump" ran everything. Memphians had neither to think nor to learn how to govern themselves. Community standards of morality and culture were set by a Crump-appointed public censor. The famous Lloyd T. Binford kept Memphians safe from movies and plays containing interracial scenes, sex, or controversial ideas. As historian Charles Crawford has suggested: "If Boss Crump ran Memphis like a rural plantation, it was because that was what he was familiar with. I don't think most people wanted Memphis to be much different from what Mr. Crump wanted, that is, conservative, not receptive to new ideas and resistant to change. Memphis was a small town with a lot of people in it."[8]

Memphis was a white man's town, but so long as blacks "behaved" and allowed themselves to be voted by the machine, race relations remained amicable. However, in the late 1930s tensions began to build in the black community, where the police were more often oppressors than protectors. On June 24, 1940, the Memphis Commission on Interracial Cooperation, a local branch of the moderate organization, was organized in response to pressure from the segregated ministerial associations. The majority of the members were white clergymen with no power. When commission members protested police harassment of black Memphians, Commissioner of Public Safety Joseph Boyle refused to meet with them, blaming local black newspapers for stirring up racial troubles and warning that such conduct

---

services nor one willing to tax itself heavily enough to improve the quality of life citywide.
8   Alfred Steinberg, *The Bosses* (New York: Macmillan, 1972), 72–233; New York *Times*, February 20, 1973, p. 8.

would not be tolerated, "for, after all, this is white man's country."[9] Although Boyle and city officials later agreed to a meeting, nothing changed and the commission itself faded after 1942.

Interracial cooperation was not attempted again until 1956 when liberal Democrats intent upon smashing all vestiges of the Crump machine organized the Greater Memphis Race Relations Committee (GMRRC). Although the GMRRC was supposed to identify community racial problems and help to solve them, its most immediate and pressing problem was the refusal of white members to meet with their black counterparts. Two subcommittees, one for each race, were created and communicated through delegates selected for that purpose. When a prominent banker became chairman of the committee, his board of directors threatened his dismissal because he advocated interracial meetings. Eventually the GMRRC went the way of the Interracial Commission and simply dissolved.[10]

In time the violence that accompanied integration in other southern cities began to frighten thoughtful Memphians. Lucius Burch, an influential lawyer and liberal Democrat, was a driving force behind the creation of the Memphis Committee on Community Relations (MCCR), which was incorporated in 1959. Spawned by the belief that race relations were too important to be left to ministers, this committee was filled with prominent business and professional people who understood that some social change was in order and wished to have a voice in its direction. Believing that the greatest gains could be made through quiet persuasion, the executive committee decided that the group would work without publicity. The leaders of the MCCR often used the argument that voluntary desegregation was the best way to defuse the NAACP, and black pressure added force to the argument. Traditionally blacks had been allowed to go to the zoo and the public library only on so-called "black Thursday" each week. In March, 1960, forty-one black college students en-

9   Marie G. Wingfield, "The Memphis Interracial Commission," *West Tennessee Historical Society Papers*, XXI (1967), 93–100; Memphis *Commercial Appeal*, December 5, 1940, p. 1.

10   Memphis *Commercial Appeal*, February 23, 1956, p. 1, February 28, 1956, p. 8; Benjamin Muse, "Memphis," Special Report of the Southern Regional Council, Atlanta, 1960, p. 18, in Mississippi Valley Collection, John Brister Library, Memphis State University.

tered two white public libraries on a Monday and were arrested. Black boycotts and picketing of white businesses followed, and in the fall the city commission agreed to end segregation on public buses, in libraries, and finally at the zoo.[11]

Although the MCCR was unable to persuade the city commission to appoint blacks to public positions, it did get some desegregation of downtown eating places and movies. The word was passed that the time had come for the change to be made. By the time the city at large became aware of the change, the flash point had passed; it was a *fait accompli*. Clearly the more progressive element in the business community and the MCCR were behind this. However, there is no record of precisely who made the decision or why it was done at this time, for the desegregation occurred voluntarily before the public accommodations act became federal law in 1964.[12]

The admission of thirteen black students brought token integration to the public school system in the fall of 1961. White Memphians congratulated themselves on the peaceful "revolution," yet neither the board of education nor the business community did anything to remove hiring barriers and the MCCR was powerless to deal with the continuing charges of police brutality. However, in comparison with other southern cities, Memphis looked good. A 1964 special report of the Southern Regional Council commended leaders of both races in Memphis for the striking changes that had occurred so smoothly. Whites never heard the warnings of men like the Reverend James Lawson, who tried to warn them that progress was too slow, too minor, too mechanical to satisfy the black community.[13]

Outsiders also complimented Memphis for solving its gov-

11   Selma S. Lewis, "Social Religion and the Memphis Sanitation Strike" (Ph.D. dissertation, Memphis State University, 1976), 71–74; David Tucker, *Black Pastors and Leaders: Memphis, 1819–1972* (Memphis: Memphis State University Press, 1975), 113–15.
12   Interview with Lucius Burch by the author, May 9, 1978. Others interviewed for this article told the same story. No one would mention the names of those involved in making the decision or say more than that the "time had come" when asked about motivation.
13   Lewis, "Social Religion and the Memphis Sanitation Strike," 76. See also "Memphis Moves Toward Racial Justice," *Christian Century*, September 9, 1964, pp. 1102–1103. Tucker, *Black Pastors*, 119–37, is particularly good in presenting Lawson's role in the integration struggle of the 1960s.

ernmental problems. Back in 1955 a group of reform-minded businessmen and the editors of the two newspapers had united to elect as mayor Edmund Orgill, a progressive Democrat whose family owned the area's largest wholesale hardware company. Although far from an integrationist, Orgill did call for the appointment of at least one black to the board of the City of Memphis Hospitals since a majority of the patients were Negro. In response, a cross was burned in his front yard.[14] Nonetheless Orgill defeated Watkins Overton, the Crump candidate, and the Crump machine went down to final defeat in the 1956 senate race. At last self-government had reached Memphis, although her lack of experience in the art would soon become painfully apparent.

Edmund Orgill was succeeded as mayor by Henry Loeb, a conservative fourth-generation Memphian and a respected member of the business community. Because of his campaign in 1959, blacks accused him of segregationist sympathies but Memphis experienced peaceful change during his years in office, 1960–1963. He was replaced by William Ingram, a lawyer and former judge who had widespread black support.

The 1967 election was the most crucial since 1955. The preceding year Memphians had replaced the inefficient commission system with a mayor-council form. The change had taken place under the auspices of an organization called Program of Progress, better known as POP. Its twenty-five-man executive committee attempted to represent all segments of the community with leadership resting with business and professional people. Downing Pryor, a local Oldsmobile dealer, led the drive and became chairman of the first city council in 1968.[15] The election was also notable for the presence of A. W. Willis, the first black member of the state legislature since Reconstruction, who was running for mayor. A wealthy businessman, Willis had five white opponents. He needed to get half the black votes to win a berth in the runoff. Mayor Ingram drained off that support and

14   Interview with Sidney Genette by the author, April 27, 1978; Burch interview.
15   Jonathan I. Wax, "Program of Progress, a Step into the Present: Change in the Form of Government, Memphis, Tennessee" (Senior thesis, Princeton University, 1968). For a concise treatment see Robert E. Bailey, "The 1968 Memphis Sanitation Strike" (M.A. thesis, Memphis State University, 1974), 1–18.

Willis finished fourth. Projecting the sort of white supremacist image he had used to defeat Edmund Orgill, Henry Loeb emerged the victor, and as one observer noted: "The mayor represented white Memphis and was alien to the blacks of the city."[16]

The first council was composed of one white woman, three blacks, and nine white males. Although idealistic and possessed with good intentions, none had prior experience in governing a city. This meant that the city had a leadership vacuum just as it was getting ready to explode.

When the new council took office in January, 1968, there was no indication that Memphis would be a very different city six months later. A typical southern city, Memphis was and is dominated by whites. The city's leaders had not realized that blacks wanted good jobs and the opportunity for advancement, respect, and involvement in the affairs of their city. It had not occurred to many whites that Memphis belonged to blacks as well as to them. No blacks were on the board of the Chamber of Commerce; none were members of the influential Future Memphis Incorporated which planned goals for the city and helped to groom young businessmen for future leadership; none served on a local bank board or on the school board. Service organizations such as Rotary were closed to them; organizations with so much as one black member were denied the use of the facilities of any country club in town. In essence there were two communities existing side by side with no communications between them.

To a degree the racial awareness of civic leadership was molded by wishful thinking about what blacks "really wanted" and blurred by the fact that Memphis had passed through the turbulent early and middle 1960s without violence. Thus most leaders felt little apprehension about the future now that public facilities and the schools had been "integrated." There had not been a race riot in Memphis since 1866 and none was expected. As Jessie Turner, president of the local chapter of the NAACP, observed, "The power structure was lulled into taking a nap

16   New York *Times*, August 9, 1967, p. 23, September 29, 1967, p. 28, October 5, 1967, p. 30, October 7, 1967, p. 58; Bailey, "The 1968 Memphis Sanitation Strike," 17.

when they should have been out there trying to stay ahead of the situation."[17]

Civic complacency came to an abrupt end in the winter of 1968. On Tuesday, January 30, more than a hundred sewer and drain workers reported for work. Twenty-one were sent home because rain made it impossible to work in the sewers; they were given two hours' "show-up" pay but lost some eleven dollars more that they normally earned. On Wednesday, T. O. Jones, local organizer of the American Federation of State, County, and Municipal Employees (AFSCME) ordered the crews off the job. The newly installed commissioner of sanitation, Charles Blackburn, met with Jones, explained that "show-up" pay was standard procedure when workers were not needed, and promised to devise a more equitable plan for the future. Jones then ordered the men back to work thinking that the twenty-one would receive a full day's pay in their next check.[18]

The next day, February 1, Blackburn met with Jones and P. J. Ciampa, a national official of AFSCME. The union now asked for grievance procedure, a checkoff for union dues, and union recognition. As Blackburn noted, only Mayor Loeb could grant the latter two demands. Even as they were meeting, the automatic compressor on an old garbage truck accidentally caught two workers who were "ground up like garbage." The men were unclassified city employees and were not covered by workman's compensation or life insurance. Mayor Loeb, with the approval of the city council, gave each of the families eight hundred dollars to help with funeral expenses. Despite the kind gesture, a bitter memory of the accident and the lack of insurance lingered in the black community.[19]

Payday, February 9, came and the twenty-one were not paid for the rainy day. At a union meeting on Sunday night, Febru-

17 Interview with Jessie Turner, 27, in the Memphis Multi-Media Sanitation Strike Project, Mississippi Valley Collection, John Brister Library, Memphis State University. All interviews followed by MSU are part of this ongoing project conducted under the auspices of the Office of Oral History at Memphis State. The MSU collection is the best available source of primary materials on the strike and the murder of Dr. King.
18 Interview with Charles Blackburn, 4, MSU; interview with T. O. Jones, 8, MSU.
19 Memphis *Commercial Appeal*, February 2, 1968, p. 14; Jones interview, 11, MSU; Blackburn interview, 12, MSU.

ary 11, a new set of demands were presented: union recognition, a dues checkoff, and an increase in the hourly wages from $1.65 to $2.35. The demands were rejected and the union members voted to strike.[20]

On paper it seems the strike should have been broken quickly. Instead it lasted sixty-five days, tore Memphis to pieces, and cost Dr. Martin Luther King his life. The local union was so small and weak that the international had to pay Jones his salary. Even the weather was against the strike as garbage neither smells nor serves as a breeding ground for disease in the winter. Still, a successful strike meant a strong black union, and the union would serve as the voice of those at the bottom of the economic ladder and force respect from the city's white leadership. The confusion occasioned by the change in municipal government provided an opportunity that could be seized only if blacks stuck together. The black response was emotional and out of proportion to the issues, but here at last was an identifiable cause and an outlet for long felt frustrations. As a result of all these factors the black community banded together as it never had before and presented the white power structure with its greatest challenge.

The actions, pronouncements, and events of the first few days set the pattern for the next two months. As several prominent Memphians have noted, Mayor Loeb's handling of the strike was a tragedy of inflexibility. He branded the strike as illegal and never budged from that position. Legally correct, and supported by the white business and social establishments, he refused to see that the strike also involved a struggle for black dignity. Mayor Loeb was willing to help the strikers' families with a city-funded food stamp program and to talk to the men on an individual basis, but he would not deal with their union. When the strikers refused to return to work, he began using supervisory personnel and hiring new workers.[21]

The nature of the strike began to change on its second day, Tuesday, February 14. Mayor Loeb's offer of personal audiences was booed and jeered as plantation paternalism by a crowd of

20 Bailey, "The 1968 Memphis Sanitation Strike," 23–25.
21 Interview with Lucius Burch, 14, MSU; interview with Downing Pryor, 47, MSU; Memphis *Commercial Appeal*, February 14–23, 1968.

one thousand strikers who had gathered at Ellis Auditorium to hear him. Furious, Loeb warned that his new administration would not be pushed around, and then stalked out.[22] When the Reverend Ezekiel Bell stood up to urge the men to stand firm, it signaled the entry of the black clergy into what had started as a labor dispute. Within a few weeks the black ministers, not the union leadership, would be running a community-wide struggle against the status quo.

Realizing that the problem was becoming racial and that Loeb was out of touch with the black community, councilman Lewis Donelson, a lawyer, invited his fellow members to a meeting in his home on Sunday, February 18, to try to find a solution. Councilman J. O. Patterson had talked to the union office that morning and found that it would settle for a small wage increase without union recognition or the checkoff. The assembled councilmen voted eleven to one (one was out of town) to authorize Patterson and the Reverend James Netters, both black, to offer the strikers ten cents an hour then and an additional five cents on July 1 when the new budget went into effect. Because the city charter denied the council any authority in administrative matters, it was necessary to get Loeb's permission to make the offer. Loeb refused. Two months later the mayor had to agree to a settlement providing for a wage increase of ten cents hourly on May 1 and an additional five cents on September 1, union recognition, and the checkoff.[23]

When the mediation efforts of the Memphis Ministerial Association failed and blacks began to boycott downtown businesses, the city council took limited action by inviting strikers to present their grievances at a special meeting of its public works committee on February 22. The emotion-charged meeting degenerated into a shouting match. When fire marshalls tried to empty the overcrowded meeting chamber, the strikers refused, sent out for sandwich makings, and settled in to wait until their demands were met. They left only after the committee agreed to present their demands to the city council.[24] The

22 Memphis *Commercial Appeal*, February 15, 1968, p. 1.
23 Interview with Lewis Donelson, 13–16, MSU; Bailey, "The 1968 Memphis Sanitation Strike," 121–22.
24 Memphis *Commercial Appeal*, February 15–23, 1968. Lewis, "Social Religion and the Memphis Sanitation Strike," 62–110, presents an authoritative analysis of the growth of the Ministerial Association and its role in the strike.

"picnic" in city hall infuriated whites, for the building was new, beautifully furnished, and a source of great civic pride. This was a turning point even for more moderate whites who had been inclined to think that some of the strikers' demands were not excessive. The white community was now solidly behind the mayor's uncompromising position.[25]

The turning point for blacks came the next day, February 23, when the strikers returned for a city council meeting in the much larger Ellis Auditorium. The council filed in, read a statement that they had voted nine to four to support the mayor, and walked out, turning their backs on the strikers, literally as well as figuratively. As the men and their leaders were marching back down Main Street to their headquarters, violence erupted. The police used nightsticks and Mace indiscriminately. Several rather conservative black ministers were Maced. They now joined the strikers' cause, which had become synonomous with the black cause. This small riot completed the alienation of blacks from whites. The gap was almost unbridgeable.[26]

Loeb reacted by breaking off any discussion and getting an injunction against the strike and its leaders. This meant that any union leader who formally negotiated as a union representative was liable to be held in contempt of court. The injunction had the indirect effect of pushing the black ministers into the leadership. On February 25, black leaders met and formed COME, Community on the Move for Equality, whose objectives were justice for the strikers and jobs for blacks. The weapons were the boycott of downtown businesses and the two newspapers, and daily marches.[27] Racial tension escalated. Still the white business community solidly supported the mayor.

The marchers carried signs reading I AM A MAN. This simple statement summed up what the strike was now all about—human dignity. A man made his own decisions about his life rather than having them made for him; a man was an individual with all the rights and responsibilities attendant thereto; a man decided for himself whether to join a union or shop at a given store. In this one sentence the black community was announc-

25   Bailey, "The 1968 Memphis Sanitation Strike," 43–50.
26   Everyone interviewed for this article made the same point as did many of those who participated in the MSU project.
27   Bailey, "The 1968 Memphis Sanitation Strike," 52–63; Memphis *Commercial Appeal*, February 23–26, 1968.

ing that henceforth blacks stood on their own feet and expected to be treated as equals and not as children. It was easier for whites to make jokes about the "necessity" for "long haired" marchers to carry a sign proclaiming their gender or to say that the trouble was about unions not sex than it was to stop to think about what lay behind the proclamation I AM A MAN. So long as garbage was being collected and the marching remained out of sight in the downtown area, whites were content to leave matters in the mayor's hands.

The strike entered its final phase in mid-March. The appearance of Roy Wilkins and Bayard Rustin, national NAACP officials, at a mass meeting on March 14, marked the beginning of a national effort to support the movement. Violence also increased. Meanwhile, the newspapers continued their total support for the mayor and police; garbage was being collected; time appeared to be on Loeb's side. At this point Martin Luther King interrupted his planning for the Poor People's March on Washington to address a rally in Memphis on March 18. He urged a general strike and promised to return to lead a march through the downtown. The papers described the meeting as rabble-rousing and branded King an opportunist.[28]

The day before the scheduled march on the twenty-second, the city council became so worried that it adopted a resolution calling for mediation of the strike. Although a record-breaking late winter snowstorm caused a cancellation of the march, mediation began. The key issue was the dues checkoff; without it the union was dead and Loeb knew it. He argued that the union was interested only in the money and that it was his duty to protect the men. Loeb increased pressure on March 27 by ending the food stamp program for strikers.[29]

Thursday, March 28, the union broke off talks and Dr. King's peaceful march ended in violence and the death of a sixteen-year-old looter. The mayor clamped a curfew on the city and called out the national guard. King's badly tattered reputation was damaged further by the fact that the riot had begun when a group of black teenagers had pulled sticks from under their coats and started breaking windows and looting stores.

28   Memphis *Commercial Appeal*, March 19, 1968, p. 5.
29   *Ibid.*, March 22–28, 1968.

Shaken, King vowed to return to lead another march and prove that nonviolence was still viable. An equally shaken but badly divided city council failed to heed Lewis Donelson's warning that the city was "sitting on a powder keg" and did nothing.[30]

It was at this juncture that the business community under the leadership of the Chamber of Commerce stepped forward to attempt to deal with one of the city's basic problems by urging the adoption of a program to provide training and jobs for the hard-core unemployed, most of whom were black. The proposal was strongly supported by the Downtown Association, whose member businesses had been badly damaged by the boycott and demonstrations. The sudden emergence of business leadership on April 2 did not involve a repudiation of the mayor or his position. Rather it was a response generated by the realization that national coverage of the strike was putting the city in the worst possible light and that this was bad for business.[31] Industries do not locate in areas torn by racial strife; Memphis desperately needed new factories. A few business leaders tried to persuade Mayor Loeb to soften his position but to no avail. Another group of top businessmen including Thomas Faires, president of the Chamber; Sam Langley, president of Future Memphis; Alvin Wunderlich, Jr., president of National Trust Life Insurance Company; and Jack Kopald, an executive with Humko Incorporated, went to see Tommy Powell, president of the Memphis Labor Council and to plan how to bring pressure on the mayor to end the strike.[32]

Mayor Loeb, fearing another riot, went into federal court to get an injunction forbidding King's return march. None of this frenzied activity mattered, for time had run out. Shortly before 7 P.M., April 4, Dr. King was murdered. Genuinely horrified by the murder, Mayor Loeb called Mrs. King to offer both his sympathy and whatever assistance the family wanted, but he did not alter his position on the strike. Not even the efforts of old friends who came to his office that night to reason with him could change his mind. A biracial ministerial delegation came the next morning to plead with him to forget the illegality of the

30   *Ibid.*; Donelson interview, 21, MSU.
31   This explanation was given by all businessmen interviewed for this article and is the view of those who commented on it for the MSU project.
32   Memphis *Commercial Appeal*, April 5, 1968, p. 12.

strike and do the moral thing—grant the union demands before more tragedies occurred. Loeb refused.[33]

On Sunday, April 7, some six thousand citizens met in Crump Stadium under the slogan "Memphis Cares." This meeting of the races had been put together by John T. Fisher, a young Chrysler dealer, as an expression of his concern about the community. It was accomplished literally between the murder Thursday night and Sunday afternoon, and without Chamber of Commerce help. Although carried live on NBC, it was buried in Monday's *Commercial Appeal*. The meeting was a tough session in which various prominent Memphians voiced their thoughts about city problems and annoyed each other. People came because they were concerned about their city; for the first time in years there was real communication between the races.[34]

John T. Fisher's involvement had begun early in March when Fred Beesom, an insurance executive and old friend, had talked to Fisher about his conviction that Memphis was headed for real trouble. Taking two like-minded friends with them, they went to see the mayor but failed to alter his position. Discouraged, they decided on March 18 to see the Reverend James Lawson, one of the major black leaders. Lawson astounded them by saying, "You are the first white businessmen to come here to ask, to listen to what our side of the story is." Although Beesom and Fisher tried to persuade other businessmen and council members to talk to Lawson, their efforts were a classic case of too little, too late.[35]

Another business leader who worked for a settlement was Edward Cook, president of Cook Industries and an aspiring Democratic candidate for Congress. A lifelong friend of Loeb's as well as one of his unofficial advisors, Cook understood that the strike had "escalated into a racial issue and ceased to be an

33   Interview with James Wax, MSU, cited in Bailey, "The 1968 Memphis Sanitation Strike," 112–13; Lewis, "Social Religion and the Memphis Sanitation Strike," 126–36; interview with Lewis McKee by the author, May 12, 1978. McKee was president of the National Bank of Commerce in 1968.
34   Interview with John T. Fisher, 3–5, MSU; interview with John T. Fisher by the author, May 10, 1978.
35   Fisher interview, 16–19, MSU; interview with Fred Beesom by the author, March 20, 1978. Beesom did not know what prompted his decision to visit Fisher nor did either remember the exact date. Both had vague premonitions of disaster and decided to try to "do something."

economic issue." Cook worked with Lucius Burch, Downing Pryor, and others to work out a settlement even though he was convinced that the strike could be broken and that the white community was solidly behind the mayor.[36]

Edward Cook was undoubtedly correct in his assessment of the situation. Prior to Dr. King's murder, probably 75 to 95 percent of the white business community had supported Loeb.[37] They tended to view the situation as one of supporting either the mayor or "them" (the blacks). The black community was not only disrupting the status quo, which is always uncomfortable, but was demanding change, and change involves thought and costs money.[38] The official reason for refusing to raise the sanitation workers' pay was that the city could not afford it without raising property taxes. Spokesmen for the business community never challenged the thinking behind that statement. "Because their business acumen was matched by their sociological ignorance, they stood back and watched as a minor labor dispute escalated into a major tragedy.[39] It was the horror of Dr. King's being murdered in Memphis and fears as to the economic repercussions that motivated businessmen to press for a quick, expedient settlement.[40] Downtown merchants, who had supported Loeb steadfastly when they thought he would win, now realized that the black boycott would end only when the union's demands were met. A delegation from the business community at large visited Loeb to tell him that the strike had to be settled at once. Too much money had been lost. Daytime boycotts and nighttime curfews had cost the city millions of dollars in lost sales and overtime pay for fire and police protection. The city was in a mess socially, economically, and politically.[41]

Business fears about the impact of the strike on the city's national image were intensified by an article in *Time*. One sen-

36   Interview with Edward Cook, 15, MSU.
37   Estimates are based on material in the MSU collection and interviews with Downing Pryor by the author, May 12, 1978, as well as with Fisher, McKee, and Burch. The two major papers, which reflect local business views, supported Loeb throughout.
38   Fisher, in his interviews at MSU and with the author, talked about the disruption of the status quo. Others interviewed agreed.
39   Burch interview, 22, MSU.
40   Everyone cited thus far expressed this opinion.
41   Cook interview, 16–17, MSU.

tence is still vividly remembered: "The proximate cause of his death was, ironically, a minor labor dispute in a Southern backwater: the two-month old strike of 1,300 predominately Negro garbage collectors in the decaying Mississippi River town of Memphis."[42] In that one sentence Memphians discovered how the rest of the nation viewed them and it hurt. Clearly Memphis was progressive only when viewed from the perspective of rural Mississippi or Arkansas.

The Chamber of Commerce reluctantly realized that as painful as was the label "decaying river town," there was a degree of truth in it, and it quickly set about trying to deal with the myriad economic problems Memphis faced. Industry had to be attracted, new jobs created, the per capita income level raised. The Chamber of Commerce raised literally millions of dollars in 1968–1969 to refurbish the city's image and to move in new directions. The Chamber's board was integrated and an effort was made to work with leaders of the black community. Many companies consciously employed more blacks and promoted those already on the payroll. When progress lagged, blacks went to the appropriate federal agencies which, in turn, saw to it that equal job opportunity laws were obeyed. As a result there was a marked improvement in the hiring of blacks for white- as well as blue-collar jobs. Even the very conservative morning paper, the *Commercial Appeal*, yielded to black pressure in 1969 and removed "Hambone," an offensive cartoon featuring a poorly dressed elderly Negro man who mouthed platitudes in a heavy dialect.

As much as the changes were needed, they did not necessarily reflect a new attitude. Hambone is now a ceramic figurine that has been a popular Christmas gift during the last few seasons. Complaints of police brutality are filed with almost monotonous regularity. In October, 1971, seventeen-year-old Elton Hayes was beaten to death; at least thirty-seven law enforcement officers were present when it occurred. No one has been convicted. Although the city dedicated a twelve-mile stretch of freeway for Martin Luther King in 1971, Mayor Loeb did not attend the ceremonies.

The Chamber of Commerce's story since 1968 has been one

42 *Time*, April 12, 1968, p. 18.

of a brief rise and a long fall. The Chamber has never been a strong organization. It almost folded in the 1950s, but in the aftermath of the strike it was able to raise between six and seven million dollars. Numerous projects were funded; advertisements portraying Memphis in a positive light appeared in national magazines. One would be hard pressed, however, to say exactly what was accomplished. Racial tensions also contributed to Chamber problems. Although federal judge Robert McRae initially ordered busing in 1971, it was not until the fall of 1973 that the plan was put into effect in a massive way. Private and church schools sprang up like weeds and spread like poison ivy. Following the example of Atlanta, the Chamber tried to calm things down, running public-service announcements on radio and television, issuing a pamphlet, and having leading members make speeches to whatever groups would listen. This small, rather ineffective effort gave the Chamber a short-lived reputation for liberalism and some companies did not renew their memberships.[43]

Support for a revitalized downtown also earned it the opprobrium of many whites who had written off the area as black-dominated and therefore not worth redeveloping. Internal, nonracial problems played a role as well in driving the Chamber of Commerce to the edge of bankruptcy early in 1978 and forcing its reorganization. The emphasis of the "New Chamber," as it styles itself, was to be almost exclusively on attracting jobs, industries, and conventions; its orientation was to business and not the community at large. Nevertheless, it was Chamber President James McGehee who took the lead in working out the settlement that ended the strike by Memphis police and firemen in July, 1978. Several prominent businessmen whose names were widely publicized were part of the negotiating group, perhaps signaling a resurgence of business leadership in Memphis.

By 1978 Memphis was legally integrated. Gone were the separate water fountains, the special "black" days at the public library and the zoo, the seats at the back of the bus. The public schools were integrated with black children in the majority by a margin of approximately 70 percent to 30 percent. There were

43 Interview with Samuel Hollis by the author, May 28, 1978. Hollis is a past president of the Chamber of Commerce and president of a large cotton warehouse company.

black members of the school board. However, white parents who could afford it or could borrow the money placed their children in private schools ranging from fundamentalist Christian to college prep. Local banks altered the way they figured car loans to take tuition costs into account. The Briarcrest Baptist Schools formed the largest private school system in the country with the result that Memphis' white children were more segregated than ever.

There were no blacks on the boards of white-owned banks and few held upper-level managerial positions in companies. None was a member of Future Memphis. Although the country clubs continued to exclude blacks from membership, they did begin to allow a few integrated groups to use their facilities. Rotary was integrated early in 1978 and the newspapers sporadically covered black social events and activities.

In the aftermath of the sanitation strike, blacks discovered that by continuing to work as a unit and by calling on the federal government when its assistance was needed, they could alter the surface of Memphis life. Only in rare instances, such as court-ordered busing, did the government intervene directly, but the threat of intervention and the presence of federal officials charged with enforcement of equal opportunity laws were constant factors speeding the pace of integration. The 1970s saw the development of a black political machine under the leadership of Congressman Harold Ford. Now when the black 40 percent speak, they are assured of a hearing. Once the business community can learn both to listen and to act, it will be able to shake off the troubled past and make Memphis into a "city of good abode" for all its citizens.

BIBLIOGRAPHICAL ESSAY

Rather than attempting to provide a complete bibliography of the American civil rights movement, this essay is designed to suggest general works that are particularly useful in understanding twentieth-century southern culture, and to point out specific studies that clarify the role of the business community in coping with the civil rights challenge to southern race relations.

The best and most informative surveys of the South in the twentieth century are C. Vann Woodward, *The Origins of the New South, 1877–1913* (Baton Rouge: Louisiana State University Press, 1951), and George Brown Tindall, *The Emergence of the New South, 1913–1945* (Baton Rouge: Louisiana State University Press, 1967). C. Vann Woodward's *The Burden of Southern History* (Rev. ed.; Baton Rouge: Louisiana State University Press, 1968), still offers a provocative analysis of southern history and culture, as does W. J. Cash, *The Mind of the South* (New York: Knopf, 1941). More recently, Charles P. Roland's *The Improbable Era: The South Since World War II* (Lexington, Ky.: University Press of Kentucky, 1975), traces southern developments from World War II to the mid-1970s.

The starting point for any analysis of race relations remains Gunnar Myrdal, Richard Sterner, and Arnold Rose, *An American Dilemma: The Negro Problem and Modern Democracy* (2 vols.; New York: Harper, 1944). The best general surveys of black life and changing racial patterns are to be found in C. Vann Woodward, *The Strange Career of Jim Crow* (3rd ed.; New

York: Oxford University Press, 1975); August Meier and Elliott Rudwick, *From Plantation to Ghetto* (Rev. ed.; New York: Hill and Wang, 1970); and John Hope Franklin, *From Slavery to Freedom: A History of American Negroes* (4th ed.; New York: Knopf, 1974), all of which have sections on the civil rights movement.

Still the most incisive study of southern politics is V. O. Key, Jr., *Southern Politics in State and Nation* (New York: Vintage, 1949). Key argues from the basic premise that "in its grand outlines the politics of the South revolves around the position of the Negro." Key's analysis has been updated by William C. Havard, (ed.), *The Changing Politics of the South* (Baton Rouge: Louisiana State University Press, 1972); Numan Bartley and Hugh Davis Graham, *Southern Politics and the Second Reconstruction* (Baltimore: Johns Hopkins University Press, 1975); Jack Bass and Walter DeVries, *The Transformation of Southern Politics: Social Change and Political Consequences Since 1945* (New York: Basic Books, 1976); and Earl Black, *Southern Governors and Civil Rights: Racial Segregation as a Campaign Issue in the Second Reconstruction* (Cambridge: Harvard University Press, 1976), although Black argues that in southern gubernatorial politics, campaigning no longer revolves around the issue of race. An excellent analysis of the involvement of blacks in the politics of the post–World War II South is Donald R. Matthews and James W. Prothro, *Negroes and the New Southern Politics* (New York: Harcourt, Brace and World, 1966). Also valuable in understanding the southern political tradition are George B. Tindall, *The Persistent Tradition in New South Politics* (Baton Rouge: Louisiana State University Press, 1975); Dewey Grantham, *The Democratic South* (Athens, Ga.: University of Georgia Press, 1963); and T. Harry Williams, *Romance and Realism in Southern Politics* (Athens, Ga.: University of Georgia Press, 1961).

For a comprehensive analysis of the *Brown* decision and the Supreme Court one should consult Richard Kluger, *Simple Justice* (New York: Knopf, 1976). The role of southern federal judges in implementing federal judicial decisions has been chronicled by Jack W. Peltason, *Fifty-Eight Lonely Men: Southern Federal Judges and School Desegregation* (New York: Random House, 1961); and Charles V. Hamilton, *The Bench and the*

Ballot: Southern Federal Judges and Black Voters (New York: Oxford University Press, 1973), which assesses the judicial treatment of blacks in the South.

Several fine studies trace the southern white response to the *Brown* decision, especially Benjamin Muse, *Ten Years of Prelude: The Story of Integration Since the Supreme Court's 1954 Decision* (New York: Viking Press, 1964), and Numan V. Bartley, *The Rise of Massive Resistance: Race and Politics in the South in the 1950's* (Baton Rouge: Louisiana State University Press, 1969). Bartley argues that the acceptance of token integration in 1960 did not represent a dramatic break with the southern past and that the strategy of massive resistance stabilized political patterns in favor of white supremacy. Neil R. McMillen's *The Citizens' Council: Organized Resistance to the Second Reconstruction* (Urbana: University of Illinois Press, 1971), contends that the decline of the white Citizens' Council was a result of the federal government's determination "to guarantee equality for black Americans." Reed Sarratt's *The Ordeal of Segregation: The First Decade* (New York: Harper and Row, 1966), suggests that biracial public schools in the South became a reality primarily as a result of federal pressure, and that even then the process was slow and laborious. Robert Crain's *The Politics of School Desegregation* (Chicago: Aldine, 1968), examines northern as well as southern schools and finds that intense conflict could have been avoided if the white leadership had been determined to prevent it.

During the past ten years several important books have been written on the civil rights movement of the 1960s. Of particular importance is August Meier and Elliott Rudwick's *CORE: A Study in the Civil Rights Movement, 1942–1968* (New York: Oxford University Press, 1973), which discusses the impact of the movement and analyzes the changes experienced by CORE during the 1960s. William H. Chafe in *Civilities and Civil Rights: Greensboro, North Carolina and the Black Struggle for Freedom* (New York: Oxford University Press, 1980) details the history of race relations in this southern community in the twentieth century. Chafe argues that Greensboro leaders used the concept of civility to block desegregation. He finds little to suggest that significant racial progress has occurred since 1965. David J. Garrow, *Protest at Selma: Martin Luther King,*

Jr., and the Voting Rights Act of 1965 (New Haven: Yale University Press, 1978) examines King's strategy of protest and suggests that he and the SCLC were fully aware that the movement had to generate violence in order to attract media attention and public support, thereby assuring passage of federal voting rights legislation. Charles Fager, *Selma 1965* (New York: Scribner's, 1974) is less critical in its assessment. Steven Lawson, *Black Ballots: Voting Rights in the South, 1944–1969* (New York: Columbia University Press, 1976) is a detailed account of the long and often frustrating struggle by blacks for suffrage, beginning with the *Smith* v. *Allwright* decision. The story of the 1964 civil rights bill's passage through the Kennedy administration is recounted in Carl M. Brauer, *John F. Kennedy and the Second Reconstruction* (New York: Columbia University Press, 1977). The role of Dr. Martin Luther King, Jr., has been sketched in his own *Stride Toward Freedom: The Montgomery Story* (New York: Harper and Row, 1958); David L. Lewis, *King: A Critical Biography* (New York: Praeger, 1970); and C. Eric Lincoln, (ed.), *Martin Luther King, Jr.: A Profile* (New York: Hill and Wang, 1970). Howard Zinn, *SNCC* (Boston: Beacon Press, 1964), is still an effective although outdated study of the student organization.

Very little has been written about the role of the southern business community in the desegregation process. Paul M. Gaston, *The New South Creed: A Study in Southern Mythmaking* (New York: Knopf, 1970), details the post–Civil War development of a southern "mythology" of opulence, innocence, and national reunification through industrialization—a process which laid the foundation for the subsequent respectability of "Whiggish" ideas in an agrarian culture. Numan Bartley's *The Rise of Massive Resistance* analyzes the role of business considerations in the southern response to desegregation; Bartley categorizes southern leaders as neobourbons, neopopulists, and business conservatives.

C. Vann Woodward's "New South Fraud Is Papered by Old South Myth," Washington *Post*, July 9, 1961, argues that industrialization in the South did not lead to increased moderation in racial attitudes and patterns of behavior; indeed, Woodward contends that industrial development in the South occurred with the assumption that racial discrimination would continue and both races would be exploited. Richard Cramer's "School Deseg-regation and New Industry: The Southern Community Leader's Viewpoint," *Social Forces*, XLI (May, 1963), 384–89, supports Woodward's argument; Cramer finds no relationship between support for new industry and the community's attitude concern-ing racial moderation. On the other hand, in examining eco-nomic developments in the post–World War II South, Ralph McGill, *The South and the Southerner* (2nd ed.; Boston: Little, Brown, 1963), suggests that there "could have been no postwar surge toward a new South without the new managerial breed, the executives who came with the new industries, and the young, especially competent Southerners." Noting this develop-ment, Jack Patterson's "Business Response to the Negro Move-ment," *New South*, XXI (Winter, 1966), 67–74, contends that these businessmen exerted an important influence on the south-ern response to the black protest; "Business managers, acting under pressure to defend their economic welfare, have joined other community groups to make concessions to Negro de-mands, especially as those demands were backed by federal leg-islation." Edward F. Haas, "The Southern Metropolis, 1940–1976," in Blaine Brownell and David R. Goldfield (eds.), *The City in Southern History: The Growth of Urban Civilization in the South* (Port Washington, N.Y.: Kennikat Press, 1977), finds that business leaders in New Orleans, Atlanta, and Birmingham used their influence to mitigate racial tensions or to prevent them from developing. Calvin Trillin has made a similar argu-ment in "Reflections: Remembrance of Moderates Past," *New Yorker*, March 21, 1977, pp. 85–97; Trillin argues that busi-nessmen in Georgia "wanted as little integration as possible but they also wanted as little trouble as possible accompanying the integration that had to come." For additional insights into the response of the business community to the civil rights move-ment see Lorin A. Thompson, "Virginia Education Crisis and Its Economic Aspects," *New South* (February, 1959), 3–8; Alfred Hero, *The Southerner and World Affairs* (Baton Rouge: Louisi-ana State University Press, 1965); and Eli Ginzberg (ed.), *The Negro Challenge to the Business Community* (New York: Mc-Graw-Hill, 1964). Of more recent interest is J. Mills Thornton's "Challenge and Response: The Montgomery Bus Boycott of 1955–1956," *Alabama Review*, XXXIII (July, 1980), 163–235.

NOTES ON CONTRIBUTORS

Carl Abbott is Associate Professor of Urban Studies at Portland State University. The author of *The New Urban America: Growth and Politics in Sunbelt Cities* (Chapel Hill: University of North Carolina Press, 1981), he received his graduate degrees from the University of Chicago.

John Quincy Adams is Associate Professor of Political Science at Millsaps College. The author of "The Mississippi Legislature" in David M. Landry and Joseph B. Parker (eds.), *Mississippi Government and Politics in Transition* (Dubuque, Iowa: Kendall/ Hunt Publishing Company, 1976), he received his J.D. from the University of Texas in 1959.

William J. Brophy is Associate Professor of History and Chairman of the Department of History at Stephen F. Austin State University. The author of "Black Texans and the New Deal," in Donald W. Whisenhunt (ed.), *The Depression in the Southwest* (Port Washington, N.Y.: Kennikat Press, 1980), he received his Ph.D. from Vanderbilt University.

William H. Chafe is Professor of History and Co-Director of the Center for the Study of Civil Rights and Race Relations at Duke University. The author of *Civilities and Civil Rights: Greensboro, North Carolina and the Black Struggle for Freedom* (New York: Oxford University Press, 1980), he received his Ph.D. from Columbia University in 1971.

James C. Cobb is Associate Professor of History and Social Studies at the University of Mississippi. The author of *The Selling of the South: The Southern Crusade for Industrial Development, 1936–1980* (Baton Rouge: Louisiana State University Press, 1982), he received his Ph.D. from the University of Georgia.

David R. Colburn is Associate Professor of History and Chairman of the Department of History at the University of Florida. The author, with Richard Scher, of *Florida's Gubernatorial Politics in the Twentieth Century* (Tallahassee: University Presses of Florida, 1981), he received his Ph.D. from the University of North Carolina in 1971.

Robert Corley is Assistant Archivist at the Department of Archives and Manuscripts of the Birmingham Public Library. He received his Ph.D. from the University of Virginia in 1979, where he wrote a dissertation on "Race Relations in Birmingham, Alabama, 1948–1963."

Alton Hornsby, Jr., is Professor of History and Chairman of the Department of History at Morehouse College, and editor of the *Journal of Negro History*. The author of *In the Cage: Eyewitness Accounts of the Freed Negro in Southern Society* (New York: Quadrangle Press, 1971), he received his Ph.D. from the University of Texas in 1969.

Morton Inger is a member of the Fundamental Planning Division of the American Telephone and Telegraph Company in Basking Ridge, New Jersey. For many years, he was an analyst of school desegregation and integration in cities throughout the United States. The author of *Politics and Reality in an American City: The New Orleans School Crisis of 1960* (New York: Center for Urban Education, 1969), he has degrees in law and political science.

Elizabeth Jacoway is Adjunct Associate Professor of History at the University of Arkansas at Little Rock. Author of *Yankee Missionaries in the South: The Penn School Experiment* (Baton Rouge: Louisiana State University Press, 1980), she received her Ph.D. from the University of North Carolina in 1974.

Steven F. Lawson is Associate Professor of History at the University of South Florida and Managing Editor of *Tampa Bay History*. Author of *Black Ballots: Voting Rights in the South, 1944–1969* (New York: Columbia University Press, 1976), he received his Ph.D. from Columbia University in 1974.

Paul S. Lofton is Professor of History at Spartanburg Methodist College. He received his Ph.D. from the University of Texas in 1977, where he wrote a dissertation entitled "A Social and Economic History of Columbia, South Carolina, During the Great Depression of 1929–1940."

Charles Sallis is Professor of History at Millsaps College. Coauthor, with James W. Loewen, of *Mississippi: Conflict and Change* (New York: Pantheon, 1974), he received his Ph.D. from the University of Kentucky in 1967.

Anne Trotter (Leonard) is formerly Associate Professor of History at Memphis State University. Author of "The Development of the Merchants of Death Theory," in Franklin Cooling (ed.), *War, Business and American Society* (Port Washington, N.Y.: Kennikat Press, 1976), she received her Ph.D. from Duke University.

George Wright is Assistant Professor of History at the University of Texas. He received his Ph.D. from Duke University in 1977, where he wrote a dissertation on "Blacks in Louisville, Kentucky, 1890–1930."

INDEX